# SPECIAL EDUCATIONAL NEEDS IN THE EARLY YEARS

*Ruth A. Wilson*

London and New York

First published 1998
by Routledge
11 New Fetter Lane, London EC4P 4EE

Simultaneously published in the USA and Canada
by Routledge
29 West 35th Street, New York, NY 10001

© 1998 Ruth A. Wilson

Typeset in Palatino by Keystroke, Jacaranda Lodge, Wolverhampton
Printed and bound in Great Britain by TJ International Ltd, Padstow, Cornwall

*British Library Cataloguing in Publication Data*
A catalogue record for this book is available from the British Library

*Library of Congress Cataloging in Publication Data*
Wilson, Ruth A.
Special educational needs in the early years / Ruth A. Wilson.
p.    cm. – (Teaching and learning in the first three years of school)
Includes bibliographical references and index.
1. Handicapped children–Education (Early childhood)–Case
studies.  2. Special education–Case studies.  I. Title.
II.  Series.
LC4019.3.W55 1998
371.9'0472–dc21      97–38917

ISBN 0–415–16382–X (hbk)
ISBN 0–415–16383–8 (pbk)

University of Nottingham
School of Nursing & Midwifery
Derbyshire Royal Infirmary
London Road
DERBY DE1 2QY

# SPECIAL EDUCATIONAL NEEDS
# IN THE EARLY YEARS

This volume adopts a holistic approach and focuses on the child with special educational needs as an active learner, rather than on how to cope with a disability. Young children with special needs can be very active learners when provided with environments that encourage alternative ways to explore and experience the world around them.

The book is divided into five sections:

- establishing a theoretical framework for understanding and working with young children with special needs;
- presenting some of the major issues and concerns related to atypical development;
- the intervention team – emphasizing the importance of the home–school partnership and professional–home–school links;
- the child as an individual – how to make the learning environment accessible;
- the professional development of the teacher.

Case-study examples are used throughout the book to illustrate different methods of intervention and relate relevant research and theory to actual practice. This is an interesting and accessible book, which will be of particular value to practicing early years teachers and trainee teachers.

**Ruth A. Wilson** is Associate Professor in Early Childhood Special Education at Bowling Green State University, Ohio (USA). She has also been involved as teacher, administrator, and evaluator of various pro-grams serving young children with special educational needs and their families. Dr. Wilson has published widely in the fields of early childhood education, special education, and environmental education.

# TEACHING AND LEARNING IN THE FIRST THREE YEARS OF SCHOOL
## Series Editor *Joy Palmer*

This innovatory and up-to-date series is concerned specifically with curriculum practice in the first three years of school. Each book includes guidance on:

- subject content
- planning and organisation
- assessment and record-keeping
- in-service training

This practical advice is placed in the context of the National Curriculum and the latest theoretical work on how children learn at this age and what experiences they bring to their early years in the classroom.

Other books in the series:

GEOGRAPHY IN THE EARLY YEARS
*Joy Palmer*

HISTORY IN THE EARLY YEARS
*Hilary Cooper*

MATHEMATICS IN THE EARLY YEARS
*Wendy Clemson and David Clemson*

PHYSICAL EDUCATION IN THE EARLY YEARS
*Pauline Wetton*

# CONTENTS

CONTENTS

CONTENTS

CONTENTS

# FIGURES AND TABLES

## Figures

## Tables

# BOXES

# FOREWORD

I should like to welcome this book as a valuable addition to UK texts on the early years/special educational needs scene.

Ruth Wilson is Associate Professor in the Department of Special Education at Bowling Green State University, Bowling Green, Ohio, USA, and her book demonstrates her sound and extensive knowledge of early years development as well as of the equally specialist area of early years special needs.

I have enjoyed reading through this book and especially like Ruth Wilson's writing style, which is clear and accessible, with a minimum of jargon. Likewise, the many case studies graphically illustrate the points and messages contained in each chapter and also serve to show the concerns and issues that our counterparts across the Atlantic Ocean deal with, many of which are so similar to our own. Indeed such commonalities transcend other cultural and educational differences and confirm that, for identified problems, there are solutions that we can relate to in the UK.

Ruth Wilson's book is also welcomed because of its timeliness. We have had, since May 1997, a new Labour government that is reviewing early years and special needs provision.

Within the early years and pre-school area, the government has asked for each locality to have an Early Years Forum, to enhance planning and communication between nursery and other pre-school providers. Centres of early years excellence will also provide beacons of good practice across the country.

At the time of writing, the government has just published its consultative Green Paper (Department for Education, 1997) on future directions for special educational needs (SEN). The document marries pre-school education and SEN in these words:

> In each LEA area, an early years development partnership will be established. Each will be fully representative of providers of early years services, including those with expertise in SEN, and will take into account the views of parents. Each partnership will

xi

draw up an Early Years Development Plan, which must show that appropriate provision will be available for children with SEN and that all providers, with support where necessary, are able to identify and assess SEN. The new emphasis we are placing on early identification will mean that many children's SEN are identified before they reach compulsory school age.

(Para. 8, p. 14)

Key themes of these reviews are a call for a greater degree of active co-operation between the various agencies, and a call for closer working partnerships between educators and parents. These too are integral themes of this book. Practitioners will welcome the practical content of the book to support their pursuit of the requisite pedagogic and curriculum goals.

There is one profound principle pursued throughout the book, which I applaud – that is, promotion of the idea of integration between regular early years educators and special needs educators. It is what Ruth Wilson refers to as "twin track", a principle she elaborates in Chapter 1. This is a message well worth reiterating for a UK readership of early years and SEN practitioners and policy makers, at a time when co-operative working is being urged.

I hope readers will be as inspired as I have been by Ruth Wilson's blend of conceptual sophistication, her "Challenges" (see Chapter 2) and her practical focus.

Sheila Wolfendale

# SERIES EDITOR'S PREFACE

Each book in this series focuses on a specific curriculum area. The series relates relevant learning theory or a rationale for early years learning to the practical development and implementation of subject-based topics and classroom activities at the infant level (i.e., Reception, Year 1, Year 2). It seems that the majority of existing books on primary education and the primary curriculum focus on pupils aged 7–11 years. It is hoped that this series presents a refreshing and much needed change in that it specifically addresses the first three years in school.

Each volume is intended to be an up-to-date, judicious mix of theory and practical classroom application, offering a wealth of background information, ideas and advice to all concerned with planning, implementing, monitoring and evaluating teaching and learning in the first three years in school. Theoretical perspectives are presented in a lively and interesting way, drawing upon recent classroom research findings wherever possible. Case studies and activities from a range of classrooms and schools illuminate many of the substantial issues related to the subject area in question.

Readers will find a similar pattern of contents in all the books in the series. Each discusses the early learning environment, transition from home- to school-based learning, and addresses the key questions of what this means for the early years teacher and the curriculum. Such discussion inevitably incorporates ideas on the knowledge which young children may have of subjects and an overview of the subject matter itself which is under scrutiny. As the thrust of the series is towards young children learning subjects, albeit in a holistic way, no doubt readers will wish to consider what is an appropriate content or rationale for the subject in the early years. Having considered young children as learners, what they are bringing into school in terms of prior knowledge, the teacher's task and the subject matter itself, each book then turns its attention to appropriate methods of planning, organising, implementing and evaluating teaching and learning activities. Crucial matters such as assessment, evaluation and record-keeping are dealt with in their own right, and are also referred to and discussed in ongoing examples of good practice. Each book concludes with useful suggestions for further staffroom discussion/ INSET activities and advice on resources.

As a whole, the series aims to be inspirational and forward-looking. As all readers know so well, the National Curriculum is not 'written in concrete'. Education is a dynamic process. While taking due account of the essential National Curriculum framework, authors go far beyond the level of description of rigid content guidelines to highlight *principles* for teaching and learning. Furthermore, they incorporate two key messages which surely underpin successful, reflective education, namely 'vision' and 'enthusiasm'. It is hoped that students and teachers will be inspired and assisted in their task of implementing successful and progressive plans which help young learners to make sense of their world and the key areas of knowledge within it.

Joy A. Palmer

# INTRODUCTION

## How young children learn

Young children learn through play and through interactions with people and objects in their environment. Young children with disabilities, however, often lack the skills and/or motivation to engage in play-based activities and to interact with the world around them (Odom & McLean, 1996). Without effective intervention their primary avenues for learning are seriously blocked. As a major goal of early intervention (EI) for young children with special needs during the first three years of school is to remove or side-step the barriers to learning, it would seem logical for EI to focus on the development of skills relating to play, social interactions, and exploration of the environment. Unfortunately, this is not always the case.

There is a tendency for programs serving young children with special needs to focus on the disability or deficit areas and to lose sight of what is most important for learning and development during the early childhood years – that is, opportunities to engage successfully in a variety of playful interactions with people and objects in one's environment. Because there is little evidence to support the idea that play *in any form* is educational (Johnson *et al.*, 1987), it is critical for adults working with young children to understand which types of play are optimal for development. This understanding becomes especially critical when working with young children with disabilities, as they are more dependent than typically developing children on the intervention of adults to make play situations meaningful and valuable to their growth and development.

Play that is optimal for development is play that reflects or slightly stretches the current abilities of the child (Johnson *et al.*, 1987). Given interesting and appropriate materials and a supportive environment, typically developing children tend to create the kind of play situations that are a good match to their abilities and potentials. They enjoy the excitement of challenge and accept with gusto problems to be solved or feats to be accomplished. Can I move this heavy rock all by myself? Can I figure out how to use these blocks to build a bridge over that road we just made in the sandbox? Can I throw the ball over the fence or run faster than Scotty, the dog? Can I paint a picture of a dragon or dinosaur, and can I write my own name at the top of the paper? Young children with disabilities, however, often have a great deal of trouble envisioning such feats and, with a history of failure and frustration, little incentive to try.

To be successful in play, young children need to manipulate objects, look for challenges in using materials, and engage in social interactions. Most children with disabilities have trouble in one or all of these areas. Some lack the motor skills to hold or control objects; others, due to vision or attention deficits, may not even notice the objects available to them. For other children, social and communication deficits may be the primary obstacles to engaging in play and other types of learning situations. Such children may not know how to join a group activity already in progress or one that is being facilitated by a teacher. They may also have difficulty inviting or involving other children in a play/learning initiative of their own. The aggressive and assaultive behaviors of some children may cause them to be disliked and shunned by their peers. For other children, cognitive delays may create developmental differences between them and their peers, resulting in widely differing interests and abilities. Due to such differences and disabilities, it is not surprising to find that young children with special needs, when served in programs with typically developing children, are often isolated and not engaged in play and other learning activities with their peers (Odom & McLean, 1996).

## Approaches to intervention

One approach to intervention might be to focus on the disability or deficit in an attempt to "fix it." This approach, however, has very limited potential for success. Many disabilities cannot be "fixed." The child who is blind, for example, may never be able to see. The child with a physical disability – perhaps due to cerebral palsy or a missing limb – may never be able to kick a ball or walk independently. While, at times, some deficit-related behaviors can be taught (such as using a spoon for feeding or saying "please" to get a second cookie), the benefits of this "fix it" approach to more generalized learning situations are usually minimal. Because young children's learning is so closely tied to competence in play and widely varying interactions with people and objects in their environment, the "fix it" approach to intervention (which tends to focus on narrowly defined goals and activities) is not recommended.

The recommended approach to intervention focuses on removing or circumventing the barriers young children with special needs often experience in their attempts at play and interactions with their physical and social environment. Circumventing these barriers is accomplished by developing competencies in the overlapping areas of play, social interactions, and exploration of the environment. It is this competency-based approach to serving young children with special educational needs (SEN) that is presented in this book.

Intervention with a competency-based approach looks at the child holistically versus focusing on deficits or disabilities. The primary thrust of this approach is on building competence and confidence in the young child and minimizing any negative impact the disability may have on development and learning. This competency-based approach, therefore, looks at the child in terms of strengths as well as areas of need. It works from the premise that the child can learn and that a major part of our challenge is figuring out which way he or she learns the best.

This competency-based approach also views the child as a learner who constructs his or her knowledge versus receiving such knowledge from adults. This approach recognizes all children as being competent to construct their own knowledge, as long as major barriers to interacting with the environment are removed or circumvented.

A competency-based approach to intervention involves creating a vision for the child. By viewing the child in terms of competencies and strengths, we acknowledge the child's potential for the future. Obviously, a vision for the child's future cannot be developed without the input of the family, nor can such a vision be developed without a consideration of the child's interests and special abilities. It is the vision for the child's future which should be a major determining factor in developing and planning educational experiences for the young child. In addition to involving the family in developing a vision for the child, the competency-based approach to intervention also works in partnership with the family to make the vision become reality. The vision for the child's future cannot be realized without the family's involvement, as it is with the family that the child spends most of his or her time from birth to adulthood. The family provides the context and continuity for the ongoing development of the life and learning goals for the child.

## Uniqueness of the field

The field of early intervention for young children with special needs is unique in a number of ways. First, a close look at the field (sometimes referred to as early childhood special education) indicates that it is relatively new and still in its early stage of development. What we currently know as "best practices" in the field is likely to grow and change over time. Our knowledge base in early childhood special education will continue to evolve, and values and conditions in society will continue to change. Thus, practices considered "best" today may not be considered such even just a few years from now. With this in mind, the term "recommended practices" versus "best practices" will be used throughout this book. This terminology is consistent with professional opinion in the field (Odom & McLean, 1996).

The field of early childhood special education is also unique in that it reflects a blend of practices and values from several different disciplines, primarily early childhood education and special education. Compensatory education, which overlaps with both early childhood education and special education, certainly plays a role as well. This role will be discussed in Chapter 1 in relation to the historical roots of the field. A brief overview of the other two contributing areas (i.e., early childhood education and special education) follows. It should be evident from this discussion that these two areas differ considerably in their major areas of emphases. A special challenge of the field is to merge these two disciplines in a way that retains the integrity of each. This challenge is discussed in greater detail in Chapter 2.

Early childhood education, or education during the early years, usually emphasizes creative play, social skill development, "pre-academics" (i.e., basic skills in English, math, and science), and the development of basic understandings about the natural and built environment. Curriculum during the early years is often planned around themes (e.g., neighborhoods, animals in our backyard, etc.) which combine concepts across different subjects, like math and science. Because young children learn best when they are curious and interested in what they are doing, a large portion of the day in many early childhood classrooms is devoted to child-initiated, child-directed, and teacher-supported play activities.

While early childhood education is usually planned around children's interests and natural curiosity, special education is more typically planned around individual needs and areas of weaknesses. One of the cornerstones of special education is an "individual education plan," which must be drawn up for each child identified as having special needs. The nature of the child's learning difficulties, as well as performance targets to be achieved in a given time, are essential components of this individual plan. This individualized focus with specified targets often results in a more teacher-directed versus child-initiated curriculum. For many children with special needs, a special education teacher is often involved in teaching the child directly or supporting the classroom teacher in implementing the child's individual education plan.

In the literature, as well as in recent practices, early childhood education and special education have followed separate and quite differing paths. Today, a merging of these disciplines is considered recommended practice. Such a merging brings with it, not only a great deal of potential benefits for young children and their families, but also some special challenges for professionals working with young children during their first three years of school. Both the potential benefits and the challenges of this merging are discussed in subsequent chapters of this book.

## Overview of the book

This book is divided into four major sections: one establishing a theoretical framework for understanding and working with young children with special needs; one presenting some of the major issues and concerns related to atypical development and programming for children with special needs, followed by separate sections devoted to the intervention team and the individual child. Case studies and/or program examples, as well as a discussion of relevant research and theory relating to the early years classrooms, are weaved into each of the chapters.

This book is written primarily for teachers and teachers in training. Others who may find this book helpful include school administrators, other professionals in non-teaching roles, parents, and the general public. The book is written in the hope that individuals will come away from the reading with a deeper understanding of young children with special needs, and ways in which their needs can be met in their early years of school. This understanding is critical to becoming partners with the child in developing competence and confidence on his or her individualized path to learning.

The understanding that young children with special educational needs are both alike and different from their same-age peers is one of the primary principles, or beliefs, running as a basic theme throughout this book. This understanding calls for services that are both integrated (i.e., provided in a mainstream environment) and individualized. It also calls for professional expertise in both typical and atypical child development. In terms of curriculum and program planning, this belief translates into a merging of developmentally appropriate practices and exceptionality appropriate practices. The material presented in this book is designed to serve as an elaboration on this basic theme.

# Part I

# ESTABLISHING THE FRAMEWORK

Special education during the early years is not about an intervention system nor a special curricular model. Special education during the early years is about children who have special needs. Such children cannot be categorized, or thought of, as an homogenous group. Children with special needs vary tremendously. Not only do they have the same type of variances as the general population (e.g., different interests, likes, dislikes, temperaments, abilities, etc.), they also vary by type and extent of disability.

There are many different "reasons" why some children have disabilities or are at risk for being handicapped. Some of these reasons, or causes, are discussed in Part I of the book. Also included in Part I is a discussion of why early intervention for young children with special needs is important and what data we have to support effectiveness claims relating to early intervention services. A brief historical overview is provided, as well as some information about social and legal support for early intervention services. Information about the team of professionals involved in providing early intervention services, what has been identified as "quality indicators" in the field, and some of the challenges related to the merging of curriculum for young children during the first three years of school with early intervention are also addressed. The discussion throughout this section emphasizes the two-fold mission of early intervention services – that of providing successful learning experiences for young children with special needs, and providing effective and timely intervention before a handicap or at-risk condition undermines the development and future capabilities of these children. The primary goals of early intervention, then, are as follows: (1) to develop competence and confidence in the child's learning ability, and (2) to avoid or minimize the development of secondary handicaps (e.g., the development of social deficits and/or emotional problems related to a hearing impairment).

# 1

# SURVEY OF THE FIELD

## Who is served

A concept often stated and rarely challenged is that "no two people are alike." While we all know and accept this statement to be true, we still seem, in some ways, to be troubled by the notion of "differences." Once differences are identified, we tend to think in terms of "we" versus "them" and begin judging individuals in relation to "better" and "worse." While some lip-service is given to "celebrating differences," many of our attitudes and behaviors fail to reflect this orientation.

It is true that people with disabilities are, in some ways, different from those who do not have disabilities. These differences challenge not only the people with disabilities, but everyone else as well. These differences challenge parents, teachers, program planners, school administrators, architects, playground designers, and peers. Rising to the challenge often requires an understanding of the conditions causing, or relating to, the disability. Rising to the challenge also requires an understanding of the potential impact of the disability on the child's overall development and learning. It is this potential impact that gives special urgency to early intervention for children with disabilities.

Teachers of children in the early years serve a wide range of students. Some of these children have obvious (i.e., readily apparent) disabilities or handicaps, some may be developmentally delayed, and others are at-risk for future academic failure. While the needs of these children differ widely, as a group they are sometimes referred to as "children with special educational needs" and require an educational program customized to their unique needs. It is estimated that nationally (i.e., in Great Britain), approximately 20% of children will have some form of special educational need at some time (Department for Education, 1994). According to the Department for Education (DFE) *Code of Practice on the Identification and Assessment of Special Educational Needs*, a child is considered to have special educational needs if he or she has a learning difficulty which calls for special educational provision to be made for him or her. The learning difficulty is manifested when the child (1) has a significantly greater difficulty in learning than the majority of children of the same age; (2) has a disability which either prevents or hinders the child from making use of educational facilities of a kind provided for children of the same age in schools within the area of local education; and (3) is under age 5 and falls within the definition of (1) or (2) above or would do so if special educational provision was not made for the child (Department for Education, 1994).

For some children, their exceptionalities, or special needs, are obvious; for others, their special needs are not immediately apparent. Many children with cerebral palsy have motor difficulties which prohibit walking. For a 4-year-old child with such a disability, his or her handicap would soon be obvious to any observer. Conversely, however, the disability of a 6-year-old who is developmentally delayed and functioning as a 4-year-old may not be immediately noticed by a visitor to the classroom.

Whether obvious or not, it is to the young child's advantage to have his or her disability identified and understood. However, it is also critically important to recognize that a child with a disability is first a young child who is more like his or her typically developing peers than different. It is for this reason that "person-first" language should be used when referring to children with disabilities. "Person-first" language puts the child first and the disability second. Instead of saying "deaf child," the preferred terminology would be "child who is deaf;" likewise, instead of saying "disabled child," the preferred terminology would be "child with a disability."

Another important understanding in relation to terminology has to do with the terms "disability" and "handicap." While the general public tends to use these terms interchangeably, they have distinct meanings. Referring to a child as having a disability indicates that he or she is unable to do something in a certain way. A disability, then, is an inability to perform as other children do because of an impairment in some area(s) of functioning (e.g., physical, cognitive, sensory, etc.). A handicap, on the other hand, refers to the problems an individual with a disability encounters when attempting to function and interact in the environment. While attention to the quality of the environment is important in all educational programs for young children, it is particularly significant for children with disabilities, in that the quality of the environment determines, in large part, the extent to which a disability becomes handicapping.

A disability, then, may or may not be a handicap, depending upon the specific circumstances or demands of the environment. For example, a 7-year-old child with cerebral palsy may have a great deal of difficulty standing by a chalkboard to draw or write. When seated at a table with support for balance, however, his or her creativity and talents may be easily recognized. In this instance, the child experiences a handicap at the chalkboard, but not at the table. One major goal of intervention is to minimize the extent to which a disability puts the child in a handicapping situation. For educators to provide such intervention, however, they need some understanding of the different types of disability and the ways the disability may impact on development and learning. Discussions throughout the book are designed to help educators develop and/or deepen this understanding.

Many people believe that all children have special needs, in that each child, regardless of abilities and background, has unique needs and deserves special adult attention (Wolery & Wilbers, 1994). The term "special needs," however, generally refers to children with disabilities or developmental delays. In this book, the terms "children with special needs" and "children with special educational needs" (SEN) will be used interchangeably with "children with disabilities" and will refer to those children whose well-being, development, and learning are compromised if special intervention is not provided.

As stated earlier, children with disabilities are similar in many ways to their typically developing peers. Yet, many children with disabilities also have special needs that children without disabilities do not have. These needs include: (1) environments that are specifically arranged to minimize the impact of the disabilities, and (2) professionals who are competent in promoting learning and the use of skills critical to the specific needs of children with disabilities (Wolery *et al.*, 1992). A listing of professionals who are often involved in early intervention services and a discussion of their roles are presented in later sections of this book (especially Chapter 7).

A discussion of who is served in early intervention cannot be complete without some reference to the families involved. All families play a critical role in the early development of a child, and are faced with many challenges in the process. These demands and challenges, however, certainly escalate when the child has a disability. Thus, while the child is usually considered to be the focus of educational programs designed for children and youth, for children with disabilities such programs should also focus on the family. This is especially necessary during the first few years of the child's schooling.

## Historical perspectives

Young children with special needs have not always been served in educational programs. In fact, there was a time when children with special needs were excluded from the public schools. It was felt that since the curriculum was not appropriate to the children, the children did not belong in the program. The understanding today is that all children do,

11

indeed, belong in school and that they have a right to an educational program which is appropriate to their individual needs. This understanding, however, is relatively recent.

Over the last twenty years, there has been a dramatic increase in awareness, services, and opportunities for young children with special needs. Factors supporting this growth include legislative initiatives, litigation, public policy, and the efforts of various advocacy groups. Historical roots of the rapidly emerging field of early childhood special education can be traced to trends and developments in early childhood education, special education, and compensatory programs for children at environmental risk. Several early contributors to the concept of compensatory programs warrant special mention, notably John Locke and Robert Owen.

John Locke (1632–1704), a seventeenth-century English physician and philosopher, was an early contributor to our understanding of the importance of the early years for later development. Locke was a strong advocate of an environmental point of view and introduced the notion that, at birth, children are very much like a blank slate (*tabula rasa*). According to this view, what children learn is a direct result of experiences, activities, and sensations; and what children become is determined by the type and quality of experiences they have, especially during their early years.

Locke's belief in the powerful influence of the child's environment and early experiences is reflected in compensatory education programs for young children living in poverty. These compensatory programs are designed to "make up" for the disadvantages experienced by children living in deprived environments.

Robert Owen (1771–1858) was another important contributor to early childhood and compensatory education. Owen, a manager of a textile mill in Scotland, was concerned about the living and working conditions of the children and their parents. He prohibited very young children from working at all and limited the number of working hours for older children. Believing that the early years represented the best time to influence a child's development, Owen established an infant school for children between the ages of 3 and 10. This infant school and others that soon followed were noted for an emphasis on basic academics (e.g., reading, math, science, etc.), creative experiences (e.g., music and dance), and mutual respect between teacher and learner. These schools were also seen as a way of compensating children of poverty for the deprived conditions they experienced at home. Owen's work was based, in large part, on the premise that poverty could be eliminated by educating and socializing young children from poor families.

The establishment of compensatory programs indicated that the belief that early intervention can make a difference in a child's development and learning was becoming more readily understood and accepted. In compensatory education, early intervention usually takes the form of "make up" or equivalent experiences which are designed to offset, or make amends, for the poverty conditions experienced at home. The rationale for special education takes this concept one step further. Maria Montessori (1870–1952) played a major role in laying the foundation for this step.

In the late 1800s, Montessori was working as a physician in a psychiatric clinic in Rome, Italy. Here, she had the opportunity to closely observe "idiot children," or children with mental retardation. Mental retardation, at the time, was viewed as indistinguishable from insanity. From her observations, Montessori concluded that educational intervention rather than medical treatment would be a more effective strategy for working with these children. This phenomenon of "physician becoming educator" is representative of the historical tradition upon which special education is built.

Montessori's work with children with mental retardation was based on the premise that intelligence is not static or fixed, but can be influenced by experiences. To provide enriching experiences for the children, Montessori developed an innovative, activity-based sensory education program involving didactic, or teaching, materials. This program proved to be highly effective. Children who were originally believed to be incapable of learning, after participating in the intervention program, successfully performed on various academic achievement measures.

Over time, Montessori expanded her educational program, and in 1907 opened the Casa dei Bambini or "children's home" in one of the slum districts of Rome. Here, she worked with children between the ages of 30 months and 7 years, who in today's terminology would be considered environmentally at-risk. Montessori based her educational program on the belief that children have a natural tendency to explore and understand their world and that they learn best by direct sensory experiences. While she envisioned child development as a process of natural unfolding, she also believed that environmental influences play a critical role in how and when the unfolding takes place.

Montessori's program emphasized three major components considered to be important in developing the child's independence, responsibility, and productivity. These three components are: (1) practical life experiences, (2) sensory education, and (3) academic education. These same three components are often found in intervention programs for children with disabilities. There follows a brief discussion of each.

- Practical life experiences, as outlined by Montessori, focus on personal hygiene and self-help (e.g., eating, dressing, etc.), motor development (e.g., walking, grasping, etc.), and responsibility for the natural and built environment (e.g., sweeping the floor, raking leaves, caring for plants and animals, etc.).

- Sensory education focuses on developing the student's various senses (i.e., seeing, hearing, feeling, etc.) and is based on the educational belief that cognitive development is dependent on sensory experiences. Montessori's sensory educational materials are designed to lead the students from concrete to abstract (i.e., real to representational) learning experiences.

- Academic education introduces the child to English, math, and science in developmentally appropriate ways. Formal or teacher-directed academic instruction is avoided. The emphasis is on self-chosen didactic (i.e., "teaching") materials and activities. The didactic materials are designed to be used independently by the children and are self-correcting, in that the children discover there is only one correct way to use them.

Other important aspects of the Montessori program which have critical implications for children with special needs include: (1) an emphasis on individual student activities rather than group work, and (2) the practice of modifying the curriculum to meet the unique, individual needs of each child. Children in a Montessori program work at their own pace, selecting learning materials of their choice. These materials are displayed on low shelves in an organized manner to encourage independent use. Montessori believed in allowing children to do things for themselves and was convinced that children are capable of teaching themselves through interaction with a carefully planned learning environment. The teacher's role in this environment is to foster the development of independence in the children. For some children, this means breaking down ideas and/or tasks into small, sequential steps that build on current levels of development and relate to previous experiences.

As is evident from the above discussion, the field of early childhood special education reflects valuable contributions from early childhood education, special education, and compensatory education. It also reflects a changing view of young children with special needs and their potential for development and learning. Rather than "writing them off" as uneducable, ignoring their special educational needs, or suggesting that they wait until they "outgrow" their learning problems, we now view young children with special needs as capable of learning, as responsive to the types of environments we provide for them, and as individuals with a unique potential for achieving the vision of their future. For individuals with disabilities, such a vision can neither be developed nor attained without support. Teachers and co-professionals have a critical role to play in this process.

## Expanded role of the teacher

Historically, there are considerable differences in the professional background and practices of teachers who work primarily with young children with disabilities and those who serve typically developing children. Teachers from these differing backgrounds are often educated through different college or university programs, tend to belong to separate professional organizations, and are familiar with different model programs and bodies of research. Until recently, they have also worked in different types of setting – the special educators in separate and specialized programs and the early childhood educators in public or private schools serving typically developing children. Today, however, recommended practices from both early childhood education and early childhood special education suggest that young children with and without disabilities should be served in the same programs. Such programs are sometimes referred to as "mainstream" or "inclusive" programs.

Recommended practices also suggest that, to be consistent with the inclusion of young children with special needs in regular early childhood classrooms, the two-track professional development model (i.e., one track for special educators and the other track for early childhood educators) is not appropriate. Recommended practices call for a merger of the two disciplines in teacher-preparation programs. This merger should retain the best of both disciplines and should go beyond the "team teaching" or multidisciplinary approach (i.e., where both an early childhood educator and early childhood special educator work side by side within the same classroom).

The recommended approach for including young children with disabilities in early childhood programs is to work within a transdisciplinary model. Transdiscipline involves a crossing of disciplinary lines, a stretching of one's professional role, and the development of additional competencies. For the early childhood educator, this means learning more about children with special needs and developing the skills to effectively modify the program for them. For the early childhood special educator, this means learning more about human development during the early childhood years, becoming more familiar with the intricacies of developmentally appropriate practices, and learning how to work with a larger group of children with varying interests and abilities.

Feedback from regular classroom teachers regarding the inclusion of children with special educational needs in their classrooms indicates that they often feel unprepared and intimidated at the thought of their role in the process. They may defer to special educators as the ones with the expertise needed for serving children with SEN and feel that they have little to offer. This way of thinking can serve as a formidable barrier to transdisciplinary teaming, which requires a "back-and-forth" versus

15

"one-way" sharing of expertise. Widerstrom (1986) addressed this concern and studied ways in which early childhood education contributes to the education of young children with special needs. She concluded: "one important contribution that early childhood education might make to special education is a renewed awareness of the benefits to young children of spontaneous play" (p. 214). The meaning and importance of play is a major area of emphasis in the professional development of early childhood educators. This is usually not the case for special educators. Thus, the role of early childhood educators is to serve as "experts" in this aspect of programming for young children with SEN and to share this expertise with other members of the early intervention team.

While the literature on how to best serve young children with SEN in inclusive settings often focuses on how the early childhood educator can include special education teaching strategies, Widerstrom (1986) suggests four areas in which special educators can incorporate effective strategies from early childhood education. These suggestions are as follows: (1) include group activities that foster peer interactions; (2) include more opportunities for free play; (3) practice being more indirect and more reactive in their interactions with the children, and (4) learn to be more comfortable with a lesser degree of teacher control. Early childhood educators, then, do have their own areas of expertise to offer to the intervention team. Early childhood educators would do well to recognize and value this area of expertise and not hesitate to defend and share it with their colleagues.

Team teaching, during all or part of the day, may occur within the transdisciplinary approach. When it does, the focus moves beyond working side by side to actually sharing roles and expertise. Transdisciplinary programming also requires skill in working with members of other disciplines (e.g., speech/language therapy, physical therapy, etc.) and parents. In recognition of the importance of the team effort to early intervention, entire chapters in this book are devoted to teaming with other disciplines (Chapter 7) and working in partnership with families (Chapter 8). Working as a member of a transdisciplinary team, then, represents one way in which the role of the early childhood teacher expands with the inclusion of children with disabilities in the regular classroom.

Because many young children with disabilities need more individual assistance than their typically developing peers, inclusive programs often make arrangements to have additional adults in the classrooms (e.g., paraprofessionals/teacher assistants, parents, and others who may serve as volunteers). The effectiveness of the paraprofessionals' and volunteers' contribution depends, in large part, on how well the teacher prepares for and develops a working relationship with these individuals (Cook *et al.*, 1996). Establishing this relationship is another way in which the role of the early childhood teacher expands when children with disabilities are included in the regular classroom.

## Rationale and effectiveness of early intervention

Based on the increased responsibilities and challenges that come with the expanded role of the teacher in an inclusive classroom, one may ask: Why implement such a model of early intervention? Is it worth it? Does early intervention make a difference, and if so, in what form has it proven to be most effective?

Before addressing the form or model most conducive to accomplishing the goals of early intervention, a discussion as to the rationale for special education services during the early years will be presented. This rationale can be developed on the basis of theoretical arguments, empirical evidence, and societal needs. Presented first, however, is a statement of the purpose of early intervention.

The primary purpose of early intervention is to provide successful learning experiences for young children with special needs, and to do so in an effective and timely manner so as to prevent or minimize the handicapping or at-risk condition from undermining the development and future capabilities of these children. As is evident from this "understanding," early intervention can be viewed as being both remedial and preventive in nature – i.e., remediating existing developmental problems and preventing the occurrence of additional ones (Council for Exceptional Children, 1988).

Both theoretical arguments and empirical evidence relate to the significance of early environmental influences on later development. In the early 1960s, this significance was brought to the attention of the professional community in Hunt's notable book *Intelligence and Experience*. After presenting a convincing argument for the impact of the early years on later development, Hunt (1961) recommends that young children be provided with optimal environments as a way of increasing their intellectual development. Hunt's argument lends strong theoretical support to early intervention in that it clearly links developmental outcomes to early experiences.

Empirical evidence in support of early intervention was provided by a number of landmark studies, including investigations by Skeels and Dye (1939) and Skeels (1966). In the Skeels and Dye study, a group of children living in an orphanage were transferred to a ward housing women with mental retardation. These women showered the children with a great deal of attention and care. Follow-up testing indicated that the children who received such attention showed impressive IQ gains when compared with children who had not been transferred to this women's ward. The new environment clearly provided more stimulation and richer learning experiences for the children and resulted in increased intellectual functioning.

Approximately twenty-five years later, Skeels (1966) did a follow-up study of these same children. He found that differences remained between the group of children who had been transferred to the women's ward and the group who were not transferred. As adults, the individuals who had been transferred (and thus received a more stimulating environment) showed higher academic education levels and more advanced levels of occupational achievement. Thus not only theory, but also research data supports the concept that developmental outcomes can be effected by early experiences.

A major premise of early intervention is that the stimulation provided through such programs will result in higher levels of functioning for individuals with disabilities than would have been achieved without such intervention. In essence, the argument for early intervention is that it does make a difference. As stated above, both theory and research support this argument.

The rationale for early intervention also relates to societal needs and the fact that such services are cost-effective. Special education is more intensive (i.e., involving more individualized programming, more professionals involved, etc.) and thus more costly than regular education. However, because children receiving early intervention services are more likely to go on to regular education later in their academic career, the net result is considerable savings in educational costs.

A number of studies indicate that these cost-saving arguments for early intervention are based on more than theory. Research relating to the Perry Preschool Project is perhaps the most impressive. The long-term follow-up of the Perry Preschool Project found that children who participated in the preschool experience were less likely to require more costly and intensive special education services in later years and that the projected lifetime earnings for program participants were greater than those of the control group of children who did not have the preschool experience. Projected benefits were estimated to be in excess of $14,000 per child over his or her life span (Schweinhart et al., 1993). Other studies focusing on the economic benefits of early intervention have arrived at similar or greater estimates of cost savings. (See Bricker (1989) and The Council for Exceptional Children (1988) for a review of such studies.)

Societal benefits, however, extend beyond cost savings and improved academic outcomes for children. Early intervention services also provide benefits for families of children with disabilities. Positive outcomes for such families include: (1) improved mother–child interactions (Ramey et al., 1983); (2) increased school and/or work attendance and performance of teenage mothers (Field et al., 1982), and (3) decreases in parental stress (Shonkoff & Hauser-Cram, 1987). Such outcomes tend to increase the child's and the family's chances of developing to their full potential (Hanson & Lynch, 1995).

Today, legal support also provides incentive for early intervention services. In the United Kingdom, Part III of the Education Act 1993 (now incorporated into the 1996 Education Act, Part 4) specifies that the needs of all students who may have special educational needs must be addressed. In response to this mandate and to provide guidance on how to implement it, the Department for Education (DFE) developed the *Code of Practice on the Identification and Assessment of Special Education Needs* (DFE, 1994). This *Code of Practice* clearly indicates that local education authorities (LEAs) are responsible for identifying and assessing children with special educational needs as early as possible (even before the age of two) and for providing them with "the greatest possible access to a broad and balanced education, including the National Curriculum" (DFE, 1994, p. 2).

## Basic understandings

During the early history of special education, it was common practice for intervention services to be provided in separate classrooms or facilities. Today, the recommended practice, supported both by theory and research, is to educate children with special educational needs alongside their peers in mainstream schools (Wolery & Wilbers, 1994). The mainstream model for the provision of special education services is also specified in the DFE *Code of Practice*:

> the needs of most pupils will be met in the mainstream. . . . Children with special educational needs, including children with statement of special educational needs, should, where appropriate and taking into account the wishes of their parents, be educated alongside their peers in mainstream schools.
>
> (DFE, 1994)

In addition to the concept of mainstreaming, the following "basic understandings" also help establish the framework around which recommended practices in the field of early childhood special education are developed.

- Children with special educational needs differ widely from one another and thus require individualized plans for intervention.
- "All children with special educational needs should be identified and assessed as early as possible and as quickly as is consistent with thoroughness" (DFE, 1994, p. 2).
- Because a disability in one area of development and/or learning is

likely to impact on other areas, intervention programs should address the needs of the whole child versus being focused only on the deficit area.

- A specific diagnosis rarely results in precise prescriptions for educational practices. While the diagnosis of a specific disability may suggest the need for certain broad categories of interventions, the nature of the interventions should be tied to a variety of other considerations, including the child's current abilities, the influence of specific environmental factors and instructional strategies on the child's learning, as well as the family's goals and resources (Wolery & Wilbers, 1994).
- In addition to focusing on the child and his or her special education needs, early intervention must also focus on providing support and assistance to the family and offer varied opportunities for their meaningful involvement.

## Case study – Patrick

### Background information

Patrick's first few years of life were quite unstable. His mother, Tammy, had just turned 16 when he was born about eight weeks prematurely. Patrick's father, Chuck, who was 17, had dropped out of school the previous year and now worked as an auto mechanic in his uncle's garage. Chuck seemed pleased and proud to be a father. Tammy, however, wanted nothing to do with Chuck. She considered giving up the baby for adoption but was hampered by Chuck's opposition. Chuck indicated that he would never consent to the baby's adoption and would raise the baby on his own if he had to.

Patrick lived with Tammy and her mother (i.e., the maternal grandmother) for the first eight months. Tammy tried going back to school after Patrick was 6 weeks old. Child care, however, was a constant concern. Tammy's mother was often too intoxicated to be left alone with the baby. Chuck was constantly angry about the situation. While he wanted to be more involved in his son's care, he was almost helpless to do so. His own parents felt that Patrick should have been given up for adoption and vowed to offer absolutely no financial or emotional support. They refused to even see the baby and demanded that as long as Chuck chose to be involved with his son, he could not live with them.

Chuck moved to a small apartment where two of his "buddies" lived. He tried, at times, to care for his son in this apartment, but conditions there were very unhealthy for an infant, including inadequate bedroom, bathroom, and kitchen facilities and loud parties lasting late into the night. Tammy talked to a social worker about these conditions; the social worker agreed that Chuck's apartment was not suitable for an infant. After repeated instances of inadequate care for Patrick – such as being left alone with Tammy's mother while she was intoxicated or spending considerable time in Chuck's apartment – Patrick was placed in a foster home. He was now 8 months old.

One of the first things his foster parents noticed was that Patrick was not demonstrating the skills expected of an infant his age. Patrick could not sit up independently, did not make "babbling" sounds, showed little interest in toys and other objects presented to him, and did not reach out to adults for comfort or social interaction. Developmental assessments requested by his foster parents indicated that Patrick was considerably developmentally delayed and was showing signs of serious mental retardation. Patrick's foster parents had never cared for a child with special needs before and requested that Patrick be moved to a different foster home.

By the time Patrick was 4 years old, he had lived in three different foster homes and had only sporadic contact with his mother. Chuck, now 21, finally got custody of his son. Chuck was engaged to Annmarie, who agreed to care for Patrick while Chuck was at work. Chuck and Annmarie were planning to get married in about six months.

Since his initial assessment requested by his first foster parents, Patrick's progress was being monitored by the local education authority, and a home-based learning program was provided. Chuck had had some involvement with this intervention program, but foster parents had been the primary contacts for the early intervention team. Now that Patrick was 4 years old, he was to be enrolled in a reception class at his local school. Special education services were to be provided in the context of the mainstream class. Chuck was feeling very optimistic that by having custody, stable child care, and enrollment in a school program Patrick would make great gains. At this time, Patrick was walking independently but had balance and coordination problems, would occasionally look at a book but could not turn the pages one at a time, was using two-word utterances but usually relied on gestures and cries to express his feelings and needs, was naming a few body parts and familiar objects, was using the toilet with assistance but only when prompted, and was showing very little interest in playing with other children.

Information about Patrick was shared with the classroom teacher prior to his first day of attendance, and arrangements were made for a special education resource teacher to assist in developing and implementing an individualized education plan for Patrick. The plan that was developed outlined three stages to be implemented sequentially. During the first stage, the emphasis would be on increasing independence in self-help skills – eating, dressing, and toileting. The second stage would focus on language and basic concept development (e.g., colors, numbers, sizes, shapes, etc.). The third stage would focus on making friends and playing coopera- tively with others. The special education resource teacher would provide direct assistance in the classroom for at least two hours per week.

The first day of school was traumatic for Patrick, his father, and the classroom teacher. Patrick clung to his father, screamed, kicked the teacher, threw the toys that were offered to him to the floor, and fell against a table while trying to run out of the classroom. Patrick's head hit the table, resulting in a small gash over his right eye. The teacher suggested that Chuck take Patrick to the emergency room to see if stitches were necessary. Not having medical insurance to cover the expense, Chuck resisted and suggested that he would just take Patrick home and monitor him closely. As Chuck had to go to work, Annmarie agreed to watch Patrick during the day. Patrick cried most of the day and refused to eat.

The next day, Annmarie went with Chuck to take Patrick to school. Again, there was a great deal of crying, hitting, and screaming. The teacher and the other children in the classroom all seemed frightened. Annmarie agreed to stay at school with Patrick while Chuck went to work. A call to the special education resource teacher brought her to the classroom by early afternoon. Patrick was still crying and refusing to eat or play. Annmarie held him and tried to comfort him throughout the morning. After consulting with the special education teacher, the decision was made to provide services to Patrick at home (primarily with Annmarie) until he developed some of the independence and social skills specified on his individual education plan.

## *Discussion*

Patrick's case is an example of a child at-risk for special education needs even prior to his birth. His parents were young, unmarried, estranged, and had little financial or social support to raise a child. Patrick was also at-risk due to a premature birth. Observation and formal assessment results indicated that Patrick was developmentally delayed and showed signs of mental retardation. Because he had significantly greater difficulty learning than other children his age, Patrick qualified for special education services. Such services commenced while he was still an infant.

Unfortunately, due in part to his inconsistent home situations, the early intervention services provided did not prepare Patrick or his family for the transition to a school-based setting. Additionally, the three-stage instructional plan developed for Patrick failed to prioritize goals in relation to the educational setting. For Patrick to succeed in a mainstream classroom, he would need to feel comfortable in that setting and would need at least some social skills in relating to peers and unfamiliar adults. Yet, according to the plan, social interaction skills would not be emphasized until after satisfactory self-help and cognitively related and language skills were in place.

The experience for Patrick might have been different if the transition had been carefully planned and more support provided during the initial entrance to school. If support had been provided on a more-to-least schedule (i.e., more at first with gradual withdrawal), Patrick may have been able to adjust to the classroom setting. By starting with a minimum of support and little attention to the social aspects of integration, Patrick did not have much chance of succeeding.

The three-stage instructional plan developed for Patrick represents a deficit- versus competency-based approach to intervention. Patrick's deficit areas (i.e., self-help, cognitive, language, and social) dictated the nature of the plan. A competency-based approach might have started with a recognition of Patrick's positive response to his father. In most situations, Chuck was able to calm and comfort Patrick. Patrick also enjoyed playing simple games with Chuck. Thus, two of Patrick's "competencies" were calming in response to his father's attention and interacting socially with a familiar adult. Building on these competencies, initial goals for Patrick could have been to respond positively to other adults (e.g., the classroom

23

teacher and Annmarie) and to interact socially with other adults and peers.

Instead of "one giant step" into the mainstream environment, smaller steps might have included one or several classroom visits with Chuck and Annmarie, with just the teacher present. Gradually, Patrick could have developed a sense of familiarity and comfort with the setting and the teacher. After that, the teacher, with one or two peers, could have played the "games" Patrick engaged in with his father. This gradual approach to integration would represent adaptations to the social environment. Rather than placing the "demands" of the environment on Patrick, the environment would be adapted to meet the needs of Patrick. The gradual approach to integration and a focus on competencies versus deficits would also reflect attention to the needs of the whole child (i.e., emotional, psychological, social, etc.) versus focusing on the more narrow self-help and academic needs. Patrick's negative experience with integration in a mainstream classroom may have been avoided – or at least minimized – if recommended practices had been followed.

# 2

# EVOLVING THEMES AND SPECIAL CONCERNS

## Contemporary research and "recommended practices"

Serious attempts have been made over the past decade – as early childhood special education has been evolving into a field of its own – to identify quality indicators that might be used as standards for the field. Some of these attempts have resulted in the identification of "critical features" of effective early intervention programs (Council for Exceptional Children, 1988) and the publication of "best practice" guidelines for the field (McDonnell & Hardman, 1988). A recent publication (Odom & McLean, 1996) presents accepted/recommended practices in fourteen strands of early intervention/early childhood special education: assessment, family participation, individual education plan/individual family service plan (IEP/IFSP), service–delivery system, curriculum and intervention strategies, cognitive competence, communication intervention, social/emotional development, motor skills, adaptive behavior skills, transition, gifted children, personnel preparation, and program evaluation. This comprehensive volume by Odom and McLean (1996) is the result of a five-year study that brought together experts/researchers, practitioners, and parents to reach consensus on best practices in the field.

The following quality indicators represent a subset of the "recommended practices" presented in the literature and might be used as initial guidelines for developing and/or evaluating programs and services for young children with special educational needs. This list is certainly not exhaustive, but is representative of the critical features which define effective early intervention programs.

- Young children with disabilities are viewed as active learners who are capable of constructing their own knowledge in environments offering alternative ways to explore and experience the world around them.
- Young children with special educational needs are generally served in inclusive settings – i.e., in regular education classrooms alongside their typically developing peers.

- The integration of young children with special educational needs is planned and implemented in *all* aspects of the program, including the physical, instructional, and social dimensions of the classrooms.
- Young children with special educational needs are best served when professionals work together as a transdisciplinary team.
- Individual instructional goals are fostered through the activities of a developmentally appropriate curriculum.
- The interests, priorities, and resources of the community are reflected in instructional materials and daily activities.
- Instructional materials and daily activities reflect an understanding and appreciation of diversity in various dimensions of the human community (e.g., gender, race, culture, etc.).
- Professionals work with parents as full partners in educational planning and decision making and, in the process, recognize and support a variety of family structures and priorities.
- Careful planning guides the process of transitioning a child from home to school and from one educational setting to another.
- An ongoing process of assessment is used to identify strengths and resources and to monitor development of each child with special educational needs.
- Child assessment is an individualized process and is shaped by child characteristics and diagnostic concerns, as well as by family priorities and information needs.

## The challenge of merging regular education and special education

The field of early intervention evolved from a medical or therapeutic model rather than from educational perspectives. As such, its focus has often been on the remediation of skill deficits in children who are not developing normally on their own. In an effort to help the child with delays to "catch up" with their typically developing peers, special education teachers have often used highly directive teaching methods, including drill, or rote learning, and the teaching of isolated skills (Widerstrom, 1986).

This approach is in direct contrast with the philosophy and practices of most early childhood programs where learning through child-initiated activities and discovery are emphasized. These philosophical and instructional differences produce "inevitable conflict" when attempts are made to embed early intervention services in typical early childhood classrooms (Widerstrom, 1986). Such conflict can be viewed as a formidable roadblock to effective programming, or as a healthy challenge with potential benefits to all involved. There follows a discussion of some of the challenges and a brief summary of the issues involved. More discussion is

26

devoted to Challenge 1 than any of the other "challenges," as it relates to the primary issue that must be addressed in serving young children with disabilities in an inclusive early childhood program and because it overlaps with some of the other challenges presented in this section.

- *Challenge 1: Integrating developmentally appropriate practices with exceptionality appropriate practices.* Developmentally appropriate practices (DAPs) are characterized, in large part, by active exploration and interactions with learning activities and materials that are concrete, real, and relevant to young children (Bredekamp, 1987; Bredekamp & Copple, 1997). Such activities and materials are designed to be both age appropriate and individually appropriate – i.e., both chronological age and developmental age are given consideration in planning activities and providing materials. Other considerations in a DAP program include children's interests, cultural backgrounds, and special abilities. DAP settings tend to avoid teacher-directed activities and direct instruction. A major goal of DAP is to enable children to construct their own knowledge.

The DAP approach is considered a good context in which inter-vention for children with disabilities can be provided (Howard *et al.*, 1994). To effectively meet the needs of children with disabilities, however, the DAP approach must, at times, be integrated with exceptionality appropriate practices. This means that, for some child-ren, the DAP guidelines may require adaptations or modifications. It also means that, at times, "children's experiences will need to be facilitated using strategies and adult behaviors not described in the [DAP] guidelines" (Wolery, 1994, pp. 100–101). Such behaviors sometimes include direct instruction.

A primary role of early childhood personnel in working with children with disabilities is to adapt the environment in ways which will motivate them to explore the environment and to experience success in doing so. This requires close observation of the child interacting with his or her environment over time and in multiple settings (e.g., classroom, home, clinic, etc.). It also requires talking with others, especially parents, about their observations of how the child interacts with his or her environment and being attentive to their concerns and suggestions about how to foster the child's competence and confidence in exploring the environment.

In the classroom, the early childhood teacher needs to facilitate the interactions children have with toys, materials, activities, peers, and adults. Such interactions, if successful, develop understandings about the world and the way it works, and helps the child gain feelings of self-worth and competency. Such experiences also help the child enjoy learning and provide incentives for further explorations. By supporting and facilitating the interaction between the child with special educational needs with his or her environment, the teacher, in essence, combines the roles of early childhood educator and special educator. The teacher uses information about the child's disability and his or her developmental level to determine the degree to which intervention is necessary to facilitate the child–environment interaction.

While the curriculum in a DAP program is both child-initiated and teacher-directed, the extent of teacher directedness is often greater for the child with special needs than for his or her typically developing peers. The degree of teacher direction or direct instruction appropriate for any one child depends on that child's need for adult support. Children vary considerably in their ability to interact meaningfully with their environment and to assume increasingly more responsibility for their own learning. Direct instruction, when used appropriately, does not negate the DAP orientation; it augments it. Some confusion exists as to how this can be so. Kostelnik (1992) addresses this and other sources of confusion relating to DAP. Myths about DAP "represent collective opinions that are based on false assumptions or are the product of fallacious reasoning" (Kostelnik, 1992, p. 1). Some of these myths evolved from attempts to simplify a complex concept. Other myths are related to a superficial understanding of child development and/or learning-related theories and research. Kostelnik (1992) outlines nine different myths. The following three seem to be especially pertinent to the merging of DAP and exceptionality appropriate practices.

- *Myth*: There is only one right way to implement a developmentally appropriate program. If this myth were true, there would be one method of teaching that suits all children and all situations. Obviously this is not the case, as the appropriateness of individual teaching episodes depends on a number of different variables, including the child's current level of development, his or her experiential background, and his or her interest and confidence in learning something new. Other variables relating to the appropriateness of individual teaching episodes include such contextual elements as the nature of the physical environment, the availability of material resources, the values and expectations of the school and community, and time available for a learning activity. For children with special educational needs, additional variables might include the child's physical, emotional, or cognitive limitations. Factoring in these limitations and adjusting the curriculum and environment accordingly is what exceptionality appropriate practices is all about. Thus the concept that there is only one right way to implement a developmentally appropriate curriculum is false.

- *Myth*: In developmentally appropriate classrooms, teachers do not teach. This myth is based on a stereotypic idea of what a teacher does – that is, provide large-group instruction primarily by telling the students what they need to know. This image of a teacher is certainly in conflict with both early childhood education and special education. Teachers in an early childhood classroom know that they "teach" in a variety of direct and indirect ways. They create physical environments and establish daily schedules that encourage children to engage in meaningful learning activities. While some large-group activities take place, teachers spend much of their time moving about the classroom and interacting with children individually and in small informal groups. The focus is on facilitating learning through self-discovery and exploration. Some of the instructional techniques which teachers use during these informal teaching episodes include: (1) posing thought-provoking questions; (2) providing information as requested and/or appropriate; (3) suggesting additional and/or extended explorations, and (4) presenting physical, social, and/or cognitive challenges. These techniques are designed to help children move beyond their current understandings and skill achievement levels.

This "early childhood" approach to teaching is quite consistent with the philosophy and goals of special education and is thus not in conflict with the merging of DAP and exceptionality appropriate practices. One of the tenets of special education is to identify the child's current level of functioning and then begin instruction at that point, with the goal of moving him or her toward more complex understandings and skill achievement levels. This approach often works best through individual and small group instruction – instruction that, while teacher-facilitated, need not always be teacher-directed. As indicated earlier, the extent of teacher-directedness is determined by the needs of individual children. Thus, teachers in DAP classrooms do indeed teach, but do so in a variety of ways to best meet the needs of all children.

- *Myth*: Developmentally appropriate programs are suitable for only certain kinds of children. Because DAP programs are designed to be both age appropriate and individually appropriate, there is "no group for whom the basic tenets of developmentally appropriate practices do not apply" (Kostelnik, 1992, p. 6), including children with disabilities. The original publication outlining DAP has been criticized for failing to provide enough guidance for meeting the needs of children with disabilities. A second edition (Bredekamp & Copple, 1997) addresses this concern. One of the concepts emphasized in this revised edition is the importance of having age-appropriate expectations which are flexible with modifications (accommodations) and/or adaptations. In this way, both the age-appropriate and individual-appropriate aspects of DAP can be honored. As such, DAP programs can be suitable for a wide variety of children, including children with disabilities. More discussion on how to adapt a DAP program for children with special educational needs is presented in Chapters 11 and 12.

- *Challenge 2: Utilizing the expertise and resources of different disciplines and agencies while maintaining integration and consistency.* When young children with special education needs are included in early childhood programs with typically developing children, special education staff and early childhood staff clearly must work together to best serve the children with disabilities and their families. For many young children with SEN, the extent and complexity of their needs require the involvement of professionals from other disciplines as well, such as speech/language pathologists, physical therapists, etc. At times, professionals from different agencies are also involved. Crossing discipline and agency boundaries often entails special challenges for early childhood personnel.

  While the quality of services provided for a child with SEN can be greatly enhanced by the involvement of professionals from multiple disciplines, there is a danger that such services can also be quite splintered and uncoordinated. This tends to be the case when professionals from different disciplines work from a multidisciplinary versus transdisciplinary model of interaction. In a multidisciplinary model, professionals from different disciplines serve the same child and family but do so without coordinating their efforts. The result, as experienced by the child and family, is a lack of integration and consistency. At times, conflicting messages and suggestions can actually result in confusion and added stress for all involved.

  In a transdisciplinary model, professionals from different disciplines not only work to coordinate their efforts, but also share their disciplinary knowledge and skill expertise with each other. Further information about the special benefits and challenges of transdisciplinary teaming is presented in Part III of this book. Suggestions on how to implement this model are also presented. (See especially Chapter 7.)

- *Challenge 3: Implementing a play-based curriculum with children with widely varying levels of play skills.* As stated, recommended practices indicate that the integration of young children with special educational needs is planned and implemented in all aspects of the program, including the physical, instructional, and social dimensions of the classroom. In a developmentally appropriate program, child-initiated play is the primary context for all three of these dimensions. Thus, a child with poorly developed, or "primitive," play skills is likely to have difficulty in the various dimensions of inclusion. While most typically developing children play with a variety of toys and materials and learn to interact with others during play situations without anyone "teaching" them how to do so, young children with SEN often require the intervention of adults to show them how to play (Widerstrom, 1986; Wolery & Wilbers, 1994).

In addition to teaching children with SEN how to play, early childhood personnel must also be concerned with the fact that there are varying levels of play and that these differing levels often determine with whom children choose to be engaged during play situations. Typically developing children tend to interact more readily and frequently with children who are similar to, rather than different from, themselves. The greater the difference in the children, the less likely are interactions (Stoneman, 1993; Wolery & Wilbers, 1994). A major challenge of early childhood personnel, then, is to plan and implement ways in which children with special educational needs can be meaningfully included in play situations with their typically developing peers using age-appropriate materials.

- *Challenge 4: Achieving social integration among a group of children with widely varying levels of social interaction skills.* Research findings indicate that young children with and without disabilities generally do not engage in high levels of social interaction with one another unless they are encouraged and supported in doing so (Odom & McEvoy, 1988; Wolery & Wilbers, 1994). Factors frequently associated with this lack of interaction include language and cognitive delays, poorly developed play skills, and behavior disorders on the part of the children with SEN. It takes a great deal of energy and creativity on the part of early childhood educators to achieve social integration between children with special educational needs and their typically developing peers, as the levels of social interaction skills of these two groups generally differ to a significant extent. Ideas on how to address these concerns are presented in various sections of this book, especially Chapters 5 and 12.

- *Challenge 5: Preserving the intensity of instruction needed to ensure educational benefit while also preserving the essential qualities of a developmentally appropriate approach.* Inclusive intervention models which rely primarily on the regular education teacher for day-to-day implementation are sometimes criticized for compromising intensity of instruction. As stated in the literature, "the intense needs of young children with severe disabilities challenge the boundaries of prac-titioner knowledge and organizational supports, and, for some, their commitment to integration and inclusion" (Salisbury *et al.*, 1994, p. 312). This concern should not be taken lightly. Children with SEN have "significantly greater difficulty in learning than the majority of children of the same age" and because of their disability are prevented or hindered from "making use of educational facilities of a kind provided for children of the same age" (DFE, 1994, p. 5). Without appropriately intense intervention, children with SEN will not reach their potential in their current learning situation nor in their life-long accomplishments.

The challenge of early childhood personnel working in inclusive settings is to integrate the child-initiation aspects of quality early childhood education with specific intervention strategies for children with SEN. Left to their own initiative, many children with SEN would not make sufficient progress toward their individual goals and objectives, nor would they experience full inclusion in the various dimensions of the early childhood classroom. Thus, early childhood personnel working in inclusive settings need to be both facilitators of child-initiated learning and intervenors for children with SEN in situations where more teacher direction is needed. By definition, children with SEN require intervention services (DFE, 1994). Such services, although somewhat different in inclusive early childhood versus separate special education settings, should not be less intensive.

A related concern, however, is to focus too exclusively on the accomplishment of individual goals and objectives and to rely too heavily on teacher-organized and teacher-directed activities. The result of this more "special education" approach tends to be isolated skill learning at the expense of child-directedness and autonomy. This approach can also result in an exclusive versus inclusive experience for the child with SEN, even though the program is organizationally designed to be a "mainstream" classroom. Another undesirable result of the more traditional special education approach is an over-reliance on external structure and an accompanying weakness in the ability to make choices (Sainato & Lyon, 1989).

- *Challenge 6: Implementing inclusive classrooms in schools and communities unfamiliar or opposed to the concept of inclusion.* To be truly effective, the process of inclusion needs to occur "within the larger context of a school where there is a clear philosophical foundation, teaming practices, and a commitment to shared decision making" (Salisbury *et al.*, 1994, p. 319). Unfortunately, not all schools and communities value the inclusion and/or teaming model of intervention. Even though national mandates and policies call for the provision of intervention services in mainstream schools (DFE, 1994), laws alone are insufficient for changing attitudes.

Opponents of inclusive classrooms often refer to barriers that inhibit effectiveness of this approach. As outlined by Odom and McEvoy (1990), such barriers include: (1) lack of adequate training in general and special early education; (2) philosophical differences between the two disciplines; (3) lack of related services in many programs (e.g., speech/language therapy, physical therapy, etc.); (4) lack of monitoring systems, and (5) negative staff attitudes. Additional barriers that have been identified by other researchers include the emphasis on academic achievement in the educational reform movement, competition for shrinking fiscal resources, lack of flexibility in teachers' contracts, and lack of clear policy directives (Strain & Smith, 1993). All of these identified barriers are, indeed, real issues, and need to be addressed in planning and implementing inclusive programs for young children with SEN. Unless these barriers to inclusion are adequately addressed, it will be difficult to convince reluctant schools and communities to move toward, or adopt, the inclusive approach.

- *Challenge 7: Documenting the positive outcomes of individualized curricular accommodations.* Curricular adaptations are usually designed to serve two main goals: (1) to promote positive child outcomes, and (2) to optimize the physical, social, and instructional inclusion of the child in ongoing classroom activities (Salisbury *et al.*, 1994). Do adaptations in an inclusive program actually achieve these goals? Results of studies relating to each of these outcomes lend support to the effectiveness of the "inclusion-with-modifications" model (Salisbury *et al.*, 1994). Further studies, however, are certainly warranted. Such studies would do well to focus on the effects and perceived value of the process by stakeholder groups, including school administrators, teachers, and parents (Salisbury *et al.*, 1994).

The following "standards" should be considered when evaluating the relative success of individualized curriculum accommodations: (1) efficient acquisition and use of important skills; (2) high levels of child engagement throughout the day; (3) parents' satisfaction with the manner and outcomes of instruction; (4) student participation in activities that are preferred or valued by the student, friends, or family members, and (5) increased participation in classroom activities (Salisbury *et al.*, 1994).

Without sufficient documentation of the positive outcomes of individualized curricular accommodations, teachers may have difficulty deciding whether or not particular strategies are working, and may thus not be consistent in the use of such strategies. Teachers may also have difficulty informing parents and other members of the intervention team about child progress toward instructional goals and objectives. Additionally, without sufficient documentation, legislators, school administrators, and other policy makers may not be convinced of the effectiveness of the inclusion model, and may thus withhold their support of such programs.

- *Challenge 8: Easing the transition from home- to school-based learning and from one school setting to another.* Transitioning a child from home- to school-based learning is often accompanied by a great deal of uncertainty and anxiety. All parents want their children to feel comfortable and competent when they enter school, yet there is no way to build in assurance that this will be the case. While this is true whether or not a child has a disability, the concerns are certainly magnified for children with special educational needs. Common concerns expressed by parents of children with disabilities relate to (1) medical fragility and/or special health conditions (e.g., seizures, asthma, immune deficiency, etc.); (2) peer acceptance and making friends; (3) participation in group activities (e.g., listening to stories, playing group games, etc.), and (4) fear and distress in separating from parents.

  The transition from home- to school-based learning places new expectations and demands on the child and family. Both child and family must become acquainted with new people in their lives and adjust to new schedules. Parents know there will be certain school-related behaviors that their child will be expected to adopt. They may be concerned about whether or not their child will follow directions, eat and toilet independently, and respond socially to other children. Parents may also be concerned about their child's safety. Will he or she be helped and supported on playground equipment? Will medications and adaptive equipment be used correctly? Will the other children play too roughly?

  Parents, too, will be faced with new expectations as their child enters school. They will be expected to be informed of and involved in their child's educational program. For some parents this can be intimidating – either because of the added time and energy investment this will entail, or because of their uncertainty or lack of confidence in how to relate to professionals.

  The transitioning of a child with SEN from one educational setting to another can also generate a great deal of uncertainty and anxiety on the part of all involved – child, family, teachers, and the rest of the intervention team. This uncertainty and anxiety can be minimized by viewing transition not as a single event, but rather as an ongoing process, beginning at least six months before a child leaves a program (the "sending" program) and continuing throughout the child's adjustment to the new program (the "receiving" program).

While most children experience some anxiety about moving on to a new classroom or school, reasons for such anxiety are usually greater for children with special educational needs. For typically developing children, emotional support, in the form of reassurance, is usually sufficient to ease the transition enough for them to move on with the likelihood of success in the new environment. Concern for children with SEN, however, "must go beyond their initial emotional adjustment to the transition" (Atwater *et al.*, 1994, p. 168). This is due, in large part, to the fact that children with developmental delays often have considerable difficulty transferring what they have learned from familiar to unfamiliar settings. In dealing with new routines, different activities, and unfamiliar people, children with SEN often fail to demonstrate competencies that they developed over time in their more familiar settings.

The consequences of transition difficulties for children with SEN should not be taken lightly. "The child experiencing such difficulties is at a serious disadvantage for learning more complex skills, being a full participant in the activities of the new setting, and forming positive relationships with new teachers and peers" (Atwater *et al.*, p. 168). Children with SEN are also at increased risk of further delays, behavior problems, and future placement in more restrictive (i.e., separate special education classes) versus inclusive settings (Hanline, 1993b).

Early childhood professionals, then, need not only to plan and implement a quality instructional program, but also to ease the transition to their program from the home setting and from their program to the next educational placement. The special needs of the children and families must be considered at each of these transitions. Unless these transitions are successful, the benefits of the program to the parents and the children will be considerably limited. Some ideas on how to ease this transition are presented in Chapter 10.

- *Challenge 9: Identifying and assessing children with special educational needs in a timely and least intrusive manner and involving the family in a respectful and meaningful way.* The term "assessment" is sometimes used interchangeably with "testing." This usage is misleading, as assessment has a broader meaning than testing. Assessment – which may include, but is not equivalent to, testing – might be defined as the "process of systematically gathering information about a child" (Wolery, 1994, p. 71). To protect the child's and the family's basic rights, certain guidelines for assessment have been developed by the early childhood profession. One such guideline relates to the purpose of conducting an assessment – i.e., unless the purpose is clear, assessment activities should not occur (Wolery, 1994).

There are, of course, a number of reasons for assessing young children, including screening them to identify developmental delays and disabilities, determining a specific diagnosis, determining eligibility for special services, planning educational programs, monitoring progress, and evaluating the effects of the early childhood services. Gathering information for one of these purposes may not be useful or appropriate for another. For example, information gathered during screening may not be useful for planning the child's educational program. Thus it is very important to clarify the reason(s) for assessment prior to initiating the assessment process.

Once the reason for assessment is clearly defined, the process of conducting an assessment must be determined. Recommended practices in the field indicate that this process should be as unintrusive as possible and should involve the family in a respectful and meaningful way. As indicated by the Department for Education *Code of Practice*, this includes conducting the assessment "in a place where the child and family feel comfortable" (DFE, 1994, p. 99). At times, this may mean the child's home, a playgroup setting, or the facility of another community program or agency (e.g., day care/nursery school, health clinic, etc.). Alternative assessment arrangements may be especially important for children under the age of two.

Parent involvement is another critical component of recommended practices for assessing young children. "The parental perspective is particularly important for children under five" (DFE, 1994, p. 99). Obtaining this parental perspective, while respecting their privacy and being sensitive to their feelings, is usually quite challenging for educators.

Recommended practices for assessing young children differ considerably from assessment practices typically used with older children. With younger children, a transdisciplinary play-based assessment is recommended (Linder, 1993). Professionals from a more traditional professional background often find the play-based approach especially difficult, in both theory and practice. This difficulty presents a special challenge for the field.

Another special challenge relating to assessment has to do with timeliness. Once the need (i.e., purpose) for assessment is determined, the process should be initiated in a timely manner, especially if the purpose is to screen for special educational needs and to determine the type of services required. According to the DFE *Code of Practice*,

> The importance of early identification, assessment and provision for any child who may have special educational needs cannot be over-emphasised. The earlier action is taken, the more responsive the child is likely to be, and the more

readily can intervention be made without undue disruption to the organisation of the school, including the delivery of the curriculum for that particular child.

(DFE, 1994, p. 10)

The process, then, of identifying and assessing children with special educational needs presents a special challenge for educators involved in early intervention. See Chapter 9 for further discussion about this challenge and related recommended practices.

- *Challenge 10: Assisting families as they cope and adapt to the challenges of having a child with a disability*. In addition to enhancing child development, family education and support are primary goals of early intervention. The rationale for family education and support is rooted in the understanding of the home as the child's first and most important learning environment. Early childhood educators and child development specialists generally recognize that the home environment plays a major role in shaping the child's overall development. Influential aspects of this environment are both physical and emotional, and include opportunities for stimulation and exploration, parent–child interactions, peer and sibling relationships, and contextual aspects of the neighborhood community.

  Having a child with a disability greatly impacts on the family and the way it functions. Family education and support activities provided through early intervention programs are generally designed to assist families as they cope with and adapt to the challenges of having a child with a disability. Many such programs are also designed to enable and empower families to be effective decision makers in relation to the special educational needs of their children in present and future circumstances (Dunst *et al.*, 1988). See Chapter 8 for more information and ideas for working with families of children with special needs.

- *Challenge 11: Recognizing and respecting the diversity of families in the types of parent education and involvement options available to them*. One of the philosophical foundations of recommended practices in early childhood special education relates to the diversity of families, and is grounded in the belief that "each family has its own culture and a unique set of strengths, values, skills, expectations, and service needs" (Bailey, 1994, p. 28). Thus, just as the individualized needs of children with SEN require an individualized educational program for them, so do the unique characteristics of families (including their priorities and values) establish the need for a variety of parent education and involvement options. To best serve the needs of the families, these options must reflect an understanding and appreciation of the diversity that exists among families. Obviously, planning parent education and involvement programs with diversity in mind is much more challenging than offering one plan which parents are expected to adopt and participate in.

- *Challenge 12: Growing with the profession.* Early childhood special education, as noted earlier, is a young and evolving field. Model programs and recommended practices are still being developed, as are teacher education and other personnel preparation programs. While research is constantly being conducted, much more is still required. Keeping up with new understandings and developments is thus one of the challenges of professionals in the field.

## Case study – Tara

### Background information

Tara's parents realized that she was not hearing well when she was 6 months old. Tara was not responding differentially to sounds (e.g., looking up when the doorbell rang or turning toward someone when her name was called), nor was she playing with the sound of her own voice (e.g., babbling, cooing, etc.). Audiological testing indicated that she had a moderate to profound hearing loss.

Through home-based early intervention services, Tara and her parents were introduced to signing (i.e., the use of sign language) before her second birthday. Tara also started wearing hearing aids by the age of two. The response to both the signing and the amplification (i.e., hearing aids) was very positive. Amplification benefits, however, seemed to be limited to discriminating high volume environmental sounds versus aiding in understanding speech.

At age 4, Tara participated in a mainstream Reception class and did quite well in making friends, playing cooperatively with others, making choices, and showing initiative in play activities. She communicated with her parents primarily through signing, and with her teachers and friends through a combination of gestures, signs, and utterances. Special support was provided by a special education teacher and Tara's mother, who each spent one afternoon a week in the classroom to help the teacher and the other children learn some signing and other ways to communicate effectively with Tara. A speech/language therapist also provided consultation and assistance on a regular basis.

After the Reception year, Tara was enrolled in a mainstream Year I classroom. A major concern at this time related to a more academically focused curriculum, with a heavier emphasis on language and literacy than that to which Tara was exposed in the Reception year. The Year 1 classroom teacher was not skilled in signing and was quite concerned about meeting Tara's special educational needs.

An intervention team meeting was held prior to the first week of school. Attending the meeting were Tara's parents, the classroom teacher, the special education resource teacher, the speech/language pathologist, and the Reception year classroom teacher. During the meeting, all shared ideas on what environmental and curricular modifications would be most helpful to Tara. Decisions were made to introduce Tara (and her parents) to computers and picture communication boards (i.e., visual devices using pictures or symbols to represent communicative ideas). It was also decided that the speech/language pathologist would work with Tara's classroom teacher and classmates to teach them about what it means to be hearing impaired and to help them learn some basic signs. Both the speech/language pathologist and the special education resource teacher would work with Tara (along with the classroom teacher) to develop beginning reading and writing skills and would encourage her to begin using these skills to enhance her communication abilities.

Discussion during the meeting also focused on how to assure full integration for Tara – i.e., in the instructional and social aspects of the program as well as the physical. Questions were raised about how Tara might participate meaningfully in music and drama as well as in classroom discussions and cooperative small group learning activities. Because of her warm and outgoing personality, there was little concern about Tara being able to make friends. All agreed, however, that this would have to be monitored carefully, with observations about such things as whether or not Tara was being invited to classmates' birthday parties and if other children were reaching out to her during both indoor and outdoor play activities.

### Discussion

In spite of the challenges that faced Tara and the intervention team as she entered Year 1, there were a number of factors enhancing

Tara's chances for success. The intervention team was working from a transdisciplinary approach where there was a back-and-forth sharing of discipline-specific information, ideas, and skills. Parents were viewed as equal-status members of this team and had been involved as such during Tara's preschool years. This transdisciplinary approach with active parent involvement contributed to consistency and intensity of instruction.

Another factor supporting Tara's chances of success in the school setting was the understanding that full inclusion means more than physical integration. For Tara to do well in the regular classroom, she would need understanding, acceptance, and ways to communicate effectively. She would also need to learn what the other children were learning (e.g., reading, writing, math, science, etc.), even though alternative methods would have to be introduced. These alternative methods included sign language, the use of a communication board individualized to Tara's situation, and computer-assisted instruction. The use of these alternative methods to help Tara benefit from the regular curriculum represents a merging of developmentally appropriate practices with exceptionality appropriate practices.

The transdisciplinary approach to teaming, efforts to assure full inclusion, and the merging of developmentally appropriate practices with exceptionality appropriate practices will enhance Tara's chances of success as she makes her way through Year 1. As planning alone is no assurance of success, the classroom teacher, along with other members of the team, are aware of the need to closely monitor Tara's progress. The combination of careful planning, effective implementation, and ongoing assessment represents a critical component of intervention services for young children with special educational needs. As these elements were in place for Tara, her chances of doing well during Year 1 are quite good.

# Part II

# IDENTIFYING THE ISSUES

How we view children and the ways in which they develop and learn influences, to a large extent, the types of educational programs we provide for them. While there are varying perspectives on how young children go through the process of development and learning, the developmental perspective lays the philosophical groundwork for what is generally viewed as "recommended practices" in the field of early childhood education and early childhood special education.

This section of the book begins with a description of the developmental perspective on human growth and development and presents a discussion of how this perspective relates to educational programming both for children who are developing typically and children with atypical development. Major principles and patterns of growth and development are presented, as are concerns relating to the impact of different disabling conditions on the process of development and learning. Because disabling conditions impact not only on the individual child with the disability but on his or her family as well, Part II addresses some of the special concerns relating to parenting, parent–child interactions, and the maintenance of a healthy home environment when faced with the challenge of meeting the needs of a child with a disability.

Also presented in this section is an outline of the different types of "risk factors," the etiologies (or causes) of disabilities, and different categories of disabling conditions. Finally, there is a discussion about how some disabilities, especially secondary handicaps, might be prevented. While most of the discussion in this section addresses complex issues relating to the nature and impact of disabling conditions, the implications for educational programming that are presented stress the importance of viewing the young child with a disability from a developmental rather than a "deficit" perspective. This means remembering that young children with special needs are children first – i.e., children who have many of the same characteristics and needs as typically developing children. They possess a set of complex skills or competencies, learn through active involvement with the environment, and need the opportunity and encouragement to explore and interact with their environment in positive ways.

# 3

# TYPICAL AND EXCEPTIONAL EARLY DEVELOPMENT

Human development is a fascinating and complex phenomenon. The most remarkable changes that occur during this process do so between the time of human conception and the first few years of school. An understanding of these changes – and the basic patterns in which they occur – is a critical aspect of what it means to be an early childhood professional.

Without sufficient knowledge of developmental patterns for physical growth, as well as cognitive, language, and social/emotional development, early childhood educators will be seriously hampered in making wise decisions for young children and their families. Knowledge of developmental patterns should guide decisions relating to such critical factors as: (1) screening and assessing young children to identify special educational needs; (2) selecting materials and activities that are appropriate for the developmental level of children while fostering maturation to the next levels; (3) selecting appropriate intervention objectives and strategies for young children with SEN, and (4) providing accurate and timely information and advice to parents.

## A developmental perspective

Cultivating a thorough understanding of how human beings develop is a complex process and cannot be accomplished in a short period of time. Fortunately, there are many quality resources available relating to human development. While professionals should not regard these resources as substitutes for their own expertise, they can look to such resources to supplement a soundly established understanding of the way human beings develop. There follows a brief discussion of a developmental perspective on child growth and development, which – according to recommended practices in the field – is the perspective with the most promise for guiding wise decision making for young children and their families (Odom & McLean, 1996).

Parents of young children are often asked about the age of their child. Age is also the determining factor for participation in many educational and recreational programs – e.g., a child must be at least 4 years old to participate in the Reception class and at least 5 to enter Key Stage 1 of the National Curriculum in the UK. While age is one aspect of child development, it is a critical error to equate development with age.

Development is far more complex than age. Age marks the passage of time – i.e., how much time has elapsed since the child's birth or, when talking about prenatal development, how much time has elapsed since conception. Development, however, occurs when the complexity of a child's behavior increases (Allen & Marotz, 1989). For example, when a child's play behavior moves from simply holding and manipulating toy dishes to pretending to cook and eat while using these toys, we can say that cognitive development has occurred. Similarly, when a child's balance and coordination improve to where he or she can kick a ball while running versus being able to kick a ball only from a stationary position, we can say that motor development has occurred.

Just as development is not the same as age, neither is it the same as maturation. Maturation refers to the universal sequence of biological changes that occur as one ages. Increased height represents one visible example of maturation. Maturation is closely related to development, in that maturation permits the development of psychological functions (Howard *et al.*, 1997). Certain psychological functions would never occur without sufficient maturation preceding it. The development of language is an example. The brain must first develop sufficiently before infants become capable of understanding and producing language. A child with severe brain damage may thus be prevented from ever developing a broad repertoire of language skills. While language stimulation plays a critical role in the development of language, sufficient neurological maturation is also required. One without the other will not accomplish the task.

Misunderstandings about the maturation/stimulation relationship sometimes lead to inappropriate practices in intervention. It would be inappropriate, for example, to avoid working toward individual goals in the area most affected by the child's disability on the premise that he or she will never achieve sufficient neurological maturation to accomplish the desired goals anyway. If the goals are important to the child's successful functioning, alternative routes to accomplishing the goals should be identified. In the case of a child with severe brain damage who may be prevented from ever developing a broad repertoire of language skills, the goal of successful communication must still be pursued. Similarly, if the severity of a physical disability prohibits a child from ever writing his or her name, alternative methods of providing a personal signature should be explored.

Just as *misunderstandings* about the maturation/stimulation relationship might lead to inappropriate practices, a clear *understanding* of this connection can provide valuable guidance to educators working with both typically developing children and children with special educational needs. When working from a developmental perspective, professionals consider both maturation and stimulation to be critical factors in identifying appropriate educational objectives and strategies. Unless children are neurologically and/or physically "ready" for certain accomplishments, it is not appropriate to expect nor "teach" related behaviors. Trying to teach a child to read before he or she can differentiate between similar but different symbols (e.g., the letters "m" and "n") is inappropriate. Elkind (1987) refers to attempts to teach young children skills before they are ready as "miseducation" and suggests that this practice puts children at both psychological and physical risk.

Developmental milestones play a role in our understanding of the developmental perspective on human development. Developmental milestones represent major indexes of developmental accomplishments and are based on the average age at which children acquire certain skills or pass through certain stages. Developmental milestones have been identified across developmental areas (e.g., cognition, language, social skills, etc.) and are often used as guides for expectations in the different areas of development. For example, a typically developing child who has learned to pull himself up to a standing position while holding on to a piece of furniture can be expected to begin "walking" with support (i.e., either the support of holding on to someone's hand or the support of holding on to the furniture) in a relatively short period of time.

For children without disabilities, a listing of developmental milestones can thus be used in relation to expected ages at which they will develop certain skills. The norm (i.e., average age) for accomplishing the developmental milestone of independent sitting, for example, is six months. Some children – even those without disabilities – take longer to develop this skill, while others accomplish independent sitting before six months of age. Thus, a "range of normalcy," versus a simple average (i.e., the "norm"), should be used in relation to expectations. While the norm for independent sitting is six months, the range of normalcy is four to eight months.

The range of normalcy for developmental milestones should be clearly understood by all early childhood professionals and should be used as a guide in talking with parents about their child's development and appropriate expectations. An understanding of developmental milestones and the range of normalcy should also be used in helping to identify children who may not be developing at an expected rate. If developmental milestones do not occur within the range of normalcy, a child may be at risk of developmental delays. When this occurs, the child should be assessed to determine eligibility for special education services.

## Normal developmental patterns

As indicated earlier, human development is a very complex phenomenon – certainly more complex than a listing of developmental milestones might suggest. Part of the complexity relates to the interaction between environment (i.e., stimulation) and maturation as experienced by the child. Through decades of observation and research, certain principles relating to normal developmental patterns have been identified. There follow six such principles with a brief discussion of each. An understanding of these principles can be critical to making informed decisions about assessment procedures, instructional strategies, and curricular materials, whether working with children with disabilities or with typically developing children.

- *Principle 1: Humans at all levels of development possess a set of complex skills or competencies.* All living organisms are competent, in that they have the capacity to react to environmental stimuli. Infants, very young children, and individuals with severe disabilties, however, are not always viewed as being competent. What they *cannot do* often overshadows what they *can do*. This perspective is not in the best interests of the child, and should certainly be avoided in intervention programs.

  While any one individual possesses competencies unique to his or her development, there are also certain competencies that are practically universal. These competencies include the ability to learn new behaviors, to solve problems, and to adapt to changes in the environment (Howard *et al.*, 1997). Professionals working with young children with special educational needs would do well to identify the skills or competencies of the child, build on these skills to enhance the child's feelings of confidence and competence, and plan educational programs that focus on competencies versus deficits. A competency-based approach to intervention recognizes and values the child's contributions to the learning process. As presented in Chapter 5, this competency-based approach is especially important in fostering the social and communication development of the child.

- *Principle 2: Humans at all levels of development are active learners.* Active learners construct their own knowledge versus passively receiving it from others; and humans at all levels of development can be active learners. This principle underscores the importance of designing intervention strategies that recognize the involvement and contributions of the child to the instructional process. Teachers should thus be viewed as facilitators of learning versus instructors of knowledge. An important aspect of the teacher's role is to encourage and stimulate children to engage in exploratory and problem-solving activities.

In her essays on teaching and learning, Eleanor Duckworth (1987) talks about "the having of wonderful ideas" as "the essence of intellectual development" (p. 1), and indicates that the role of the teacher is to provide occasions for children to have such ideas. The "wonderful ideas" that Duckworth refers to need not necessarily look wonderful to the outside world. She sees "no difference in kind between wonderful ideas that many people have already had, and wonderful ideas that nobody has yet happened upon" (p. 14). The nature of the creative intellectual act remains the same. Duckworth does go on to say, however, that "the more we help children to have their wonderful ideas and to feel good about themselves for having them, the more likely it is that they will some day happen upon wonderful ideas that no one else has happened upon before" (p. 14).

- *Principle 3: No area of functioning develops in isolation from other areas.* We often refer to different developmental domains (e.g., social, physical, cognitive, etc.) as if they were separate areas of development. This reference, however, can be misleading and may contribute to inappropriate practices in intervention. Assessment and instructional strategies should be based on the understanding that "independent areas and skills cannot be examined separately or in isolation; rather the whole of the child's development and the interrelatedness of developmental areas must be considered" (Hanson & Lynch, 1995, p. 6). Thus, if a child shows developmental delays in the area of social skills, other areas that should be carefully assessed include language and cognitive development. This recommendation is based on the fact that the child's social difficulties may be due primarily to deficits in the use of language – e.g., not knowing how to use language to express feelings and ideas. Cognitive delays may also play a major role in how a child relates to others. For example, if adults and peers use vocabulary and sentence structure that the child does not understand, or they use representational materials in play and other instructional activities that the child cannot relate to, he or she may respond by withdrawing or "acting out." In either case, the child may be labeled as having "social problems," whereas the concerns with social development may be in response to language and/or cognitive deficits. Focusing on the development of language skills and/or considering the child's level of cognitive functioning in relation to expectations and learning activities may allieviate the child's social problems much more effectively than implementing a "behavioral intervention" plan.

Understanding that no area of functioning develops in isolation from other areas also lends support to the rationale for early intervention. By intervening early, the likelihood of secondary impairments developing in related areas is reduced. For example, a child with language delays may become so frustrated in his attempts to communicate effectively that he may begin using physical force to express his feelings of frustration and to get what he wants and/or needs. The pattern of using physical force may become an established form of behavior that, before long, this child is not only language delayed, but "behavior disordered" as well. The behavior disorder is an example of a secondary impairment that developed in response to an earlier existing disability. Early intervention focusing on the development of more effective communication skills may have prevented the development of this secondary impairment.

- *Principle 4: Skill development proceeds from unspecialized to specialized functioning.* The pattern of human development has been likened to that of a tree (Lewis, 1984). The trunk of the tree – with primarily an undifferentiated functioning role – develops prior to the branches and leaves which perform more differentiated roles. Likewise, in human beings the pattern of skill development moves from unspecialized to specialized functioning. Thus, for a young child, generalized skills (e.g., whole-hand grasping) develop prior to specialized skills (e.g., holding small items with thumb and forefinger).

  Understanding that human development moves from unspecialized to specialized functioning is of considerable importance when working with children with disabilities (Hanson & Lynch, 1995). It can be particularly useful in determining appropriate goals and objectives for children with special educational needs and planning intervention strategies that focus on present and emerging stages of development. Without an understanding of this pattern of development, parents and professionals may base their intervention efforts on unrealistic expectations and involve the child in inappropriate instructional strategies. For example, milestones in language development include "naming familiar objects" and "describing objects." An analysis of these two skills indicates that "naming familiar objects" is less specialized than "describing objects." If a child has neither of these skills in his or her language repertoire, it would be unrealistic and inappropriate to make "describing objects" a current instructional goal for the child. A realistic goal might be for the child to begin naming objects with which he or she is familiar.

- *Principle 5: Human development occurs in a predictable pattern.* This principle of human development builds on the understanding presented in Principle 4 – i.e., skill development moves from unspecialized to specialized functioning. The predictable pattern or sequence of human development is applicable to both children with and without disabilities. What varies is the individual timing of reaching certain developmental milestones. An understanding of this principle also has important implications for individual goal setting, as discussed with Principle 4.

- *Principle 6: Human development represents an interactive process between an individual's status at any point in time and the environment in which the individual is immersed.* Because the environment plays a critical role in human development, the quality of the environment in which an individual is immersed can determine, in large part, the extent to which his or her potential is reached. "Favorable conditions enable children to reach the high end of their potential, while unfavorable conditions can depress development toward the lower end of the range of a child's potential" (Howard *et al.*, 1997, p. 46). What are favorable or unfavorable environmental conditions, however, can vary in some instances from child to child. An environment rich in visual beauty or imagery may be favorable for many children. A child who is blind, however, may receive very little or no benefit from such an environment.

  This principle, then, has considerable importance for serving young children with disabilities. As already indicated in Chapter 1, a disability may or may not be a handicap for a child, depending upon the specific circumstances or demands of the environment. If the demands of the environment create problems for the child in his or her efforts to function and interact with that environment, then the disability becomes a handicap and gets in the way of allowing the child to reach his or her potential. Professionals working with children with disabilities need to adapt the environment in ways which allow the child with special educational needs to experience, explore, and interact with the environment in positive ways. An enriched environment means nothing to a child who cannot interact effectively with it.

## Atypical developmental patterns

A major difficulty in describing the development of a young child who is developing atypically (i.e., in a way that is not typical or not normal) begins with the problem of trying to define "atypical." The literature on atypical development includes children who range from those born prematurely to those with multiple and severe disorders. Thus, children with atypical developmental patterns "represent an extremely heterogeneous group, one from which clustering for the purposes of testing and analysis becomes difficult at best" (Hanson, 1996, p. 162). The most that testing and analysis generally offer is an indication that some children are not developing normally, rather than identifying how their developmental processes differ (Hanson, 1996).

49

By definition, children with special education needs fail to develop in concert with their typically developing peers. In one or more areas of development, children with SEN fail to accomplish developmental milestones within the range of normalcy. As indicated earlier, for many children with SEN, the sequence of skill development is the same as their typically developing peers; what differs is the age at which such skills are developed. At times, however, the nature of the child's disability prevents the child from ever accomplishing certain skills. An obvious example is a child who is profoundly deaf who will never be able to accomplish certain auditory discrimination skills. The important thing to keep in mind, however, is that such a child can develop other sensory discrimination skills and accomplish many related cognitive and adaptive living goals through alternative routes.

Atypical developmental patterns are sometimes grouped into three general categories: delays, disorders, and giftedness. Individual children may experience just one or a combination of these conditions. Many children with developmental delays and/or disorders are eligible for special education services for all or part of their academic careers. For some children with SEN, participation in an early intervention program minimizes the impact of the delay and/or disorder, to the point where they can later function successfully in a regular education program without any further special support services. While giftedness represents an atypical developmental pattern, it does not qualify children for special education services. The special needs of children who are gifted, however, should not be overlooked. There follows a brief discussion of the three general categories of atypical development (i.e., delays, disorders, and giftedness).

### Delays

Children with delays are those who experience delayed or slow progress in reaching developmental milestones in one or more areas of development, such as communication, cognition, adaptive behavior (i.e., feeding, dressing, toileting, etc.), physical development, and social/emotional development. The extent of delay is determined by comparing the child's actual performance level with his or her chronological age. For example, a child who is 50 months old (i.e., 4 years and two months) but receives an age-equivalent score of 40 months (i.e., 3 years, 4 months) in the area of communication is considered to have a ten-month delay in communication development.

In addition to using an age differential (e.g., the ten-month delay) to describe the extent of a child's delay, other quantitative descriptions sometimes used include (1) percentage of delay, and (2) standard deviations from the mean. For the child who is 50 months old but scores at

40 months on an age-equivalent measure of performance, the extent of delay would be 20%.

Determining a standard deviation from the mean requires the use of an assessment instrument where standardized scores are obtained. A standardized score is a score that has been transformed to fit a normal curve of development, with a mean (i.e., average) and standard deviation that remain the same across ages. In the overall population, most individuals score at or near the mean. As scores deviate from the mean (either greater than or less than), fewer instances of those scores will be observed. At a certain point, such deviations indicate atypical development.

The term "standard deviation" is used to describe how far a score is from the mean (either above or below). As displayed in Figure 3.1, within the normal curve model, one standard deviation on either side of the mean encompasses approximately 34% of individuals in a group. Two standard deviations on either side of the mean would encompass 48% of individuals in a group. Thus, for a child to score at one standard deviation below the mean would suggest that his or her performance was better than 16% of the total population, while a score of two standard deviations below the mean would suggest that his or her performance was better than only 2% of the total population. While standard deviations are sometimes used in the process of determining eligibility for special education

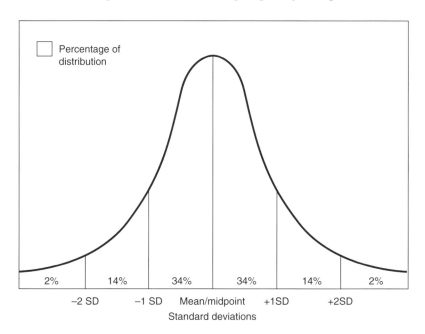

*Figure 3.1* Normal curve

services, the use of standardized assessment measures to get standardized scores is under a great deal of criticism, especially for young children (NAEYC, 1986, 1988; NAEYC & NAECS/SDE, 1991; Raver, 1991). Reasons for this criticism and other issues related to screening and assessment are presented in Chapter 9.

How delays are quantified or referred to is certainly not as important as how to provide the most advantageous educational program for children with developmental delays. Such programs should be designed to minimize the extent of delay and to ward off the development of secondary handicaps.

## Disorders

A "disorder," in terms of growth and development, refers to a condition that disrupts or changes the order of a child's developmental progress. A disorder differs from a delay, in that a child with a developmental delay falls significantly behind developmental norms but still proceeds through the normal sequence of development. A child with a disorder, however, will not experience the same order of development in one or more developmental domains. Due to the disruption to normal development, a child with a disorder may require alternate routes for achieving certain basic living skills. For example, a child with a serious motor impairment (i.e., disorder) may never be able to walk. He or she may still achieve independent mobility, however, by learning to use a motorized chair.

Disorders for which there is documented, descriptive information on child development include visual impairment, hearing impairment, motor impairment, and Down syndrome. Most children with any of these disorders will also experience developmental delays in one or more areas of development. Educational programs should consider both the disorder and the accompanying delay(s) in planning and implementing intervention strategies. While intervention programs cannot remove the disorder itself, they can minimize the negative impact of the disorder on the child's development.

## Gifted

Atypical development includes not only children with developmental delays or disorders who tend to fall below the norm in one or more areas of development, but also children who perform significantly above the norm or have the potential for such performance. While nearly every early education program has children who are gifted, identifying such children is often difficult (Cook et al., 1996). Characteristics to look for in identifying children who are potentially gifted include a large vocabulary, a high level of curiosity, a good memory, and an ability to concentrate intensely and for long periods of time. Such children also tend to learn rapidly, show a mature sense of humor, and enjoy the challenge of problem solving and abstract thinking (Cook *et al.*, 1996). While the needs of many young children who are gifted can be met through the enrichment of a quality regular early education environment, special encouragement from adults can add depth and breadth to their experiences.

Early recognition and nurturance of children's special talents and abilities may foster not only their cognitive and creative abilities, but their mental health as well. A substantial body of research indicates that "the optimal years for child development in such areas as self-esteem and self-image, social competence, specific cognitive abilities, and achievement motivation are birth through 8 years" (Stile, 1996, p. 310). Without appropriate early intervention, young children who are gifted may be at increased risk of poor self-concepts, the development of behavior problems, and underachievement, or failure to perform in relation to their potential. Early intervention for young children who are gifted should include activities and materials that enhance creativity, promote higher cognitive processes, engage the child in problem solving and inquiry, and promote affective and social development (Cook *et al.*, 1996).

## Risk conditions

Certain conditions place children at increased risk of experiencing atypical development in the form of delays and/or disorders. These "risk conditions" are sometimes grouped into three general and overlapping categories: established risk, biological risk, and environmental risk.

- *Established risk* refers to medical and/or neurological disorders and includes such conditions as Down syndrome and Fragile X syndrome. These conditions often have a known etiology (source) and a relatively predictable pattern of development that is associated with some level of developmental delay.
- *Biological risk* includes those conditions in which there is a history of complications and/or concerns in prenatal, perinatal, neonatal, or early development. Prenatal refers to the time of conception to birth, while perinatal refers to the time immediately before, during, and soon after birth. Neonatal represents the period from birth to 30 days of age, while early development refers to the first few years of life. Complications or concerns during any of these periods often relate to some type of insult or injury to the central nervous system. Children with biological risk include those born prematurely, those who are small for gestational age, and those who were prenatally exposed to harmful substances (e.g., drugs, alcohol, etc.).
- *Environmental risk* refers to situations and conditions in the child's life

that tend to interfere with healthy development. Examples include poor nutrition, physical or psychological abuse, and conditions normally associated with living in poverty (e.g., overcrowding, frequent moves, increased exposure to environmental toxins, minimal access to stimulating materials, etc.).

There are a number of disabling conditions which may be due to established risk, biological risk, environmental risk, or a combination of these different areas of risk. Such conditions include motor impairments, sensory impairments (e.g., deafness, blindness), delayed development, and chronic health problems. These and other types of disabilities, along with their impact on development, will be discussed further in Chapters 4, 5, and 6.

---

## Case study – Michael

### *Background information*

Michael, age 7, lives in a small apartment of an older building in the "slum" section of a city with his mother and twin siblings who are just one year younger than Michael. Michael has cerebral palsy and has considerable difficulty with mobility and balance. He wears a leg brace and uses a walker to enhance his mobility skills. At school, he also uses special adaptive equipment for positioning and balance while seated. Michael does well at school, his favorite subjects being reading and science. He also enjoys computers and has been communicating with a pen pal in Australia by way of e-mail. Michael and his pen pal like to share information about the natural environment in their respective countries and about special environmental concerns in their local communities. In addition to being identified as a student with special educational needs due to his physical disability, Michael has also been identified as being gifted.

The intervention team working with Michael recognized his special talents and interests during his Reception Year of school. They decided at that time to introduce him to computers and use his interest in science and the environment to motivate him to learn computer skills. Michael caught on quickly and was soon reading and writing at a level far beyond his classmates.

*Discussion*

Michael was environmentally at risk for special education needs even before he was born. His mother was young, single, and living in poverty. The cerebral palsy, evident soon after birth, placed him in the established risk category as well. But Michael's exceptionalities also included giftedness. To help Michael achieve his potential, the intervention team looked at all aspects of Michael's situation. They knew that, due to his cerebral palsy, Michael would have motor difficulties. Not wanting this to interfere with reaching his potential, the early intervention team made sure that Michael had the appropriate adaptive equipment to provide the necessary support while working at the computer and using other instructional materials. Computer-assisted instruction allowed Michael to pursue his special areas of interest in greater depth than most of his peers could benefit from. While motor control problems prevented him from doing well at "paper work" assignments, an enlarged keyboard made it possible for him to type his work on the computer. Thus, both curricular and physical adaptations were used in the classroom to meet Michael's special needs in the areas of motor development and giftedness.

# 4

# SENSORY, PHYSICAL, AND NEUROLOGICAL CONCERNS

Sensory, physical, and neurological concerns represent a variety of areas that place a child at risk for special educational needs. Conditions relating to these concerns are often present at, or soon after, birth. Such conditions include significant infection and genetic syndromes (e.g., Down syndrome).

Presented in this chapter are discussions relating to some of the more common sensory, physical, and neurological concerns, including vision problems, hearing problems, orthopedic impairments, and other health-related problems. Chapter 5 will address concerns in other areas of development, namely social/emotional, speech/language, and cognitive domains. While separate sections are devoted to each of these concerns, an important concept to keep in mind is that development across domains does not occur in isolation. Thus, a concern or impairment in one area will often affect development and functioning in another area. Additionally, what is sometimes considered a skill or milestone in one developmental domain can also be viewed as a skill or milestone in one or more areas of development. For example, asking for help when it is needed is often considered a milestone in the language/communication area of development, but it can also be viewed as having significance for social/emotional development. Discussions presented in Chapters 4 and 5 relating to various areas of development should thus be viewed as only one of several possible ways to categorize areas of disability. The overlapping aspects of development should also be kept in mind. The two areas of sensory impairments – i.e., vision and hearing – are presented first. While vision and hearing impairments are considered to be "low incident" handicapping conditions for the general population, among young children with SEN they are common findings (Howard *et al.*, 1997).

# Vision problems

## *Types of vision problems*

Vision problems take many forms, with widely varying implications for a child's development and academic performance. Such problems range from relatively minor and remediable conditions to total blindness. The time of onset also varies and plays a major role in the child's ability to adapt socially and psychologically, as well as to achieve academic success.

Vision problems can be related to visual acuity and/or peripheral field of vision. Visual acuity refers to the distance at which a person can discriminate an object in relation to the distance at which a person with average visual acuity (20/20) can discriminate the same object. An individual with 20/90 visual acuity, for example, would be able to see accurately only up to 20 feet (6 metres) what a person with average visual acuity could see as far away as 90 feet (27 metres). A person is considered legally blind if his or her visual acuity is 20/200 or less in the best eye with correction. A person is also considered legally blind if his or her peripheral field of vision is 20 degrees or less, even though visual acuity might be normal.

Legal blindness is a relatively low incidence disability, occurring approximately only once per one thousand people. Blindness, however, is not the only vision problem causing a child to have special educational needs. Low vision (where visual acuity is 20/70 or less in the best eye with correction) can also be a significant factor negatively affecting a child's development and learning. In fact, approximately 30% to 70% of children with severe visual loss experience special educational needs (Kirchner, 1988).

The incidence of both visual impairment and blindness seems to be rising (Kirchner, 1988). This may be due, in part, to the increased survival rate of premature and low birth weight infants and to the increased numbers of children living in poverty. Many cases of blindness and serious visual impairment – especially in instances where the condition seems to be related to poor environmental conditions – are considered preventable. In fact, as many as two out of three cases might be prevented through control of infection and malnutrition (Howard *et al.*, 1997).

Although assessing actual visual acuity in infants is very difficult, there are indications that newborns do not have 20/20 vision. In fact, the average visual acuity of newborns is estimated to be about 20/200. Acuity gradually improves but probably does not reach 20/20 until about the age of 5. The term "developmental visual impairment" is sometimes used in reference to the vision status of children under the age of 5 (Howard *et al.*, 1997).

## Impact on development

Children who are visually impaired often experience delays in other areas of development as well. Delays in cognitive development are common. This is due, in part, to the fact that children with visual impairments cannot rely on their sense of vision to give them reliable information about their world. Without such information, it is difficult for children to construct knowledge about the world in which they live.

Another factor negatively affecting the cognitive development of children with visual disabilities is the fact that by not seeing what is available for exploration and manipulation, they are not adequately motivated to become engaged with the world outside themselves. Thus, they "miss out on" not only the information available through the medium of vision, but information from other channels of learning as well. For example, if a child with a visual impairment cannot see the funnel and cup in the sandbox or what other children are doing with them, he or she may not be motivated to explore the potential of these materials.

Normal vision is thus a significant factor in encouraging or motivating a child to explore his or her world. Additionally, seeing the world around them fosters the development of visual memory in young children and enables them to feel "'safe' in exploring their world" (Howard et al., 1997). Children with visual impairments do not have the opportunity to develop this visual memory and may thus feel unsafe or insecure in relating to new materials, new places, and new circumstances. The reluctance often observed in children with visual impairments suggests that this may be true.

In addition to the negative impact on cognitive development, visual impairments tend to imperil other areas of development as well, especially language and social development. Eye contact, so critical for social and language interactions, is often absent or only minimally present for children with visual impairments. Also absent is the ability to see mouth movements involved in producing speech. Thus young children who are blind or visually impaired often experience speech delays and/or disorders. Because children with visual impairments have difficulty seeing the nonverbal aspects of communication, they also experience difficulties associated with both the expressive and receptive aspects of effective conversation. These speech, language, and social interaction difficulties can lead to self-orientation and/or social isolation, which are typical characteristics of children with visual impairments (Hoon, 1991).

Motor difficulties are also common in children who are blind or visually impaired. These difficulties are usually evidenced in both gross motor and fine motor development. Gross motor skills involve the movement and control of large muscle groups and affect such activities as walking, kicking, jumping, etc. Fine motor skills involve the movement and control of small muscle groups to perform such actions as grasping and manipulating a variety of materials. Children who are visually impaired are usually hampered in such fine motor activities as working switches, folding paper, and buttoning buttons. As normal mobility is impeded for children who are blind or visually impaired, they sometimes develop hypotonic muscle tone (i.e., low muscle tone leading to "excessive" versus "controlled" joint movements), stereotypical behaviors (e.g., rocking), and postural abnormalities (e.g., leaning to one side when standing and/or walking, tilting the head, etc.).

### Intervention strategies

Early intervention for children who are blind or visually impaired should focus primarily on helping them make the best use of their residual vision (i.e., the visual ability remaining to an individual with a visual loss) (Howard *et al.*, 1997). Related instructional strategies should teach children with visual impairments to "pay attention" to relevant visual stimuli as they seek new information (Morse, 1991). Children with visual impairments must also learn to apply previously gained information to new situations. For example, if a child with a visual impairment discovers that some doorways mark a change in elevation (i.e., a step up or a step down) or type of floor covering (e.g., from carpeting to tiles), he or she should learn to take this into consideration when walking through unfamiliar doorways.

One of the ways adults can help children with visual impairments to use their residual vision is to limit the amount of assistance they provide. Generally, assistance should be provided only in situations where safety and/or success call for intervention (Howard *et al.*, 1997). If assistance is provided when the child would be able to figure things out on his or her own, a form of "learned helplessness" may hinder the child from exploring his or her environment and moving about independently.

Special instruction in orientation and mobility skills can also help children with visual impairments to make use of their residual vision and increase their ability to explore and move about independently. Orientation involves an awareness of space and the environment, especially in terms of one's own body position in space. Through orientation training, children are taught to take advantage of their other senses (i.e., touch, hearing, smell, etc.) to replace sight in learning about their environment and their body's position in that environment. For example, by becoming more aware of the breeze across the face and the sound of wind in the trees, a child with a visual impairment may deduce that he or she is near an open window.

By pairing orientation with mobility training, children are taught to move about their environment with confidence, independence, and a sense of purpose. For example, a child who is blind can learn to move from the classroom to the cafeteria independently by orienting him- or herself in the right direction (e.g., turn left when leaving the classroom) and then using his or her hand against the wall to "follow the path" to the cafeteria (e.g., perhaps going past two more doorways before entering the cafeteria). In addition to using one's hand and other body parts, other types of aids that can be used to increase mobility for children with visual impairments include canes, "walking ropes," and large push toys.

Walking ropes consist of one or two ropes running horizontally that serve as tactile guides for individuals moving from one place to another. While one could be used along the wall to help a child find his way to the cafeteria, it would have the disadvantage of "broken space" when crossing open doorways. Additionally, the walking rope may provide more assistance than the child really needs. If the child can learn to use his or her hand along the wall, the walking rope should not be installed. In fact, the use of walking ropes has been criticized as an example of "overmodification" of the environment. The presence of walking ropes "may interfere with the children's awareness of normal environmental features, which can provide generalizable clues for orientation to the environment and independent mobility" (Lang & Deitz, 1990, p. 4). However, for some children, the wall alone may not provide enough assurance that they are on the right path. Masking tape along the wall could serve as a modified and less intrusive guide. Out of doors, however, walking ropes may be necessary to help children with visual impairments feel safe and "oriented" to their surroundings.

Large push toys, such as sturdy toy grocery carts, can be used to provide support while walking. Using a push toy when moving from one place to another can help a child feel safe from falls and bumps. The use of a push toy instead of a cane or walker for this purpose is less intrusive, in that when used appropriately, it does not make the child with a visual impairment appear different from the other children.

To prevent or minimize the development of secondary disabilities, intervention should also focus on fostering motor, language, and social skills. A variety of enriching experiences with activities, materials, and interactions that involve residual vision as well as the other senses (i.e., auditory, kinesthetic, tactile, and olfactory) should be provided. At all times, the goal should be to increase the child's confidence and competence in interacting with his or her physical and social environment.

### Classroom/school adaptations

Adaptations in the classroom and other areas of the school will certainly have to be made for children with visual impairments to enable them to be active learners in a fully inclusive way. Classroom teachers working with children who are blind or visually impaired will usually have access to a qualified teacher of the visually impaired and/or a mobility officer qualified to work with visually impaired children. Such specialists can be of considerable assistance and should become an integral part of the transdisciplinary team serving the child who is visually impaired.

In addition to the use of mobility devices (such as the examples provided above), other adaptations and suggestions that may be helpful for children with visual impairments include the following:

- When moving through unfamiliar or crowded areas, pair the child who is blind with a sighted guide (either an adult or peer).
- Use handrails, lighting and contrast application, uncluttered pathways, and more tactile and auditory stimuli to help the child orient to his or her surroundings.
- Provide modified eating utensils to prevent or minimize spillage.
- Provide appropriate information technology, such as voice synthesizers linked to computers.
- Allow the child more time to accomplish certain tasks.
- Define classroom areas (e.g., block area, book area, etc.), work space (e.g., portion of a table top, etc.), and personal space (e.g., "cubbie," "locker," etc.) with easily identified cues, as needed. Such cues could include brightly colored tape, carpet squares, concrete objects, and "work trays."
- Provide additional tactile, auditory, and olfactory cues to materials, activities, and communicative exchanges, as needed. For example, in addition to putting your finger over your mouth to ask for quiet, use an auditory signal as well. One way to adapt materials is to add "texture" cues to games or toys, such as a sandpaper square glued next to the "start" button for a music box.
- Place objects at the child's level and encourage him or her to examine them tactually. The other children in the class could be involved in a similar activity by having them feel and describe items in a "feelie" bag.

## Hearing problems

### *Types of hearing problems*

A significant number of young children experience some degree of hearing problem. These problems may be temporary or permanent, but either way are likely to cause learning difficulties. Temporary hearing losses are usually caused by otitis media (middle ear disease), which is believed to affect over 75% of children within the first two years of life (Northern & Downs, 1984). Permanent hearing losses are usually sensori-neural (i.e., resulting from damage to the cochlea or auditory nerve) and vary from mild to profound. Children with a severe hearing loss usually experience major communication problems. They often experience other significant academic and social problems as well.

The two major types of hearing loss are conductive and sensori-neural. With a conductive hearing loss, there is a disruption of the mechanical conduction of sound as it is transferred through the outer ear to the middle ear. Most causes of conductive hearing loss (which in most instances is otitis media) can be treated through medical intervention. To avoid developmental and learning problems, however, educational intervention is also warranted in many cases. A comprehensive model for addressing the developmental and educational concerns relating to otitis media has been developed by Johnson (1981) and seems to offer some promise of positive long-term benefits (Mandell & Johnson, 1984).

While serious sensori-neural loss is related to genetic inheritance in approximately 70–80% of cases, noise pollution can also lead to sensori-neural loss. There are some indications that even the ambient noise in incubators – if not closely monitored – can cause some hearing loss in premature infants (Howard *et al.*, 1997).

## Impact on development

Due to the strong, positive relationship between hearing and language development, early detection of hearing loss is critical. Such detection, however, does not occur on a regular basis. Even though the critical period for language development is during the first three years of life, as many as 50% of infants with hearing impairments are not identified until much later (Howard *et al.*, 1997). By then, serious language and learning problems may already exist.

Indicators of a hearing loss in young children include failing to react to loud noises, difficulty in localizing the source of sound, and delayed acquisition of language milestones. Hearing losses are sometimes mis-diagnosed as cognitive delays, as children with hearing losses fail to respond to language stimuli (e.g., questions, commands, greetings, etc.) and to use age-appropriate expressive language (e.g., naming and/or describing things, providing information, etc.). When tested on nonverbal measures, however, children with hearing losses generally score within the normal range of intelligence.

## Intervention strategies

Decisions about medical and educational interventions should be based on a number of different factors including etiology, location, severity of damage, and time of onset of the hearing loss. The educational intervention for young children with hearing impairments should focus on both the use of residual hearing and on language development. In many cases, an augmentative communication system should be introduced early. An augmentative communication system augments, or adds to, a traditional or mainstream communication system (e.g., the English language). Sign language and the use of "communication boards" are examples of augmentative communication systems often used with individuals who are hearing impaired. Sign language, which uses hand gestures to communicate, is widely used by individuals who are deaf. It is very important that children with hearing losses who are introduced to sign language also learn to make use of residual hearing, lip-reading, and oral speech to communicate. The method of combining manual signs with oral means of communication is referred to as "total communication" and is the method most frequently used when introducing children to an augmentative communication system.

Communication boards are visual devices utilizing pictures or symbols to represent communicative ideas. Communication boards can be elaborate and expensive electronic devices or simple, home-made constructions. Some teachers and parents make communication boards by using a flat piece of cardboard and a set of pictures representing simple items, places, and activities familiar to the child. Once the pictures are attached to the board, the child simply points to individual pictures to tell others what he or she needs or wants. Thus, by pointing to a picture of a bathroom, a child can inform the teacher that he or she needs to use the bathroom. Similarly, by pointing to a picture of a TV, a child can ask his or her parents if he or she can watch a TV program.

In addition to the use of an augmentative communication system, auditory assistive devices can also be used to enhance the development and learning of a child with a hearing loss. Hearing aids and sound field amplification systems represent two different types of auditory assistive devices. Both hearing aids and sound field systems amplify sound but do not replace natural hearing.

Hearing aids amplify sound for the individual person wearing the aid. Most hearing aids have the disadvantage of amplifying all environmental sounds, including distracting or interfering noises. Hearing aids also tend to distort sounds. Thus, for a young child still learning the intricacies of spoken language, the sounds amplified through his or her hearing aid may include the dog barking, the fan humming, and the mother talking. In this case, the child may have great difficulty attending to the sound of the mother's voice. Even when the child does attend and can discriminate between relevant and irrelevant sounds, he or she may still not hear the mother correctly, due to sound distortions. If the mother says "now" the child may hear only the "ow" sound and not understand the intent of her message. He or she may thus choose to ignore the fact that she is speaking to him or her. When adults are unaware of the child's hearing difficulties (even after amplification), they may mistakenly read this response (or non-response) as misbehavior. This, of course, will be frustrating for both the child and the adults working with that child.

Sound distortions, which often accompany the use of hearing aids, may lead to speech and language problems as well. If a child cannot hear a word correctly, he or she has no consistent model on which to base the pronunciation of words. Additionally, the child often has difficulty learning the rules of language, including sentence structure, the use of pronouns, plurals, etc.

Sound field amplification systems differ from hearing aids in that they amplify sound throughout a designated space, such as a classroom, rather than to just one specific individual. When sound field amplification is used in the classroom, the teacher wears a small wireless microphone, which can be switched on and off as needed. Two or more speakers are placed strategically in the classroom. When the microphone is on, the teacher's voice is amplified throughout the room. The extent of amplification is usually about 10 decibels, which is just enough to help the students attend to the teacher's voice while disregarding irrelevant environmental sounds (e.g., students coughing, carts moving in the hall, nearby traffic noise, etc.).

One of the major disadvantages to the use of sound field amplification in the classroom is that only the speaker's voice is amplified. While this may be fine for instruction at higher grade levels, for instruction with young children this raises some concerns. As much learning occurs through interactions with other students, amplifying only the teacher's voice provides limited assistance for a child with a hearing impairment.

Because classroom use of sound field amplification has only recently been made feasible through advances in technology, the body of research related to its effects is limited. However, most of the studies investigating the effects of sound field amplification in classrooms provides support for its use as an instructional tool (Linton, 1995). Research findings suggest that the use of sound field amplification can (1) improve the academic performance of children with learning disabilities in mainstream settings (Ray et al., 1986); (2) improve the test-taking skills of students, including students with minimal hearing loss (Burgener, 1980); (3) reduce the number of children referred for special education services (Osborn et al., 1992); (4) have a positive effect on students' behavior (Linton, 1995), and (5) reduce teacher stress in the classroom (Linton, 1995; Wilson, 1988). As articulated by Wilson (1988) and Linton (1995), a major caution in using sound field amplification with young children relates to the appropriate use of this technology. Young children need to be engaged in active, hands-on experiences and not be expected just to sit and listen. The teacher's voice should thus not dominate the classroom throughout the day. If sound field amplification is used with young children, teachers should be clearly aware of when to use it (e.g., during a large group activity) and when it is not appropriate to do so (e.g., when children are working alone or in small groups).

## Classroom/school adaptations

Serving children with hearing impairments in the regular classroom does require some special accommodations. In addition to the possible use of amplification systems (i.e., hearing aids and/or sound field amplification), other recommendations presented in the *Code of Practice* (DFE, 1994) include:

- taking the advice of appropriate external specialists, including teachers of the deaf;
- positioning the child in the class for maximum auditory reception;
- arranging paired activities with hearing children or adults;
- alerting all teachers and adults in the school to the child's hearing difficulty and making them aware of basic measures they should take to overcome or circumvent that difficulty;
- seeking the views of and involving the child's parents at each stage of educational programming;
- exploring "the possible benefits of, and where practicable secured access for the child to, appropriate information technology, for example word processing facilities, painting programs and other software which uses the visual power of the computer, providing training in the use of that technology for the child, his or her parents and staff, so that the child is able to use that technology across the curriculum in school, and wherever appropriate, at home" (DFE, 1994, p. 63).

Additional recommendations suggested by Harrington and Meyers (1992) include:

- obtaining oral interpreters and/or sign interpreters as needed for children with profound deafness;
- adapting classrooms so that ceilings and walls use acoustical tiles, floors are carpeted, and visible fire alarm systems are installed;
- furnishing classes with captioning equipment and telecommunication devices (TDD) to interact with parents who are deaf and members of the deaf community.

## Orthopedic/neurological impairments

The term "orthopedic" refers primarily to bones and joints, while the term "neurological" is used in reference to the nervous system. Impairments in these two areas are addressed together in this section as they both represent body systems that affect physical functioning.

Many orthopedic and neurological impairments experienced by young children are present at, or soon after, birth. Such impairments include seizure disorder, cerebral palsy (CP), autism, attention deficit disorder (ADD) and attention deficit hyperactivity disorder (ADHD), and such syndromes as Down syndrome. There follows a brief description of each of these conditions along with some information as to how these conditions may impact on development. While some recommendations on how to adapt a program for children with such impairments are also presented, more detailed discussion relating to program adaptations can be found in Chapters 11 and 12.

### Seizure disorder

Seizure disorder is a chronic disorder of the nervous system often characterized by seizures (i.e., sudden attacks of involuntary muscle spasms) associated with abnormal electrical activity of the brain cells. Seizures can range from mild to severe and can occur either frequently (e.g., several times a day) or infrequently (e.g., once or twice a year). While seizures can occur at any time over the span of one's life, they tend to occur more frequently during the neonatal period than at any other time (Ensher & Clark, 1986; Raver, 1991).

A person who has a seizure may have epilepsy, but this is not necessarily the case. Epilepsy is a condition in which seizures are recurrent and where the seizures are not provoked by external stimuli (e.g., exposure to toxins, insult or injury to the central nervous system, metabolic disturbances, etc.). For persons who do not have epilepsy, seizures are sometimes triggered by such external events. It has been suggested that all human beings have a threshold for seizures, beyond which a clinical seizure will occur (Brunquell, 1994). For most, these thresholds are so high that the experiences of normal life will not push them past these limits. Individuals with very low thresholds, however, sometimes experience multiple daily seizures (Howard *et al.*, 1997).

Approximately one in ten people will have a seizure at least once in a lifetime. In childhood, approximately one in a hundred children has recurring seizures (Laybourn & Hill, 1994). Children with a seizure disorder often experience some other form of neurological damage as well. Conditions associated with seizure disorders include congenital and postnatal infections, fetal distress, perinatal trauma, head injuries, and chromosomal abnormalities (Howard *et al.*, 1997).

While not all children with seizure disorders experience cognitive impairments, children with seizures do tend to have diminished concentration and mental processing (Dam, 1990). Additionally, each seizure can cause further brain injury, especially when they last for 15 minutes or more. Various drugs used to treat seizure disorders can also have a negative impact on a child's development. Undesirable side-effects of some of these drugs include a tendency for children to be hyperactive and a reduction in cognitive functioning (Dichter, 1994).

Parents and teachers are sometimes inclined to treat children with seizure disorders differently. They may, for example, try to keep children with seizure disorders away from such potentially dangerous situations as traffic, water, and crowded areas. While careful monitoring is always important, children with seizure disorders should generally participate in the same activities as their siblings and peers.

When seizures do occur, adults should respond by remembering that the typical seizure is not a medical emergency. The best response is to remain calm and protect the child from getting hurt. To do this, carefully lower the child to the floor and clear the area of anything that might cause injury to the child. Place something flat and soft under the child's head, turn the child on his or her side, and then wait until the seizure is over. Do not interfere with the child's movements and do not try to put anything in the child's mouth. When the muscle spasms stop, let the child rest for a short period of time. Assure the child and those around him or her that everything will be all right.

### Cerebral palsy

Cerebral palsy (CP) occurs in about 1.5 to 2.7 per 1000 live births, making it one of the most common disabilities in our society (Howard *et al.*, 1997). CP results from brain injury sustained during the early stages of development and affects muscle tone, movement reflexes, and posture. The nature and extent of disability resulting from CP differs considerably from one individual to another. CP can affect one or both sides of the body and can result in high muscle tone (hypertonia), low muscle tone (hypotonia), or spasticity (the tendency to have sudden, involuntary contractions of the muscles). Conditions related to high muscle tone, or hypertonia, include shortened muscles and ligaments, with eventual restrictions on joint movement. Over time, this can lead to joint dislocation, deformities of the spine, and contractures (Bigge, 1991).

Low muscle tone, or hypotonia, is usually characterized by weakness, "floppiness," poor posture, and hypermobile joints. Children with low muscle tone sometimes need external support for positioning and mobility and are usually delayed in motor skill development.

Spasticity is characterized by a tightening of the muscles and a resistance to movement. Spastic movement has been described as a "jack-knife" response, where joints first express hyper-resistance to extension or flexion up to a certain threshold, then a sudden release of resistance.

CP is not a progressive disease, in that the damage to the brain does not get worse over time. Related physical deformities, however, can get progressively worse, especially if appropriate intervention is not provided early in life.

Children with CP are usually diagnosed as having a severe, moderate, or mild disability based on the severity of involvement. Thus, "a diagnosis of cerebral palsy is almost meaningless unless it is also paired with a description of the degree . . . to which a child is affected motorically" (Howard *et al.*, 1997, p. 158). With a diagnosis of severe CP, the child will usually experience total dependence in meeting physical needs, is likely to have poor head control, and will often be prevented from achieving academic and age-appropriate motor skills. With moderate CP, the child will usually achieve some independence in meeting physical needs, will have functional head control, and will probably experience some perceptual and/or sensory integrative deficits. Such deficits often interfere with achieving academic and age-appropriate motor skills. With mild CP, the child will likely achieve independence in meeting physical needs and, with therapy intervention, have the potential for improving the quality of motor and/or perceptual skills. Without effective intervention, however, regression in motor and perceptual skills may occur.

Most children with CP experience some difficulty with self-help skills. Feeding difficulty is an especially common and troublesome problem. Estimates are that approximately 50% of children with CP experience feeding problems and 48% have growth retardation (Thommessen *et al.*, 1991). Some of the problems related to feeding include poor swallowing and chewing, poor self-feeding skills, and long, tiresome feeding sessions. Due to the feeding difficulties, it is not unusual for children with CP to be on restricted diets, consisting in large part of pureed or powdered foods. Such diets are often unappealing and offer little incentive for expending energy for self-feeding and/or cooperation in assisted feeding: "Subsequently, children's energy intake and nutritional status are frequently compromised" (Howard *et al.*, 1997, p. 159), often leading to problems with growth patterns and developmental progress.

Because CP is caused by damage to the brain, some people mistakenly believe that CP inevitably involves mental retardation as well. This is not true. While children with CP are more likely to experience some cognitive deficits and/or delayed development in sensorimotor behaviors than children without CP (Cioni *et al.*, 1993), it is important to understand that not all children with CP have intellectual deficits. It is also important to consider that the motoric limits to exploring and interacting with the environment experienced by children with CP may be as much a factor in the delayed development in sensorimotor behaviors as mental retardation resulting from brain damage. A critical consideration in intervention for children with CP, then, is finding ways to facilitate their interaction with the environment, so as to enhance their opportunities for cognitive development and other types of learning.

Another important consideration when working with children with CP is appropriate handling and positioning. High muscle tone and spasticity can make certain activities, such as dressing, very difficult. Appropriate handling for children with high muscle tone may involve strategies to relax the child's muscles, including gentle stroking, soft lighting, music, and a soothing voice. Appropriate handling for a child with low muscle tone usually involves strategies to support the child during an activity. In feeding, for example, proper head positioning and support may make a notable difference as to how well the child eats and how he or she feels about the experience.

Other important considerations in working with children with CP include:

- working closely with occupational and physical therapists as members of the intervention team;
- positioning the child for maximum safety, support, and inclusion in the instructional and social dimensions of the program;
- arranging cooperative learning activities with opportunities for all children to make contributions to the learning tasks;
- alerting all teachers and adults in the school to the child's support and positioning difficulties and making them aware of basic measures they should take to overcome or circumvent the difficulties;
- seeking the views of and involving the child's parents at each stage of the educational programming;
- exploring the possible use of, and where practicable secured access for the child to appropriate technology, including computer assisted instruction, and providing training in the use of that technology for the child, his or her parents, and staff, so that the child is able to use that technology across the curriculum in school and, where appropriate, at home;
- adapting toys and other instructional materials to enhance independent use. Adaptations to materials (e.g., pencils, crayons, puzzle pieces, feeding utensils, etc.) are often used to help stabilize the materials and to assist in grasping and controlling them;
- adapting the physical environment and using adaptive equipment in the classroom and other areas of the school (e.g., bathroom, playground, etc.) to encourage and support exploration, involvement, independence, and inclusion on the part of the child with CP. Such adaptations may call for the installation of handrails and ramps,

wider-than-usual passageways and work areas both inside and outside of the classroom, support straps or "bolsters" on indoor and outdoor gross motor toys and equipment, and the use of therapeutic equipment, such as corner chairs and standing boards.

- Keep adaptations as non-intrusive as possible so that the child with a disability is not seen as "more different" than the other children. For example, adaptive seating should be used only when necessary and then should be arranged so as not to put the child with a disability at an unequal height with the other children. Additionally, because wheelchairs and wheelchair trays tend to isolate individual children from the group, such adaptive equipment should be used on a limited basis. For children in need of additional support for balance and/or safety, adaptations should be devised so as to enable them to use floor space or table tops alongside their peers.

### Autism

Autism is a complex syndrome with no known cause. One of the defining characteristics of young children with autism is the delayed and/or atypical way in which they interact with other people (Strain & Danko, 1995). Because the social interactive behaviors of people with autism are puzzling and the condition generally not understood, they have sometimes been labeled as deaf, retarded, disturbed and/or insane (Williams, 1992).

While few people with autism are able to describe what they feel or experience, a recent autobiography by Donna Williams (1992), an individual with autism, provides valuable insights into the condition. In a section dealing with her own thoughts and experiences of autism, she explains that "autistic people are not mad, not stupid. They are not fairies, not aliens – just people trapped in invisible, crippled emotional responses" (Williams, 1992, p. 205).

While autism seems to be closely linked to emotional development, it is more complex and pervasive than many other emotional delays or disorders. While the American Psychiatric Association (1987) classifies autism as a pervasive developmental disorder (PDD), this classification does little to suggest etiology or treatment; and much controversy remains regarding both cause and appropriate intervention (Howard et al., 1997).

Perhaps the words of one who is autistic can add as much insight into the condition as anyone else. Thus, Donna Williams' own voice is quoted at some length (copyright © 1992 by Donna Williams. Reprinted by permission of Times Books, a division of Random House, Inc.):

> I believe that autism results when some sort of mechanism that controls emotion does not function properly, leaving an

otherwise relatively normal body and mind unable to express themselves with the depth that they would otherwise be capable of. Perhaps before an autistic child is even born it is unable to receive or make sense of any message that says there is a connection between itself and its mother. This inability to comprehend closeness constrains the formation of attachments and inhibits efforts to make sense of one's environment in infancy. Without this, perhaps the child creates within itself what it perceives as missing and in effect becomes a world within itself to which all else is simply irrelevant, external, and redundant.

(Williams, 1992, p. 203)

Many of the stereotypic behaviors associated with autism seem strange and meaningless to the general public. Donna Williams, however, refers to these gestures as the language of "her world," and in an attempt to help others understand this language "laid out a rough analysis" of what some of them meant to her (Williams, 1992, p. 211). There follows a listing of some of the more familiar behaviors or characteristics associated with autism and Donna's explanation of what they mean.

- *Obsessive fascination with patterns*: Patterns represent continuity; "the reassurance that things will stay the same long enough to grasp an undeniable guaranteed place within the complex situation around me." When patterns take the form of surrounding circles or border-lines, they serve "as a means of protection from invasion by that which exists outside, in 'the world' " (p. 212).
- *Blinking compulsively*: Blinking seems to "slow things down" and make them seem more detached, "and therefore less frightening" (p. 212).
- *Switching lights on and off*: Similar to blinking, with the addition of a clicking sound which represents "an impersonal and graspable connection with things outside oneself. . . . It gives the pleasure of sensation denied by almost all touch, and provides security. The more patterned and predictable, the more reassuring" (p. 212).
- *Rocking, hand-shaking, flicking objects, chin-tapping*: These rhythmic behaviors provide security and release. As such, they decrease "built-up inner anxiety and tension, thereby decreasing fear" (p. 213).
- *Laughing*: "Often a release of fear, tension, and anxiety" (p. 212).
- *Staring into space or through things, also the spinning of things or oneself and running in circles*: "A means of losing awareness of self in order to relax or cope with boredom caused by an inability to express one's self or feel for the things one did. In a more extreme sense, it is a form of mental suicide used when one gives up hope of being able to reach out or be affected" (p. 214).
- *Fascination for colored and shiny objects*: This fascination seems to be

related to the concept of beauty in simplicity and is a tool for self-hypnosis. It is "needed to help calm down and relax." These objects also represent closeness to the lives of particular people "whether or not they were actually given by the other person." Such connections are "assigned . . . because they captured 'the feel' of these people" (p. 215).

To what extent Donna's experiences and thoughts represent those of other people with autism is unknown. What does seem to be known from the study of many people with autism is that autism is present at birth and is a life-long condition. Most children with autism (i.e., about two-thirds) are identified in infancy when such characteristic behaviors as avoidance of eye contact, resistance to physical closeness, disinterest in most toys, and considerable irritability are noted. The remaining one-third of children with autism are usually identified at around 12 to 18 months of age when deficits in language and social skills become evident (Howard *et al.*, 1997).

Helping children with autism is difficult and frustrating. According to Howard *et al.* (1997), however, the "first steps to treatment is the exclusion of other potential causes of autistic behavior" (p. 212). Autistic-like behaviors are sometimes associated with other syndromes (e.g., Rett and Tourette), hearing impairments, and mental retardation. Before plans for intervention are put in place, the condition(s) associated with the behaviors should be identified to the extent possible. Of course, a child can be autistic and have other developmental concerns as well. In fact, most persons with autism have some degree of mental retardation; and for between 30% and 35% of persons with autism, this falls in the severely mentally retarded range (Howard *et al.*, 1997). It has been suggested by some that autism, as such, does not exist, but represents many different brain disorders (Mauk, 1993).

Specific guidelines for helping children with autism are few and controversial. While behavioral intervention with systematic training has been used somewhat effectively in reducing some socially troublesome behaviors (e.g., violence toward self and/or others, excessive screaming, etc.), the methods are slow, rigorous, and difficult to maintain over periods of time (Howard *et al.*, 1997). Such methods also tend to be quite intrusive and are often not consistent with developmentally appropriate practices. Therefore, before systematic training is initiated, other strategies should be explored. Perhaps a good place to start is with the suggestions offered by Donna Williams (1992). There is no assurance that what she feels would have been most helpful to her would be of benefit to others with autism. However, we have no assurance that other methods are any better. We do know that much of what she offers is consistent with recommended practices in early childhood education. There follow some of her recommendations.

- "Gain the child's trust and tell him or her that you accept who and where he or she is" (p. 201).
- Help the child make the "transition from the child's sense of itself *as* the world to a new sense of itself *in* the world so-called normal people share" (p. 201). Realize that the child must trust "the world" before he or she can show interest in it.
- When giving things to the child, place them near him or her "with no expectation of thanks and no waiting for a response" (p. 216). As Donna explains, "to expect a thank-you or a response was to alienate me from the item that prompted the response" (p. 216).
- Use indirect contact (such as looking out of a window) versus direct contact (such as looking directly at the child) when you want the child to listen to you. "This seeming indifference," Donna says, "would actually demonstrate awareness and sensitivity to the child's problem in coping with directness" (p. 216). This strategy only works, however, once the child has achieved the ability to cooperate. Once the child has achieved this ability, this indirect strategy can then help the child "develop more of a self knowing it has reached out to the other person for the meaning of what is being said, rather than being in the role of a passive object being imposed upon at a pace it cannot keep up with when confronted with direct and often emotive interaction" (pp. 216–217).
- Speak out loud to yourself about the child or about someone like the child. According to Donna, this would have inspired her to show that she could relate to what was being said.
- "Speak through" objects or use visual symbols to explain things, especially in relation to social relationships, directions, or abstract concepts. This strategy represents "a way of communicating with personal distance without having to be at such a physical distance" (p. 217).
- Let the child initiate physical touch or, at the very least, be given a choice about physical contact. For very small children, Donna indicates that they "would need to be challenged to learn that they can choose" (p. 217). Regarding physical contact, Donna indicates that she never experienced the withholding of touch as neglect. She experienced it as respect and understanding. There follows an example of how Donna initiated contact and the type of response that was most helpful to her (p. 217):

When I came to them [people] and sat in front of them with the hairbrush or put my forearm out across their lap to be tickled, I appreciated a freely and casually given response that asked me nothing about what I was getting out of the action.

- When the child speaks, be sure to indicate that you are listening and that you understand the seriousness of what he or she is trying to communicate. It is also good to let the child know that you are aware of the courage it took to speak. At the same time, however, Donna indicates that the listener should not make the child too aware of his or her own efforts. In her efforts to communicate, Donna indicates that she "was only able to do so by letting my conscious mind believe that nothing of any significance was happening" (p. 218).

• In play and symbolic action, stand calmly by, without looking intently at the child, perhaps even replaying the child's actions a few feet away from him or her, without directing these efforts at the child. Such actions, Donna indicates, confirmed understanding of what she was trying to communicate and gave her hope and courage to keep trying.

• Allow the child sufficient privacy and space. According to Donna, the unthreatening nature of privacy and space inspired the courage to explore the world and get out of her personal world under glass step by step.

Donna strongly recommends starting with "non-forceful" strategies in intervention but feels that if the indirect strategies are not effective over time, a more forceful approach should be used. As she says, "sometimes people must love you enough to declare war" (pp. 218–219). There follows Donna's description of what this means (p. 217).

> For children who have not yet achieved the ability to cooperate by these [indirect] strategies, I must, against my own feelings, suggest a strongly persistent, sensitive though impersonal approach to teach the child that 'the world' will not give up on it; that it will relentlessly make demands of the child. Otherwise, 'the world' will remain closed out. Teaching the value of what 'the world' has to offer will probably have no meaning or significance, but the concept of a war that won't go away can force interaction.

Early and intensive intervention has proven to be effective in remediating some of the pervasive social skill deficits of children with autism (Brown & Kalbli, 1997; Strain & Danko, 1995). Key ingredients of these intervention efforts have been outlined by Strain and Danko (1995) and include "(a) regular and planned access to typical peers, (b) multiple-setting opportunities to practice emerging social skills, and (c) intensive data collection in order to make midcourse corrections to existing intervention plans" (p. 2). Drawing from the work of several researchers (Brown & Kalbli, 1997; Strain & Danko, 1995; Strain *et al.*, 1995) as well as the suggestions offered by Donna Williams, the following additional recommendations for intervention for young children with autism have been generated:

- Provide intervention services within the context of a mainstream or inclusive setting and encourage the child with autism to participate in the same activities as their typical peers at whatever their ability level.
- Use "narration" to reinforce appropriate social behaviors. When using narration, adults state out loud what they see the child attempting to do during explorations. The narration is used to provide support as well as information related to the child's actions. Narration might be used, for example, to help the child become more aware of cause and effect and to promote the opportunity for increased social interaction. Such narration may be perceived by the child as a form of approval and validity (Brown & Kalbli, 1997).
- Teach classmates in the inclusive setting to make persistent social overtures toward the child with autism (e.g., get the friend's attention by tapping him or her on the shoulder and calling by name; invite the friend to play by handing him or her a toy; give play ideas to a friend; offer the friend assistance or ask for it; make encouraging comments to the friend by saying that he or she is doing a nice job).
- Train parents to prompt siblings and/or the child with autism to interact socially. Parents can provide prompts by suggesting, directing, or asking for such social interactions.
- Train siblings to serve as intervention agents in the home. Their role as interventionists should focus, in large part, on engaging in persistent social overtures toward their sibling with autism. Such overtures as presented above for classmates in the school-based setting are recommended.
- Identify and work toward specific versus general intervention goals. "For all practical purposes, teaching young children with autism remains a behavior-by-behavior undertaking" (Strain *et al.*, 1995, p. 108). "Accepting a toy from a friend when offered" is an example of a specific behavior, while "socially responding to other children during play" is a more general description of a targeted behavior.
- Recognize nonverbal attempts at social interaction as meaningful communicative attempts. For example, if a child with autism moves into an area where one or more other children are playing, interpret this behavior as an attempt at establishing social interaction. Trying to get the child to then also verbalize his or her intentions will likely lead to withdrawal or escape from the situation. Brown and Kalbli (1997), therefore, suggest that teachers and teacher assistants carefully observe and document antecedent behaviors that may be linked to a child's decision to flee or stay.
- Critically examine the actions demonstrated by a child with autism and the social interaction potential that the situations may offer. Brown and Kalbli (1997), who have studied the potential for such

"reflection," suggest using the following sets of questions to guide the process.

*Self-initiated play*
1  Does the child attempt to pick up an object or toy?
2  Does the child attempt to manipulate an object or toy?
3  Does the child have gross motor skills that would allow him/her to play with an object or toy successfully?

*Social interaction potential*
1  Is the child staring at another peer or group of peers for more than 3 seconds?
2  Can the child play independently with a peer or a group?
3  Can the child tune out external distractions when making an attempt to enter into a group?
4  Can the child tune out external distractions when playing with a peer or group of peers for an extended time period?

*Environmental variables*
1  Does the child prefer to play in a particular area?
2  Does the child prefer to play with a particular toy or object?
3  Do certain sounds cause the child to leave an area?
4  Are certain sounds relaxing to the child?

As was stated earlier, autism remains with an individual throughout the duration of one's life. While treatment, especially early in life, can greatly improve the chances of that individual being able to live and function in the mainstream of society (Strain & Danko, 1995), many individuals with autism will require some form of assisted living throughout their adult life. Assisted living can take many different forms – from very restrictive (with no or very little independence) to assistance paired with independence and/or interdependence. One example of a positive approach to pairing assistance with interdependence exists in a small community in northwest Ohio (USA) in the form of Bittersweet Farms. Bittersweet Farms is an 80-acre farm which serves full-time and daytime residents with autism. Through holistic, integrated programming, individuals with autism have expanded their educational, vocational, and social development in this interdependent community. At Bittersweet Farms, individuals with autism grow vegetables, care for domestic animals (e.g., cows, chickens, etc.), assist in preparing their own food (e.g., baking bread, making cookies, canning fruits and vegetables, etc.), and participate in making crafts and baked goods that they then sell to the community. The philosophy of Bittersweet Farms is to provide as much assistance as needed while expecting as much independence as appropriate.

Bittersweet Farms is modeled, in part, on Somerset Court, the first community for autistic adults in England. Somerset Court was founded in 1974 and serves approximately forty people with autism. Today, there are several other specialized centers in Great Britain which serve as living, learning communities for adults with autism. One such center is situated in a suburb of Liverpool. Here, residents live in a large house on a road with similar houses. The property includes an acre or so of land and some additional buildings. The vocational and recreational curricula are similar across the programs in England and the United States.

### Attention deficit disorder/attention deficit hyperactivity disorder

While there is some controversy and disagreement as to the utility and meaning of the terms attention deficit disorder (ADD) and attention deficit hyperactivity disorder (ADHD), the descriptions of behaviors associated with these conditions have been recognized for over fifty years. Such descriptions include aggressive, defiant, resistant to discipline, little self-control (or impulsivity), inattention (or "poor attention span"), and overly active (or hyperactivity).

With ADD, the primary concern is inattention, which is manifest when children fail to attend and concentrate on the activity, or task, at hand. Young children with ADD often move quickly from one activity to another and, when asked, often cannot explain what they should be doing or attending to. Children with ADD seem to be easily distracted by what is going on around them – e.g., other children playing, people talking, movement in the hallway, sounds from the next room, etc.

Children with ADHD also exhibit inattention but demonstrate impulsivity and hyperactivity as well. Children who act with impulsivity seem to be unaware that their actions have consequences. They respond to situations quickly and with apparently little thought as to the appropriateness or results of their actions. Thus, they tend to interrupt others in conversation and in work or play activities, have trouble "waiting their turn," and seem to base decisions on emotion or impulse versus reflection or thought.

Hyperactivity is the primary symptom associated with ADHD. It is also the most widely known and easiest to recognize of the characteristics associated with this disorder. Children who are hyperactive tend to be always moving about, making noise, and fidgeting. As such, they are often referred to as being disruptive in the classroom. Not surprisingly, secondary characteristics associated with ADHD include poor school performance, learning disabilities, and poor problem-solving skills. Additional characteristics include delays in speech and language development, slightly more difficulties in sensory and motor skills, and low self-concepts.

Research as to the etiology, or cause, of ADD and ADHD "has been somewhat inconsistent and conflicting in outcomes" (Howard et al., 1997, p. 170). Much of the research seems to suggest that there are multiple etiologies, with both hereditary and environmental influences. Such influences seem to include exposure to environmental toxins (Marlowe, 1986) and problems with the brain's ability to use glucose fast enough to maintain normal patterns of thought (Zametkin et al., 1990).

ADD/ADHD generally starts during the early childhood period and continues throughout one's life (Barkley, 1990). Stimulant medication therapy is the primary treatment for this disorder. The two most common medications are Cylert and Ritalin. While both drugs have proven to be quite effective in dealing with the symptoms of ADD/ADHD (Barkley, 1990), there are some concerns relating to the side-effects, including weight loss, insomnia, headaches, dizziness, reduced speech, irritability, sadness, and nightmares.

Behavioral interventions (e.g., reward systems, behavioral contracting, and self-management techniques) have also produced some positive outcomes for young children, especially when used by parents in the home (Barkley, 1990). As students become older, behavioral interventions – alone or in combination with medication – have also been effective in the school setting (Abramowitz et al., 1992).

It is important to keep in mind that most young children tend to be quite active, impulsive, and easily distracted. This is normal and should be viewed as such by adults working with young children. Early childhood educators, then, should arrange the environment and introduce activities that match the way young children function, rather than trying to shape the behavior of the students into patterns that are not "natural" to their developmental level. As articulated by Widerstrom (1986), many teachers seem to be overly concerned about classroom control, and this seems to be especially true for teachers in special education rather than early childhood settings. One of Widerstrom's suggestions is for teachers to give some thought to the "comfort/control index." According to this index, there tends to be a direct relationship between levels of comfort and control on the part of most teachers. A high level of control tends to result in a high comfort level for the teacher. However, the opposite may be true for the children – i.e., a high level of teacher control may result in a less comfortable environment for the children. Widerstrom thus suggests that early childhood educators work toward lowering the level of teacher control while maintaining a high comfort level.

Aspects of the comfort/control index might also be useful in working with children with ADD and ADHD. While symptoms can be exacerbated or ameliorated by environmental factors, children with attention deficit disorders cannot be expected to behave in the same way as children without this disability. Thus, teachers would do well to prepare the environment with the special needs of children with ADD and ADHD in mind and be willing to accept a higher level of activity than what is normally preferred.

There follow some specific classroom adaptations that may be helpful in working with children with ADD and ADHD:

- Carefully monitor the amount of visual and auditory stimulation present in the room. Because many children with ADD/ADHD have difficulty filtering out extraneous sights and sounds, teachers should take care to limit the noise level and visual stimuli surrounding these children (Cook *et al.*, 1996).
- Provide a "quiet place" where children can retreat and have some time away from the larger group.
- Provide ample equipment and materials to minimize the need for waiting and/or sharing desired objects and activities.
- Space work areas (e.g., tables, learning centers, etc.) far enough apart so that children working in one area are less likely to disturb children working in an adjacent area.
- Make directions extremely clear and easy to follow. For example, instead of telling a child to clean up the art materials, give step-by-step directions, such as "Put your finished work in your folder, and then throw the scrap paper in the waste basket."
- Analyze tasks and present them in small, sequential steps.
- Use the child's name often when working with a group to help focus his or her attention on the task at hand.
- Maintain a calm voice and calm behavior, as anxiety tends to heighten the child's level of activity.
- Provide clearly defined work spaces (e.g., carpet squares or pieces of tape on the floor) and definite locations for individual belongings.
- Keep materials in the classroom well organized. Storing learning materials and other supplies in clearly marked sturdy containers can help adults and children find and return materials in an orderly way. Storage containers used by the children can be marked with both words and pictures to help them easily see where items belong.
- Establish and maintain a regular routine. Children with ADD/ADHD tend to thrive in a predictable environment. While children should have choices throughout the day, their choices should fit within the structure of the daily routine.

### Down syndrome

Chromosomal disorders are a common cause of disabilities, with Down syndrome representing the most recognizable and commonly known of such disorders. Down syndrome is a non-inherited chromosomal abnormality and is usually (in 95% of cases) associated with an extra chromosome. Developmental and educational outcomes for children with Down syndrome vary widely, from only mild to very severe implications for development and learning.

Children with Down syndrome are usually recognized by certain physical features evident in infancy. Such features include a small head with a flattened back, extra skin at the inner corner of the eyes making them appear to be slanted, low muscle tone, a single crease across the palm and soles of the feet, a flat nose bridge, and short, wide hands with an inward curve of the little finger. Additionally, a high palate and a small oral cavity often lead to tongue protrusion and/or drooling. Medical conditions also tend to accompany this disability, to the point where in the early part of the century, the life expectancy of children with Down syndrome was only 9–12 years. Today, unless there are significant associated health problems, the life expectancy of individuals with Down syndrome is greater than 50 years (Hanson & Lynch, 1995).

Children with Down syndrome tend to function closest to their age-mates during the first two years of life. As they get a little older and are faced with the demands of language and higher order cognitive skills, the discrepancy between the performance of children with Down syndrome and their typically developing peers usually widens (Batshaw & Perret, 1992). Even with this increasing gap, serving children with Down syndrome in mainstream programs is usually quite beneficial to them. "Playing and learning alongside typically developing peers often provides the motivation that children with Down syndrome need to increase motor and communication skills, as well as opportunities to practice social interactions that form the foundation for later relationships" (Hanson & Lynch, 1995, p. 22).

In addition to providing a stimulating environment designed to enhance development across developmental domains, intervention for children with Down syndrome should also include a close monitoring of their hearing and vision. Well over 50% of children with Down syndrome have vision and hearing impairments. The hearing impairments are often related to middle ear disease, which is more common in children with Down syndrome than in the general population. Thus, to prevent or minimize the development of secondary handicaps, the vision and hearing of children with Down syndrome should be routinely assessed.

It is also critically important that an interdisciplinary team of professionals work closely together in planning and implementing an intervention program for young children with Down syndrome. Physical and occupational therapists should be involved, as should communication specialists.

## Health concerns

A number of medical conditions and health concerns may significantly impact on the child's ability to succeed in school. While such conditions can severely limit the extent to which the child is able to participate in the school curriculum and wider range of school activities, these conditions can also lead to serious emotional and behavioral difficulties. Common medical/health conditions found in young children which tend to impede their participation and/or success in school include asthma, cystic fibrosis, congenital heart disease, sickle cell anemia, diabetes, rheumatoid disorders, eczema, leukemia and other forms of cancer. Some of these conditions affect the child's school participation and performance on an intermittent basis, others continuously. In either case, the long-term negative impact on school performance can be profound, especially if appropriate action is not taken as early in the child's life as possible.

In addition to the medical/health conditions themselves affecting young children, medical treatments for such conditions can also have negative implications for the child's development and education. Medications required to control such conditions as seizure disorders and cancer can impair concentration and cause children to tire easily. Some medications also cause lethargy, loss of appetite, and drowsiness. Hospitalizations, too, can negatively impact on children's success in school. Hospital stays not only interrupt the child's school attendance but can also lead to social, emotional, and behavioral difficulties, due in part "to their conditions and the associated restrictions on everyday living and the nature of the treatment required" (DFE, 1994, p. 67).

Serving children with medical/health concerns in the regular classroom calls for a number of special considerations, including (and perhaps most importantly) the involvement of a multidisciplinary team of professionals representing not only education, but also medical personnel. Parents, of course, should be consulted, informed, and involved at each stage of educational programming. The Department of Education in the *Code of Practice* addresses these intervention priorities by indicating that the LEA (Local Education Authority) should ask whether:

  i the school has, with the parents' consent, notified and sought the assistance of the school doctor, the child's general practitioner or any specialist child health service, as appropriate
  ii all staff have been fully informed of the child's medical condition and a consistent approach of managing the child's education has been taken across the school
  iii the school has sought the views of, and involved, the child's parents at each stage
  iv the school has sought the cooperation of those within the local

education authority responsible for the education of children who are at home and, as appropriate, in hospital, as a result of illness.

(DFE, 1994, p. 68)

At times, the medical conditions of young children are so serious as to prevent them from participating in a regular education setting for all or part of the time. For some children, this means that their educational program is provided in a hospital setting; for others, in the home. As such arrangements tend to deprive the child with special educational needs of the benefits of interacting with typically developing peers, some communities have developed special programs that combine educational intervention services and medical care in school settings. One such program is the Prescribed Pediatric Care in Toledo, Ohio (USA). The Prescribed Pediatric Care (PPC) program offers daycare/treatment for children with chronic or temporary health problems, but with a special focus. The program is designed to integrate professional medical care into the normal structure of a regular preschool environment and non-institutional skilled care center. The family-centered PPC, which serves children aged 12 and under, offers an alternative to a long stay in the hospital or at extended care centers. PPC is a natural extension of hospital-based care and home-care settings in that it uses pediatric nurses to care for the children, based on a physician's prescribed care. Nurses not only work with the children during parents' daytime work hours, but teach parents proper home care and offer respite care so that parents can rest and deal with other family concerns.

The children in the PPC program spend their day in a bright, cheerful, school-like atmosphere, and when their health status permits, they may transfer to a continuing regular early learning group with typically developing peers in the same building. Children with such conditions as cystic fibrosis, spina bifida, or premature developmental problems can spend much of their time in the regular early childhood classroom and "check in" with the nurses at the PPC when periodic care is needed, such as tube feedings and dressing changes.

Children served through the PPC program have a variety of medical situations: ventilator dependency, gastrointestinal problems, or neurological impairments. The PPC is also for children with temporary health problems, including children undergoing chemotherapy or premature babies who need continuous monitoring.

# Case study – Mary

### Background information

Mary is the middle child in a family with three children. The other two children are boys and appear to be developing normally. Mary, however, has Down syndrome, and at the age of 6 is functioning more like her 4-year-old brother than her age-mates. Both of Mary's parents are teachers and were in their early thirties when she was born. All seemed to be going well throughout the pregnancy, so no special tests were done. Her disability at birth, then, came as a complete surprise. At the time of birth, Mary was blue and inactive. She didn't cry much and never learned to nurse.

During her preschool years, Mary seemed to enjoy being around other children and adults. She laughed easily and loved to hug people. Her language development was seriously delayed, with her first combination of words not appearing until she was about 3½ years old. Her motor development was also noticeably delayed. Mary took her first independent steps when she was nearly 2 years old.

When Mary entered her Reception year of school at the age of 4, she was still not toileting on her own. She also needed considerable help in dressing and eating. When Ms. Forman first heard that Mary would be in her Reception year class, she objected strongly. Ms. Forman had no previous experience working with a child functioning so far below typically developing children and had many concerns. How would she have time to provide the kind of individual assistance Mary needed? How would the other children react to Mary, and what would the other parents say? Additionally, Ms. Forman felt that she had neither the knowledge nor skill for meeting the intervention goals outlined on Mary's statement of special educational needs. After considerable discussion among members of the intervention team, it was decided that, in addition to consultation from a specialist teacher and other specialists on the team, a teacher's assistant would also be assigned to the classroom to facilitate Mary's integration into the program.

Three months after the beginning of the school year, the intervention team assembled again to review the status of Mary's placement and progress. At this meeting, Ms. Forman was proud to report on Mary's accomplishments. Mary's language and self-help skills had improved considerably. She was well liked by her classmates and followed the classroom rules as well as anyone. While Mary still required special assistance on many tasks, the classroom assistant was excellent in working with her in a non-intrusive way. She also used the one-on-one time required for many self-help tasks, to work with Mary on individual goals in self-help, cognitive development, and language. The specialists on the intervention team (i.e., the specialist teacher, the physical and occupational therapists, and the communication specialist) made regular visits to the classroom. They often worked with Mary in small group settings, where she could interact with her classmates and learn a variety of skills by watching them. The specialists also provided pertinent information and demonstrated intervention strategies to Ms. Forman, the classroom assistant, and Mary's parents, so that they could use these same strategies throughout the day. Mary loved school and was always eager to show her parents and brothers what she had learned or accomplished at school each day.

## *Discussion*

Ms. Forman's initial concerns about having Mary in her classroom are understandable and probably similar to what many other teachers would feel in similar situations. Without ongoing assurance, information, and support from members of the intervention team, Ms. Forman's story after the first three months might have been entirely different. With such assistance and support, however, Ms. Forman's feelings about working with a child with special educational needs changed considerably over a short period of time. In addition to feeling more open and confident about having children with SEN in her classroom, Ms. Forman had also grown professionally by learning how to implement intervention strategies in developmentally appropriate ways. While Mary was clearly not performing at the same level as her classmates during her Reception year at school, there was no doubt that she was benefitting from the mainstream experience.

# 5

# SOCIAL/EMOTIONAL, SPEECH/LANGUAGE, AND COGNITIVE CONCERNS

## Social/emotional concerns

Humans are social beings. Even as newborns, they have the neurological system to selectively attend to the social responses of people around them and to engage in behaviors that illicit social responses from others (McEvoy & Odom, 1996). Initially, the behaviors in infants that generate social responses are not consciously purposeful – i.e., infants do not engage in such behaviors as crying and fussing *for the purpose of* getting a social response. They cry or fuss because they're uncomfortable, hungry, or feeling distressed. Such behaviors, however, do tend to illicit social responses from others, usually in the form of positive attention, food, and/or other sources of comfort. Infants gradually perceive the connection between their signals of distress and the accompanying social responses. They then begin using such behaviors in a purposeful way – e.g., they cry to "tell" adults that they're uncomfortable or hungry. Attentive adults understand the infants' messages and respond by tending to their needs. Over time, infants learn that social behavior is structured around certain predictable patterns. This predictability tends to foster feelings of security and attachment and thus the emotional development of young children.

The predictable pattern of social behavior also provides incentive for infants and young children to engage in further social interactions. They have learned that participation in this pattern can prove beneficial to them. This predictability also provides incentives *for adults* to engage in further social interactions with the child. Adults feel good about being able to "read" or interpret the infant's messages and successful in providing appropriate responses. For example, adults hear the infant's cry, interpret the cry as "hunger," provide food for the infant, and then see that he or she is comforted by the food. The adult is rewarded by being able to comfort the child, and the child is rewarded by having his or her needs met.

While mid-century social learning theory placed the emphasis on the

85

caregiver's contributions to the social development of the child, new understandings about the reciprocal nature of social interactions indicate that the child's contributions also play a major role (Rothbart, 1996). Our understanding of the child's contributions has been influenced by a number of factors, including the following:

- Piaget's study of cognitive development indicates that children individually "construct" their own understanding of the physical and social world from their experiences with it.
- The work of psychoanalytically oriented investigators (e.g., Escalona, 1968; Spitz, 1965) have called attention to the impact of infant biology on social and emotional development.
- Studies on attachment indicate that the infant's contributions play a major role in the nature of the caregiver–infant attachment, and that as the child's maturational status changes, so does the nature of the child's relation with the caregiver (Ainsworth et al., 1972; Ainsworth et al., 1978).
- Studies in infancy research indicate that even young infants possess a set of complex skills or competencies (Howard et al., 1997).

As children get a little older (but still during their preschool years), interactions with peers become an important part of the child's social development (Kemple & Hartle, 1997). The confidence and competence with which young children engage in peer social interactions seem to be positively related to the robustness of their social competence and secure attachment relationships acquired earlier with their caregivers. A similar relationship seems to exist between early social competence and more advanced development in cognitive and communication skills (Odom et al., 1992). It should not be surprising, then, that the early childhood literature repeatedly stresses the importance of social competence to the overall development of the child (McEvoy & Odom, 1996).

While most typically developing children learn to interact confidently and competently with adults and peers without any special intervention or instruction, the same is not true for many children with disabilities. Because of the critical nature of social competence to overall development, early intervention programs often make the promotion of social development an essential aspect of their program (Guralnick, 1994).

As stated earlier, the social development of young children proceeds in a transactional manner, with both the caregiver and the child playing critical roles. Characteristics and/or behaviors of both the caregiver and the child will thus influence the nature of the transactions (i.e., social interactions) that occur between them. If one side of the social transaction is ineffective or unresponsive, the other side will certainly be negatively affected.

If the caregiver is absent, unable to interpret the child's "cries," or unresponsive, the child's incentive and opportunities for learning to be socially competent and emotionally secure will be diminished. While maternal responsivity to infants' behavior appears across cultures and seems to be a universal principle of early child development, some research indicates that socioeconomic and demographic variables (e.g., maternal education level) influence the degree to which maternal responsivity occurs (McEvoy & Odom, 1996). Low levels of responsivity (e.g., not recognizing and/or responding to the infant's social cues) can lead to delayed development of social and emotional competencies in the infant and young child. A high level of responsivity, on the other hand, encourages infants and young children to engage in positive social interaction with caregivers (Lussier *et al.*, 1994) and leads to healthy attachment relationships in the first year of life (van Ijzendoorn *et al.*, 1995). Secure attachment relationships, in turn, foster the development of many social behaviors and the formation of healthy peer relationships (Lyons-Ruth *et al.*, 1993).

The competencies and behaviors of the child also influence the nature of the social interactions that occur between adult and child. If the child is unable to "receive" or interpret the adult's responses, he or she cannot provide the expected feedback or "rewards" that serve as incentives for the adult to provide the consistency or predictabiltiy of response. Children with disabilities are often unable to provide the same kind of positive social feedback to their caregivers and other adults – or even to their peers – as can children without disabilities. A child who is deaf, for example, cannot hear the mother's comforting voice as she prepares a bottle in response to the infant's cry. This child may then cry longer and be more difficult to calm than a child who is not deaf. Similarly, a child who is blind cannot see the teacher's smile and outstretched arms and may thus be less responsive to invitations to let go of the mother's hand and join the group of children around the science table. This reluctance may be viewed as a problem in social and/or emotional development. The underlying problem, however, relates directly to the child's disability – i.e., not being able to see.

In addition to sensory impairments, other factors within the child that can hinder social and emotional development include medical problems, physical disabilities, and mental retardation. Young children with medical problems are often irritable, tend to tire easily, and have irregular sleep patterns. In trying to deal with their child's medical problems and related concerns, parents may feel stressed and frustrated. They may also have difficulty reading their child's social cues and have a tendency to withdraw or become passive in interacting with their child (Yoder, 1987).

Medical problems can also negatively affect the child's social inter-actions at school. The child with medical problems may miss school frequently and may not feel as comfortable as his or her classmates about the daily routine, the proper use of materials, etc. Due to absences, it may also take the child with medical problems longer to get to know his or her classmates and to make friends. Additionally, medical problems may cause the child to tire easily and thus be less inclined to join the other children in group activities.

A similar pattern of diminished interaction may occur if the child has a physical disability or mental retardation. In either case, the child's response to adults' attempts to engage him or her in social interaction may be delayed and less gratifying. Parents and teachers may then withdraw from the child with special needs and be less inclined to expend the time and energy required to engage him or her in social interaction.

Children with disabilities often face similar problems in peer relationships. During early childhood, peer interactions occur primarily through the vehicle of play. Children with disabilities, however, tend to engage in more solitary and less social play than their non-disabled peers (Kopp *et al.*, 1992). Children with disabilities, who often engage in less competent interactions with their peers, also tend to receive lower peer-rating scores than do children who are more socially competent (Guralnick & Groom, 1988). As a result, children with disabilities tend to be less involved in interactions with peers than children without disabilities. This situation puts the children with disabilities in a special bind. As social skills are learned primarily through social interactions, fewer interactions result in fewer opportunities for learning the very behaviors young children need to become more socially competent. Fostering the social competence of young children with disabilities, then, should be one of the major goals of early intervention programs (Guralnick, 1990).

Strategies that might be used to foster the social competence of young children with disabilities include (1) supporting children's participation in social interaction with peers, (2) fostering the acquisition of specific social skills, and (3) fostering the development of peer relationships (McEvoy & Odom, 1996). There follows a brief discussion of these recommendations, along with some specific ideas on how to implement them.

### *Supporting children's participation in social interaction with peers*

For some children, simple inclusion in a program with socially competent peers may be sufficient intervention for supporting peer interactions. Other children, however, will require more intense intervention with carefully planned opportunities to interact with their peers (McEvoy & Odom, 1996).

In planning opportunities for children to interact, the physical characteristics of a setting should be carefully considered. Studies have found that certain types of play materials and classroom activities are more likely to enhance peer–peer interaction than other types (Kemple & Hartle, 1997; Sainato & Carta, 1992). Play *materials* that tend to foster peer–peer interaction include such "social toys" as balls and wagons. Play *activities* that encourage interactions include sociodramatic theme play (e.g., housekeeping, camping, traveling, etc.) and group play involving partners or buddies. McEvoy *et al.* (1988) devised a special type of group play called "friendship activities" to increase the social interaction rates of children with disabilities. These activities consist of typical early childhood games and songs that are modified to include prompts for social interaction – e.g., handshakes, smiles, etc. Not only do children seem to enjoy these activities, but they also learn to use the targeted social skills at other times during the day. These benefits seem to apply to all young children, even children with such complex conditions as autism (McEvoy *et al.*, 1988).

The emotional climate of the classroom also influences peer–peer interaction. A democratic style of discipline is considered more conducive than other styles of discipline to helping children interact positively and peacefully with one another (Kemple & Hartle, 1997). Adults working within a democratic style of discipline set firm limits on inappropriate behavior and rely largely on explanations to help children learn appropriate behavior. The democratic style of discipline falls in between a laissez-faire, or highly permissive, approach and an authoritarian approach which relies on harsh, punitive practices. A democratic style of discipline allows children "to feel listened to, to understand the rules and the reasons behind the rules, and to feel confident that they will be protected" (Kemple & Hartle, 1997, p. 140). Directive and coercive interactional behaviors, on the other hand, tend to impede the social/emotional development of young children (Dunst *et al.*, 1996).

### Fostering the acquisition of specific social skills

In addition to carefully planned opportunities to interact, some children with disabilities also need directed prompts (i.e., directives or suggestions) on how to interact. Prompts from both adults and peers have proven to be effective in helping children with disabilities interact successfully with their typical peers. Prompts have also been used to help typically developing children recognize and respond to the social interaction attempts of their peers with special needs (McEvoy & Odom, 1996). Prompts may focus on such specific social interaction skills as making eye contact, looking at the person speaking, giving and responding to greetings, etc.

Prompts can be direct or indirect. They can also involve intensive teacher involvement or less intense involvement. The extent of directedness and involvement should always be determined by the needs of the child, with less direct and less intense involvement being the ultimate goal. The following examples illustrate varying degrees of directedness and involvement.

During learning center time, Amanda always chooses an activity that requires little or no interaction (e.g., looking at books, putting a puzzle together, working at the art center, using headphones at the listening center, etc.). If another child joins her or attempts to interact with her, Amanda usually turns away or leaves the area.

- *Approach 1. Indirect and less intense involvement.* When Hilary walks over to the art table where Amanda is drawing, the teacher comments on that fact and suggests that Amanda show Hilary what she is doing. ("Amanda, Hilary is coming to work with you. Maybe you would like to show her what you are doing.") This is an indirect prompt, in that the teacher is not directing either child's behavior. It is designed to raise Amanda's awareness of the opportunity for interaction and to give her an idea of how to initiate such interaction. It does not represent intense involvement, as it took very little of the teacher's time and was not specifically planned in advance, nor does it require any special materials or adaptations to the regular routine. This approach may or may not be effective with Amanda, who may choose to ignore the information and suggestion offered by the teacher.

- *Approach 2. More direct and somewhat more intense involvement.* When Hilary walks over to the art table where Amanda is drawing, the teacher joins the two girls, comments on the fact that she and Hilary would like to work with Amanda, and then tells Hilary to ask Amanda what she is doing. ("Amanda, Hilary and I are coming to work with you at the art center. Hilary, why don't you ask Amanda what she is doing?") In this case, the teacher was confident that Hilary could and would follow her suggestion about addressing Amanda. If Amanda ignores Hilary's question, the teacher is present and prepared to offer further prompts (e.g., "Amanda, show Hilary what you are doing.") Here, the prompts are more direct, in that the teacher tells both a peer and the child with a disability (i.e., Amanda) how to interact. This case also represents more intense involvement, in that the teacher physically joins and orchestrates the social interaction. It thus requires more time and attention on the teacher's part and tells the children exactly what to do versus offering a suggestion. This approach, too, may or may not be effective with Amanda; but because the teacher has entered the situation, she can continue to offer prompts until Amanda participates in some type of social interaction. The teacher is also present to extend and reward any interactions that occur (e.g., "Amanda, Hilary really likes your picture. Here's some tape to hang it on the wall. Hilary can hold it for you while you cut the tape.")

- *Approach 3. Very direct and intensive involvement.* The teacher talks to Hilary before learning center time and asks her to be "Amanda's friend" for the day. After Amanda goes to the art table, Hilary joins her and says, "Hi, Amanda. Can I work with you?" As the two children work together, the teacher stands nearby, making suggestions to both Hilary and Amanda as to what they might say and do to continue the interaction. The teacher also interprets the children's messages to each other, as needed. For example, if Amanda simply turns away when Hilary asks, "Can I work with you?", the teacher might move close to Amanda, put her hand on Amanda's shoulder, and say, "Amanda, Hilary asked if she can work with you at the art table. Tell her 'yes.'" In this case, the teacher pre-planned the intervention and prepared Hilary for her role. This is an example of very direct prompts and intensive teacher involvement. This level of intervention requires more time and preparation on the teacher's part than do the previous two approaches. Because of its intrusiveness on the children's activities, it should only be used if the first two approaches are not effective. In cases where Approach 3 is used, plans should be made for gradually reducing the directedness and intensity of the teacher's involvement.

### Fostering the development of peer relationships

Social and emotional development requires more than the acquisition of a set of social skills and the feeling of confidence in using such skills. Young children also need friends and positive relationships with their peers. As many young children with disabilities are not readily accepted by their non-disabled peers (Peterson & McConnell, 1993), it is incumbent upon classroom teachers to foster such acceptance. Teachers can do this by helping the child with a disability to learn specific social competencies associated with being liked or disliked by peers. One such competency is the ability to "read" other children's emotional responses (Kemple & Hartle, 1997). Teachers might foster this skill by calling attention to the emotional aspects of social interactions and helping children to state their feelings, ideas, and desires clearly. For example, if one child pushes another, the teacher might intervene by saying, "Jamil, look at Vanessa. Her face is sad because you pushed her." The teacher can also help children to find appropriate words to express their needs and wants versus resorting to physical approaches for such expressions. For example, the teacher might say, "Jamil, don't push Vanessa. Ask her if you can work at the table with her."

While teachers can plan some cooperative learning activities in advance as a way of promoting peer interaction and acceptance, teachers should also realize that one of the most important means by which they can help children learn to interact effectively is through "teachable moments" that occur throughout the day. Such moments often occur when children are in the midst of a difficult or challenging interaction. Teachers can guide children through the process of resolving differences through such strategies as: (1) paraphrasing each child's view to the other; (2) defining the problem in mutual terms; (3) helping the children to generate alternative solutions; (4) offering her own ideas when needed; (5) facilitating discussion of the merits of suggested solutions, and (6) acknowledging the effort and emotional investment each child contributes to the situation (Kemple & Hartle, 1997).

"Teachable moments," however, do not always involve moments of conflict. Incidental teaching should also occur in situations where children need assistance in initiating and/or maintaining social interaction. By closely observing children and identifying moments when they need support in interacting with others, teachers can help children experience success and satisfaction in peer relationships. Not only will children then be more likely to engage in similar interactions in the future, they will also feel good about having friends and knowing how to be a friend to others. These feelings and competencies serve as cornerstones to healthy social/ emotional development during the early childhood years. Serious "behavior problems" are often related to delays or deficits in social/ emotional development and present special challenges for teachers working with young children with SEN.

## Speech/language disabilities

Without effective communication skills, young children are at considerable risk of serious social and academic difficulties, as well as emotional and behavioral problems. Children with speech/language disabilities should be identified as early as possible and receive appropriate intervention services while they are still quite young, as "it is unlikely that individuals are apt to fulfill their potential unless efforts to maximize their communication skills are taken" (Goldstein et al., 1996, p. 197).

There was a time when intervention services for children with speech/language disabilities focused primarily on the speech aspects of communication. In fact, the primary interventionists in the field were referred to as "speech therapists." This orientation stresses expressive language (giving messages) without giving due regard to receptive language (receiving messages). It also focuses on the form (structure) of language at the expense of function (use).

Today, the intervention focus is much broader. Instead of focusing on just speech – or speech and language – the emphasis is on communication. Speech and language are viewed as tools for communication rather than as ends in themselves, and communication is understood to encompass both oral and non-oral modes of expression.

A similar shift of focus has occurred in the study of children's development of communication. Until about twenty years ago, the focus of study was on the form and structure of language. Today, the emphasis is on the purposes of children's communicative behavior within meaningful social contexts (Cook *et al.*, 1996). A context is considered to be meaningful only if both a communication partner and a reason to communicate are in place. For this reason, speech therapy focusing on isolated skills development apart from the child's natural environment (e.g., classroom or home setting) is rarely considered to be appropriate for young children.

Speech/language concerns can take many different forms and relate to both the expressive and receptive domains of language. Concerns in speech and language are usually assessed in relation to certain subskills of language. These subskills include pragmatics, semantics, syntax, morphology, and phonology. Knowing which subskills are involved in the breakdown of successful communication can provide valuable insights into the type of intervention strategies that may be most effective for an individual child. Many children with speech/language disabilities have deficits in more than one of these subskills.

### Pragmatics

Pragmatics refer to rules and conventions that govern how language is used for communication in different situations. Pragmatics encompass both verbal and nonverbal aspects of communication, as well as the expressive and receptive domains of language (Cook *et al.*, 1996). Receptively, while children with deficits in the area of pragmatics may understand the meaning of individual words that are spoken, they may still "miss" the message intended by the speaker. For example, if a teacher announces that it would be nice to have all the parents attend an open house at school, a child with pragmatic language difficulties may not understand that the teacher is suggesting that students invite or urge their parents to come to the open house. Unless the teacher specifically says, "Vickie, ask your mother to come to the open house," Vickie may not know that this would be an appropriate response to what the teacher just said.

In addition to "missing something" in reading other people's messages, children with pragmatic language skills may have trouble with expressive language as well. There follow some examples of how pragmatic language deficits in the expressive domain might be manifested: (1) not knowing how to initiate, maintain, or terminate conversations; (2) not knowing how to introduce new topics for conversation; (3) having difficulty adjusting communicative style to the speaking context, and (4) failing to consider the emotional impact of certain types of messages. Children with such deficits may fail to adjust the volume of their voice to different settings (e.g., libraries, hospitals, etc.), may make remarks that hurt the feelings of others (e.g., telling a classmate or an acquaintance "You're too fat" or "I don't like you"), and interject statements and questions completely unrelated to the topic of conversation.

When assessing a young child for possible pragmatic language deficits, expectations for his or her age must be taken into consideration. A summary of the developmental stages of pragmatic language skills is presented in Table 5.1 and might be used to help identify children with pragmatic language difficulties.

A tool for assessing the pragmatic language development of young children is presented in Figure 5.1. This checklist of pragmatic language skills includes a rating scale which could be helpful for establishing a baseline (i.e., where the child performs prior to intervention) of an individual child's performance. This scale could also be used for periodic reevaluation.

## Semantics

Semantics refers to the meaning of words. Young children generally learn word meanings through direct experience with objects or events relating to what the words stand for. For example, children learn to associate the word "book" with the actual object it represents when they have books read to them and available to them for their inspection. Children may have a great deal of difficulty, however, associating the word "desert" with the type of geographical region it stands for if they have never been to a desert. Failure to understand the meaning of words may thus be directly related to the child's lack of experience. Adults can enhance a child's development in semantics by pairing vocabulary with actual objects and experiences. For example, when talking about a basket, adults can make a variety of baskets available for the children's exploration. Adults can also assist young children in the area of semantics by using the names of objects and events when talking to the children versus using unspecific terminology. For example, saying "Put the book on the table" is more instructive than saying "Put this over there."

At times, a child's problems in the area of semantics does not become evident until he or she is challenged to understand the meaning of words in combinations, such as "more juice?" or "yellow book." To help a child understand words in combination, adults should continue pairing actual objects with words and avoid speaking too rapidly.

Table 5.1 Developmental sequence of pragmatic language skills

| Age | Communicative functions | Conversational competence |
|---|---|---|
| 0–5 mos. | Uses crying and cooing to express pleasure and pain | Responds to talking by looking at speaker<br>Makes vocal sounds when played with |
| 6–11 mos. | Begins using first words | Responds to mother's communicative acts by smiling and maintaining eye contact<br>Plays games like "peek-a-boo" and "pat-a-cake"<br>Responds with appropriate gestures to some words (e.g., waves when hears "bye-bye")<br>Responds when addressed (e.g., coos or gurgles in response to his or her name) |
| 12–23 mos. | Uses voice and gestures to obtain a desired object<br>Follows two or three consecutive commands<br>Begins using simple sentences to give information or manipulate the listener (e.g., "Me go.") | Looks at mother or father when asked "Where is Mommy?" or "Where is Daddy"<br>Uses and imitates more words instead of using gestures<br>Refers to self by name |
| 24–35 mos. | Understands some complex sentences<br>Asks for help when needed | Understands and uses a vocabulary of about 20 words<br>Uses at least three words in sequence (e.g., "Me want cookie.") |
| 36–47 mos. | Asks questions<br>Uses directive speech (e.g., commands, requests, threats) | Talks about experiences from recent past |
| 4–6 yrs. | Gives useful information | Begins to be less egocentric and more social in conversations |
| 7–8 yrs. | Understands purpose for doing something when given an oral explanation | Recognizes the close relationship between making friends and being accepted by adults and peers and having the ability to communicate effectively with others<br>Identifies various emotions and implied meanings expressed through nonverbal communications<br>By being courteous and attentive begins to respect the right of others to give their opinions |

Child_____  Birthdate _____

Person completing form _____  Relationship to child _____

Date _____

*Key  1 Needs no improvement  2 Acceptable  3 Needs improvement  4 Critical need for improvement*
*5 Non-existent*

## RECEPTIVE AREA

1. *Attending behavior*

| | | | | | |
|---|---|---|---|---|---|
| Makes eye contact | 1 | 2 | 3 | 4 | 5 |
| Maintains attention to speaker | 1 | 2 | 3 | 4 | 5 |

2. *Auditory listening skills*

| | | | | | |
|---|---|---|---|---|---|
| Attends to sounds | 1 | 2 | 3 | 4 | 5 |
| Responds to sounds | 1 | 2 | 3 | 4 | 5 |
| Localizes source of sounds | 1 | 2 | 3 | 4 | 5 |
| Listens actively to sounds | 1 | 2 | 3 | 4 | 5 |
| Attends to significant auditory information in presence of background noises (*selective attention*) | 1 | 2 | 3 | 4 | 5 |
| Maintains attention over a period of time (*sustained attention*) | 1 | 2 | 3 | 4 | 5 |

3. *Comprehension of meaning*

| | | | | | |
|---|---|---|---|---|---|
| "Reads" typical nonverbal cues (e.g., frowns, gestures) | 1 | 2 | 3 | 4 | 5 |
| Carries out requests or commands | 1 | 2 | 3 | 4 | 5 |
| Understands much of what is said to him or her (i.e., relates spoken language to what it represents) | 1 | 2 | 3 | 4 | 5 |
| Understands verbal hints (*implied messages*) | 1 | 2 | 3 | 4 | 5 |
| Understands questions | 1 | 2 | 3 | 4 | 5 |
| Interprets environmental sounds | 1 | 2 | 3 | 4 | 5 |

## EXPRESSIVE AREA

1. *Communicative functions*

| | | | | | |
|---|---|---|---|---|---|
| Imitates sounds | 1 | 2 | 3 | 4 | 5 |
| Requests assistance | 1 | 2 | 3 | 4 | 5 |
| Requests information (i.e., asks appropriate questions) | 1 | 2 | 3 | 4 | 5 |
| Uses directive speech (e.g., commands, threats) | 1 | 2 | 3 | 4 | 5 |
| Expresses desires | 1 | 2 | 3 | 4 | 5 |
| Uses the names of objects, events, etc. | 1 | 2 | 3 | 4 | 5 |
| Formulates questions | 1 | 2 | 3 | 4 | 5 |
| Offers assistance | 1 | 2 | 3 | 4 | 5 |
| Disagrees verbally or argues | 1 | 2 | 3 | 4 | 5 |
| Justifies own actions (i.e., gives reasons) | 1 | 2 | 3 | 4 | 5 |
| Recognizes problems and offers solutions | 1 | 2 | 3 | 4 | 5 |
| Makes self understood (i.e., is able to get a point across) | 1 | 2 | 3 | 4 | 5 |

2. *Conversational competence*

| | | | | | |
|---|---|---|---|---|---|
| Uses good voice habits (i.e., neither too loud nor too soft) | 1 | 2 | 3 | 4 | 5 |
| Answers questions | 1 | 2 | 3 | 4 | 5 |
| Talks about experiences | 1 | 2 | 3 | 4 | 5 |
| Varies speech according to setting and other speakers | 1 | 2 | 3 | 4 | 5 |
| Acknowledges what another speaker has said | 1 | 2 | 3 | 4 | 5 |
| Demonstrates appropriate turn-taking behavior | 1 | 2 | 3 | 4 | 5 |
| Initiates conversational topics | 1 | 2 | 3 | 4 | 5 |
| Makes conversational transitions in an appropriate manner | 1 | 2 | 3 | 4 | 5 |
| Participates willingly in social conversations | 1 | 2 | 3 | 4 | 5 |
| Makes suggestions and shares ideas | 1 | 2 | 3 | 4 | 5 |
| Provides sufficient (but not too much) information when answering questions | 1 | 2 | 3 | 4 | 5 |
| Communicates about self | 1 | 2 | 3 | 4 | 5 |
| Communicates about things outside self (i.e., describes objects) | 1 | 2 | 3 | 4 | 5 |
| Communicates about concrete experiences | 1 | 2 | 3 | 4 | 5 |
| Communicates abstract ideas | 1 | 2 | 3 | 4 | 5 |
| Describes an object or explains how something works | 1 | 2 | 3 | 4 | 5 |
| Tells a simple story in proper sequence | 1 | 2 | 3 | 4 | 5 |

3. *Social interactive skills*

| | | | | | |
|---|---|---|---|---|---|
| Expresses feelings in socially acceptable ways | 1 | 2 | 3 | 4 | 5 |
| Honors established social conventions | 1 | 2 | 3 | 4 | 5 |
| Adapts a message to the social context | 1 | 2 | 3 | 4 | 5 |
| Initiates contact | 1 | 2 | 3 | 4 | 5 |
| Responds to contact | 1 | 2 | 3 | 4 | 5 |
| Engages in interactive play | 1 | 2 | 3 | 4 | 5 |

*Figure 5.1* Checklist of pragmatic skills

Sometimes, a child's difficulty with semantics is revealed as much in their expressive language as it is in their receptive language. If a child tends to use "indefinite descriptors," such as "that thing" or "this one," instead of using the names of things (book, cup, chair, etc.), he or she may have semantic language problems.

## *Syntax*

Syntax refers to rules determining correct word order in sentences. Certain patterns of words form the structure for statements, while other patterns form the structure for questions and commands. For example, in making a statement, we might say, "Jon is working at the computer." In asking a question, the word order might be, "Is Jon working at the computer?" and for a command, "Jon, work at the computer." Obviously, for children to give and receive messages effectively, they must be able to express and interpret a variety of sentence structures.

## Morphology

Morphology refers to rules for changing the form of individual words, such as changing a word from singular to plural or using a different verb tense. While there may be other reasons why children have difficulty with morphology, a hearing loss would certainly contribute to the problem. Even a mild to moderate hearing loss can cause a child to miss the ending sounds on words such as "s" or "es" to form plurals, or the "ed" and "ing" used with different verb tenses.

## Phonology

Phonology refers to the sound systems of speech and language and involves not only individual speech sounds (i.e., phonemes), but the pitch and rhythm of language as well. There are forty-four phonemes in the English language, and most children learn to produce all of them by the time they are 4 years old. Articulation errors in the production of certain consonants (especially "l," "r," "s," "j" and "z") and many consonant blends (e.g., "sh," "ch," "th"), however, are still within the range of normalcy for four-year-olds and should not be cause for alarm.

## Recommended practices

Interventions to promote communication skills usually focus on enhancing the ability of children with special needs in one or more of the following areas: (1) to receive information from others; (2) to share information with others; (3) to use language to mediate their actions and cognition, and (4) to control their environment (Odom & McLean, 1996). To be consistent with this focus, assessment for communication concerns should consider the comprehension and production of content, form, and social functions of the child's performance. Recommended practices also suggest that the child's communicative performance be assessed in a variety of situations (e.g., home, classroom, playground, etc.) and "with a variety of communicative partners represented in the child's everyday life, including peers without disabilities" (Odom & McLean, 1996, p. 394).

In working with young children to enhance their communicative skills, adults should recognize and respond positively to the child's communicative attempts and build on the child's interests, requests, and comments. Speech/language therapy for young children should usually be done within the child's natural environment (i.e., classroom or home setting) and should include typically developing peers as well as familiar adults (Odom & McLean, 1996). Additionally, the environment should be arranged "to enable and accommodate children's unique receptive and

expressive modes of communicating" which may include properly functioning assistive devices such as hearing aids, glasses, communication
boards, etc. (Odom & McClean, 1996, p. 396).

## Cognitive delays

Cognitive development involves progressive changes in children's
perceptions, knowledge, understanding, reasoning, and judgment.
Another important aspect of cognitive development – which is sometimes
overlooked – is the application of cognitive competencies to daily life
experiences. Such application enables the individual to become gradually
more independent in dealing with a broad range of environmental
demands and challenges (Dunst *et al.*, 1996). Efforts to promote cognitive
development, then, should focus not just on the acquisition of knowledge
and understanding, but the application of such knowledge and understanding to daily living situations as well.

While listings of cognitive competencies needed for meeting the
challenges of daily life experiences vary across theoretical models, "cognitive abilities considered hallmarks of the first 6 years of development
. . . include but are not limited to, perception, memory, comprehension,
symbolic representation, problem solving, purposeful planning, decision
making, discrimination, and idea/intention generation" (Dunst *et al.*,
1996, p. 161).

Observations of children's play behaviors indicate that the cognitive
competencies of young children with disabilities and the way such
competencies develop are more alike than different compared to those
of typically developing children. What differs is the rate of development.
Findings from these observations suggest that efforts to promote the cognitive competencies of young children with disabilities "need not differ
much from practices used with typically developing children" (Dunst *et
al.*, 1996, p. 164).

The process through which young children (i.e., especially throughout
the first six years of life) learn is closely tied to their interactions with
people and objects in their environment. Rather than learning primarily in
terms of perceptual attributes (e.g., color, size, shape, etc.), young children
learn through the actions they perform or are engaged in. Such actions
include manipulating, exploring, and practicing.

### The role of play

Play activities offer many opportunities for manipulating, exploring, and
practicing and are thus highly recommended as avenues for fostering the
cognitive competencies of young children (Dunst *et al.*, 1996). While
the value of play to the social and emotional development of young

children has long been recognized, an understanding of its role in cognitive development has been steadily growing, especially since the cognitive theories of Piaget and Vygotsky came into prominence in the late 1960s (Johnson *et al.*, 1987). While at play – especially when engaged in "make-believe" or "pretend" play – children frequently use one thing to stand for something else or they adopt the role of another person. According to Vygotsky, such use of "representations" or symbols fosters the development of abstract thought. While at play, children often practice newly acquired mental as well as physical skills. Mental skills involved in play may include discrimination, problem solving, and decision making. According to Piaget, engaging in play behaviors can not only provide practice for such skills, but lead to consolidation of skills as well.

Due to the "high merits" afforded to play for young children, some educators are beginning to plan their entire program around play activities, with extended periods of time allotted to "free play." For them, a word of caution is in order. Not all forms of free play contribute to cognitive and/or social development. In fact, "there is little evidence linking gross motor play or nonsocial forms of dramatic play with growth in intellectual or social skills" (Johnson *et al.*, 1987, p. 18). Characteristics of play that seem to contribute to development include: (1) adult and peer involvement (Johnson *et al.*, 1987); (2) activities that reflect or slightly stretch the child's current social or cognitive abilities (Johnson *et al.*, 1987), and (3) activities that are initiated by the child (Dunst *et al.*, 1996).

### Recommended practices

Recommended practices for cognitive-based intervention are consistent with the research into the value of play and the characteristics of play most conducive to development. There follows a presentation of several of these "recommended practices," along with a brief discussion of each.

- "Intervention activities should be planned and implemented so that they complement and encourage child-initiated play and interactions with people and objects" (Dunst *et al.*, 1996, p. 178). As previously discussed (see Chapter 3), children are active participants in the learning process. They acquire cognitive skills through the construction of their own knowledge rather than as passive recipients of what is handed to them. Planning educational programs around child-initiated play reflects an understanding of children as active learners and competent beings. When given meaningful choices, the activities that children self-initiate usually reflect their current interests and level of competence. As research indicates, children tend to participate more actively and intensely in child-directed versus adult-directed activities and "are more likely to attend to and retain information that relates directly to their interests and that is within their range of competence" (Dunst *et al.*, p. 178).

Many teachers find it challenging to utilize play and child-initiated activities as a primary context for accomplishing individual child goals. They find that children do not always initiate activities related to their intervention targets (i.e., individualized objectives). Rather than "giving up" on child-initiated activities and working from a different approach, Dunst *et al.* (1996) suggest identifying intervention targets that are consistent with the child's interests and current levels of competence. "Intervention targets that build on what children already do and how they behave in various settings will naturally lead to intervention procedures and strategies that lead to activities that are competence enhancing" (Dunst *et al.*, 1996, p. 179).

While intervention for cognitive development should be based on child-initiated activities, the environment in which this intervention takes place should be arranged so as to elicit the desired behaviors (i.e., the targeted goals for the child). Research findings indicate that both physical and organizational characteristics of the environment influence the nature of children's activities in the early childhood classroom, but that the "interventive" impact of environmental determinants are often neglected by early childhood teachers (Dunst *et al.*, 1996). Because of the importance of the environment to the curriculum, a more detailed discussion about the "environment as curriculum" is presented in the first section of Chapter 11.

- "Responsive teaching methods are the instructional strategies of choice when promoting cognitive competence" (Dunst *et al.*, 1996, p. 180). The term "responsive teaching" describes an instructional approach that utilizes social responsiveness (e.g., smiles, praise, hugs, and other forms of positive attention) as a reinforcer to maintain or evoke further desired behaviors from the child. Positive social reinforcers tend to exert powerful influences on the acquisition of early cognitive competencies for both typically developing children and children with special educational needs.

Elements of responsive teaching include: (1) identifying and attending to materials and circumstances which elicit and maintain a child's engagement with objects and people; (2) arranging the physical and social environments in ways that invite and reinforce child-initiated activities; (3) using contingent social responsiveness to support and encourage elaboration of targeted behaviors; and (4) capitalizing on "teachable moments" that arise naturally in unstructured or semistructured situations. There follows a case study of James and examples of how each of the responsive teaching elements listed above might be incorporated into his intervention program for fostering cognitive competencies.

## Case study – James

### Background information

Seven-year-old James is in a Year 2 class at Dorr Primary School. James has had frequent bouts of otitis media (middle ear infection) during his early childhood years, with accompanying hearing loss. While the medical condition seems to be under control, related social and academic concerns make him eligible for special education services. In the areas of cognition and speech/language development, James seems to be functioning one to two years behind his age-mates.

James is fascinated with living things, especially animals. He spends a considerable amount of "free time" watching the birds around the bird feeder and the fish in the aquarium. His favorite books are about dolphins, dogs, and insects; and play outdoors for James usually involves digging in the ground or poking around in leaves and grass.

- *Strategy 1: Identifying and attending to materials and circumstances which elicit and maintain a child's engagement with objects and people.* Ms. Smith, the Year 2 teacher, notes James's interest in living things and decides to join him in some of his explorations. She finds a large chart depicting the various songbirds that frequent the bird feeder. She talks with James about the different birds he has already seen at the feeder and "wonders out loud" which birds are there most often. She suggests "keeping track" of the different birds seen at the feeder over the next three days. With James, she constructs a simple chart with pictures to record the information. Ms. Smith helps James write his name on the chart, attaches it to a clipboard, and hangs it near the observation window.

  James shows great interest in this project and eagerly records information about the different birds he sees. After the third day of observation and recording, Ms. Smith suggests that James might like to "write" a report about his project. She offers to do the printing if he tells her what to write. James likes the idea, but suggests they write a book instead of a report. Ms. Smith readily agrees and the two begin the process.

  In this scenario, Ms. Smith identifies what James is interested

102

in and then provides materials and devises related activities to extend his understanding about the topic (i.e., birds). In addition to providing information and new understanding, Ms. Smith also introduces James to different ways of thinking about the topic. Instead of simply learning the names of birds, Ms. Smith encourages closer observation and data collection skills. She does this, not by showing and telling, but by engaging James in an interesting and meaningful activity. By working with him, Ms. Smith is able to elicit and maintain his engagement with objects and people (which at this point is primarily herself).

- *Strategy 2: Arranging the physical and social environments in ways that invite and reinforce child-initiated activities.* In the process of writing the "Book of Birds" with James, Ms. Smith brings in several library books about birds. James spends time examining these books and then suggests that "their book" should include some pictures. Ms. Smith and James look at the library books and notice that some pictures are photos and others are drawings of birds. James says that he would like to have both photos and drawings in his book, so Ms. Smith looks for ways to facilitate this.

  In addition to bringing in a camera and helping James get "some good shots" of the birds, she also introduces bird-related materials to the art center, including some feathers. She makes a rubbing of a feather and suggests that it might be used to decorate some of the pages in the book. James agrees and decides to make some rubbings of his own. James also dips a feather in some paint and discovers that the feather works like a paint brush. James is excited about his discovery and calls Ms. Smith over to the table to share it with her.

  The physical environment, in this instance, was arranged to include new materials relating to the bird project, while the social environment (especially Ms. Smith's availability and support) reinforced James's own initiatives. In the process, James was exposed to various forms of representation and discovered interesting properties about such materials as books, feathers, and paints. He also gained confidence and competence in purposeful planning and decision making.

- *Strategy 3: Using contingent social responsiveness to support and encourage elaboration of targeted behaviors.* Ms. Smith praises James for his discovery at the art table and suggests that he share his discovery with the rest of the class. She alerts the class by ringing the "discovery bell" – a small bell that is used only on special occasions when something new or especially interesting has been discovered by one child, or a small group of the children. After the other children gather around the art table, Ms. Smith invites James to show them what he has discovered. As one of the intervention goals for James is the sequencing of information related to his own experiences, Ms. Smith has just incorporated a targeted goal in the activities of the moment. The other children are impressed by James's discovery and several of them choose to work at the art table with him. In this instance, positive responses from both teacher and peers provide support to James's emerging cognitive development skills.

- *Strategy 4: Capitalizing on "teachable moments" that arise naturally in unstructured or semistructured situations.* After the "Book of Birds" by James is completed, Ms. Smith suggests they add it to the classroom library. She even suggests that it become the "featured book" of the week. Each week a different featured book (either commercial or student made) is displayed on a special book stand and the text recorded on an audio tape, so that individual children can listen to it with headphones during "learning center" time.

  One of the other children, Lynette, recalls that several weeks previously a local author visited the classroom and that the children had the opportunity to interview her. Lynette suggests that they interview James about his book. Concerned that a "whole class" interview might be intimidating to James and that he may not handle it well, Ms. Smith suggests that the interview be conducted as a news report, with Lynette serving as the interviewer. The children love the idea! Ms. Smith uses this opportunity to introduce the class to different types of interviews done on the radio and TV and involves them in interviewing each other with "pretend" microphones. Ms. Smith thus used a "teachable moment" (i.e., the moment Lynette suggested interviewing James) to plan a class activity that would involve the whole group while focusing on several of James's targeted intervention goals, including memory and sequencing of information related to personal experiences.

# 6

# ORIGINS, PREVENTION, AND IMPACT OF DISABILITIES

## Origins/causes of developmental disabilities

The origins or causes of developmental disabilities are varied and complex. For some children with disabilities, the origins are known; for others, unknown. At times, the origins relate to conditions and/or circumstances existing prior to or near the time of birth. At other times, the origin of a child's disability relates to conditions and/or circumstances experienced during the early childhood or later years. Some disabilities that are present at birth are due to maternal and/or genetic conditions over which the parent has little or no control. Some disabilities, however, are caused by conditions within the physical or social environment experienced by the developing fetus or young child over which adults may have some control. Many of the disabilities caused by environmental conditions are preventable.

### *Maternal conditions*

Certain health-related conditions of a pregnant mother can put a fetus at risk of developmental disabilities. These conditions include diabetes, hypertension, drug and alcohol addiction, heart disease, and eating disorders. Of these conditions, alcohol addiction is perhaps the most damaging, in that it is the leading known cause of mental retardation and usually leads to life-long disabilities (Howard *et al.*, 1997).

While the negative effects of alcohol on the developing fetus have been known for a long time (Weiner & Morse, 1988), it was not until the 1970s that the term fetal alcohol syndrome (FAS) was first used to describe a set of characteristics associated with this syndrome. The three primary characteristics of FAS are growth deficiency, central nervous system dysfunction, and abnormal facial features, including a short upturned nose, thin lips, wide-set eyes, and a flat midface (Burgess & Streissguth, 1992). Many young children with FAS also have serious behavioral problems. They tend to be hyperactive, impulsive, non-compliant, have language and communication difficulties (especially in pragmatics), and have problems with self-regulation, judgment, and decision making (Burgess & Streissguth, 1992). Dealing with the behavioral problems of children with FAS can be especially challenging in that the types of consequences that are usually effective with most children seem to have little effect on children with FAS. Parents and teachers who have tried the consistent use of such consequences as praise, smiles, reprimands, withdrawal of privileges, etc. generally find that these strategies are ineffective with children with FAS. Children with FAS seem to miss the connection between their actions and the consequences that follow.

Age and certain genetic conditions (e.g., cystic fibrosis, PKU, etc.) of a pregnant woman can also put a fetus at risk. Mothers younger than 20 years and older than 40 years have an increased risk of a premature delivery and congenital abnormalities in their fetus. Intervention programs that focus on educating women in these conditions and encouraging them to seek health care and counseling before becoming pregnant can significantly reduce the risk of having children with developmental disabilities.

### Socioeconomic conditions

A number of socioeconomic factors also influence the relative health and developmental status of infants and young children. Young, single mothers with few support networks, for example, have a higher incidence of premature delivery and low birth weight infants than the general population (Report of Consensus Conferences, 1987). Poverty is another significant factor putting children at risk of developmental disabilities. Conditions of poverty make both direct and indirect attacks on children's development (Bowman, 1992). As many low-income families lack the resources to ward off these attacks, children living in poverty are far more likely to experience developmental disabilities than children from other segments of the population. Even children from middle- or upper-class homes who experience serious perinatal stress are less likely to experience developmental disabilities than poor children who have not experienced such stress. Aylward (1990) found that "by age 18, adolescents who lived in poverty were ten times more likely to have serious learning and behavioral problems than were those who had survived severe prenatal stress" (p. 3). Obviously, not all risk factors are equal in terms of probable impact. In fact, children living in poverty are considered to be the most at-risk population (Bowman, 1992).

Health-related problems make direct attacks on children living in poverty, and include such risk factors as inadequate food, shelter, and care. According to professional estimates, health problems (including low birth weight, lead poison, anemia, and hearing problems) may account for as much as 30% of the variance between the cognitive development of poor and middle-class children (Bowman, 1992).

Children with borderline nutritional levels, especially when compounded by poor health services, often experience chronic and acute viral and bacterial illnesses, which in turn foster irritability, distractibility, and passivity. Children suffering from these conditions are less likely to engage in active exploration of the environment and are less receptive to environmental feedback. This situation represents an indirect, but formidable, attack on development and learning. Other indirect attacks include a sense of hopelessness, despair, and, at times, disorganized family functioning – all of which tend to be exacerbated by the conditions of poverty. Additionally, living in a depressed community tends to make life dangerous and unpredictable, resulting in added stress for young children and their families (Bowman, 1992).

### Environmental assaults

While "within-family" problems can certainly put a young child at risk of developmental delay or disability, there are many other risk factors outside the family which can be equally problematic. Such risk factors are more prevalent in low-income and racial minority communities (Blahna & Toch, 1993; Collin, 1993) and are usually outside the family's realm of control. Such risk factors include exposure to toxic pollutants in the air, water, and food. Children living in low-income and racial minority communities experience higher than average exposure to such pollutants. A study done in the United States indicates that three out every four toxic waste dumps that fail to comply with the Environmental Protection Agency regulations are in Black or Hispanic neighborhoods (Environmental Protection Agency, 1992). In response to this unequal distribution of environmental assault conditions, an environmental justice movement has been initiated. A major goal of this movement is to create public awareness of these unjust conditions and to stimulate action to rectify such conditions (Bullard, 1994; Chavis, 1992).

Most families living in low-income and environmentally degraded neighborhoods do so not by choice, but because they lack the mobility to escape such areas (Rogue, 1993). Parents who live in these areas pay a high price for doing so – not in terms of financial costs to them, but in terms of increased health and learning problems for their children. Health problems linked to exposure to high levels of toxic wastes and other forms of environmental degradation include a higher incidence of deformed fetuses, cancer, respiratory illnesses, childhood leukemia, and immune deficiency (Adeola, 1994). Children exposed to environmental hazards are also at greater risk of mental retardation and other forms of learning disabilities.

## Social toxicity

James Garbarino (1997) uses the term "social toxicity" in reference to the harmful social climate that is domoralizing families and communities throughout the world. The social environment of children today, he says, "has become poisonous to their development – just as toxic substances in the environment threaten human well-being and survival" (pp. 13–14). Social conditions that Garbarino refers to as the "social equivalents" to lead and smoke in the air, the PCBs in the water, and pesticides in the food chain, include violence, poverty, the disruption of family relationships, despair, depression, paranoia, nastiness, and alienation. Such conditions mean that "more and more children are in greater and greater trouble" (Garbarino, 1997, p. 13). The children who are most likely to be seriously harmed by these socially toxic conditions are those who have accumulated the most developmental risk factors.

# Focus on prevention

While a *preventive* framework has been proposed for intervention services with young children and their families (Meisels, 1991; Simeonsson, 1991b), an *intervention* perspective seems to be the dominant force driving the field. Efforts in early childhood special education are usually focused on identifying the problem and then providing services to minimize the negative impact of the disabling condition. A preventive framework would focus on preventing the occurrence of a disabling condition before children are in a situation that tends to cause the problem. A preventive approach would certainly be preferable to trying to "fix it" (i.e., the problem) or minimizing the impact "after the fact."

The importance of prevention is reflected in a story told by Slavin (1996) in an argument on preventing learning disabilities. In this story, there was a town with a playground on the edge of a cliff. Periodically, a child would fall over the cliff. Discussion on what to do about the problem resulted in two possible solutions – one to put up a fence at the top of the cliff; the other to put an ambulance at the bottom. The fence certainly represents the preferred approach to prevention.

## Levels of prevention

Efforts to keep a problem from occurring are referred to as prevention. Prevention can be provided at three different levels: primary, secondary, and tertiary. Primary prevention usually means preventing problems from occurring before a child is born (or, as reflected in the story, putting up a fence before a child enters the playground). Secondary prevention involves preventing problems which have a high probability of occurring even though a disabling condition is not evident at the present time. In relation to the playground story, this might mean providing a safety net or cushion for a child who falls over the cliff. The net or cushion is intended to soften the blow. Tertiary prevention, on the other hand, involves providing services after a problem has already occurred (e.g., providing medical care after the child has hit the ground and suffered bodily harm). The purpose of tertiary prevention is to prevent secondary or related problems from developing (e.g., setting the broken bones before the body becomes deformed or stopping the bleeding before the child dies).

The majority of intervention programs in education exemplify a secondary prevention framework, where the goal is to reduce the duration or severity of developmental delays through the provision of habilitative and therapeutic interventions for the child (Simeonsson, 1991). Services for families linked to this goal are typically designed to help the family cope with the initial shock of the child's diagnosis and to support the family in meeting the special needs of the child. There is no doubt that this form of prevention warrants a great deal of attention and resources. Considerable effort, however, should also be devoted to primary prevention initiatives, where the emphasis is on promoting health, safety, and optimal development of young children – before they experience the fall over the cliff.

If lead is detected in a child's home and/or neighborhood playground, for example, primary prevention steps should be taken to keep the child out of harm's way before he or she ingests any or much of the harmful substance. Primary prevention services, in this case, might consist of on-going monitoring of the child and his or her living situation, home visits by early intervention specialists, educational materials for the parents, and advocacy efforts in the community to remove the environmental hazard.

Recommended practices in early intervention for young children with special needs call for a close linkage between early identification and prevention (Meisels, 1991). While intervention programs are certainly needed that attend to the special needs of young children with disabilities, programs are also needed for children who are still healthy but, because of certain biological or environmental risk factors, have a higher likelihood of experiencing developmental delay than children not exposed to such risk factors. Programs are needed for the children playing at the top of the hill, often precariously close to the edge. Effective prevention services should be provided soon enough and with sufficient foresight and care to keep the children from falling over the cliff and suffering physical, social, and/or academic damage.

## The great divide

Too often, a "great divide" exists between what is known about risk factors and what is provided in the way of educational or developmental prevention and intervention services. In many cases, we know the cliff is there, and we know the likely impact of the fall. Yet children often continue to play at the very edge and some fall.

While we build fences or provide cushions for some of the factors placing young children at risk, there are other risk factors that go largely unaddressed. One major area of concern is that of exposure to environmental assaults, such as exposure to lead poisoning, incinerator smoke and ash, crowding and congestion, and exposure to other problematic biomedical substances and conditions. As studies have shown, exposure to such conditions is associated with a wide variety of health problems, learning disabilities, restlessness, attention problems, and antisocial behavior (Adeola, 1994).

While it is unrealistic to suggest that educators need somehow to resolve the issues relating to poverty and other risk conditions, they should be aware of factors placing children at risk of developmental delays and become advocates for children in speaking against such conditions. A likely starting point to bridging this divide is to initiate dialogue between professionals in the environmental health/environmental justice fields, and professionals in early intervention. While it has been stated that "at risk does not mean doomed" (Ramey & Ramey, 1992), this may be true only in situations where risk factors are identified and acted upon. Some factors, such as environmental assaults, are less obvious and more problematic than others. It is around these risk factors that dialogue and collaboration between special educators and environmental health/ environmental justice professionals should take place.

The concept of cross-disciplinary dialogue and collaboration matches well the transdisciplinary teaming approach that is generally considered to be reflective of "recommended practices" in early intervention. With the transdisciplinary approach, individuals work together toward common goals, and members of the team share knowledge and skills across traditional disciplinary boundaries. Disciplines often involved in early intervention services include child development and early childhood education, speech/language and hearing services, special education, educational psychology, physical and occupational therapy, health and nutrition, and social work. An important, but often overlooked area, is environmental health.

One indication of silence instead of dialogue between early intervention and environmental health professionals has been identified through a recent review of the early intervention literature (Wilson & Reid, 1996). This particular review consisted of a study of all the articles in three major publications in the field of early intervention and early childhood special education published from January 1990 through January 1996 in the United States. The journals reviewed were the *Journal of Early Intervention*, *Topics in Early Childhood Special Education*, and *Infants and Young Children*. From this entire review, there were no articles identified that focused on the risks of environmental assaults on young children. In fact, there was only one article even mentioning any type of environmental assault (as this relates to the physical versus social environment) as a possible risk factor for infants and young children. When environmental concerns were mentioned, the risk factors listed related almost exclusively to deficiencies or problems *within the family* or the family situation (e.g., poor parenting skills, drug or alcohol abuse, illiteracy, poverty, homelessness, teen pregnancy, mothers with limited intelligence, etc.). One article analyzed for this particular study listed thirty different variables that put young children at risk (Dunst, 1993). Only one out of the thirty variables relates to environmental assaults (i.e., toxic substances). The other twenty-nine suggest that the problem lies within the family or the family situation.

A review of several early intervention/early childhood special education textbooks indicate that they also fail to adequately discuss the impact of environmental assaults on infants and young children. Four texts published since 1989 were carefully reviewed. Each of these texts include sections on prevention and risk factors, yet there was very little mention of environmental assaults. As Table 6.1 indicates, almost all the risk factors mentioned relate to deficiencies or problems within the family.

Garbarino (1997) addresses the "blaming-the-parent" issue in his discussions on social toxicity. He uses the example of a city plagued by cholera, where all parents face grave danger for their children. The ability to ward off this danger, however, varies in relation to the competencies and resources available to the parents. Some parents would have more success delivering drinkable water to their children than would other parents. Yet, at times, even the more competent parents would fail. Garbarino asks, "Would we blame them, or point the finger at the community's failed water purification system?" and notes that "in a socially toxic environment, the same principle holds" (p. 15).

### Related recommendations

In addition to expanding the early intervention team to include environmental health professionals and considering more than the "within family" variables that put young children at risk, three additional recommendations for prevention are as follows:

*Table 6.1* Text review of environmental risk factors

| Text (date of publication) | Risk factors mentioned |
| --- | --- |
| Text 1 (1995) | lack of social and or learning opportunities<br>mother with low IQ<br>poor nutrition<br>physical or psychological abuse<br>poor housing<br>poverty and related concerns including exposure to toxic environment<br>non-nurturing milieu<br>exposure to violent situations<br>socially isolated families<br>non-nurturing family<br>families who are psychologically unavailable to their children<br>limited learning opportunities<br>poor parenting<br>neglect |
| Text 2 (1996) | limited maternal and family care<br>limited health care<br>limited opportunities for expression of adaptive behaviors<br>limited physical and social stimulation |
| Text 3 (1991) | poverty/low SES<br>single parenthood<br>drug exposure<br>alcohol abuse<br>teenage parents<br>mental illness in parents<br>limited or dysfunctional parent–infant interactions<br>parental disabilities<br>parental maladjustments and/or psychiatric disorders<br>dysfunctional or disorganized parental behaviors<br>extended family members who are substance abusers, contribute to an atmosphere of family violence, or display other dysfunctional interaction patterns<br>unsafe or inadequate housing conditions and poor sanitation facilities<br>lack of safe play areas |
| Text 4 (1989) | poor or abusive homes<br>lack of prenatal care<br>poor nutrition of pregnant teenager<br>poverty |

- Define early intervention within the context of a prevention framework. Working from a prevention framework would require an understanding of risk factors that exist both within and outside the family unit. Early intervention efforts and resources would then be mobilized to address these concerns, preferably before the young child is negatively impacted by them. Working from this perspective would mean conceptualizing, prioritizing, and planning early intervention programs from a "levels of prevention framework," as suggested in the literature by Simeonsson (1991b). Such a framework would allow for a wide range of services to be provided for children and families at each level of prevention (i.e., primary, secondary, and tertiary). This framework represents an inclusive versus exclusive model, in that services are not exclusive to a given level of prevention (Simeonsson, 1991a). As such, this framework represents a level-of-concern model "that focuses on the needs of children as the basis for prevention, rather than eligibility defined by threshold criteria" (Simeonsson, 1991a, p. 54). Within this framework, a comprehensive continuum of early intervention services is provided, rather than separate categories of services – often understood to be under the domain of some *other* agency or program.

- Match intensity and breadth of prevention/intervention services to the extent of risks experienced by young children. As indicated earlier, not all risk factors are equal in terms of possible or probable impact, with children living in poverty representing the most at-risk population. To be effective, prevention and intervention services for young children living in poverty should therefore be intense. Providing such services requires a commitment of extensive resources, both human and material (Bowman, 1992). Without such a commitment, early education programs for poor children remain severely compromised.

  As the study by Wilson and Reid (1996) indicates, there is a tendency for intervention programs to focus on problems within the family, such as irresponsible and/or unresponsive parenting, disorganized home life, and inadequate child care arrangements. There is also a concomitant tendency to target interventions to particular children and/or their parents. This approach, in effect, attempts to cure sociological problems with treatments aimed at conditions within an individual and/or his or her family. Such efforts are generally futile, and may be immoral as well (Bowman, 1991).

- Establish a system for identifying and tracking/monitoring children who are most at risk of experiencing environmental assaults and for those who have already experienced such assaults. Special ongoing child identification efforts should be directed toward children living in areas that are environmentally compromised or suspected of being environmentally degraded. In too many cases, even after neighborhoods and individual homes are identified as fraught with environmental hazards, the young children living in these communities and homes receive no special attention until irreparable damage has been done. In other cases, the environmental risks within communities go unidentified or unreported. For the safety and well-being of all involved – but especially for young children – efforts should be made to identify the incidence, prevalence, and relative risk of environmental hazards in individual local communities. Once these risks are identified, systems for monitoring vulnerable children should be established and efforts to remove the hazards immediately initiated.

As suggested by Shonkoff and Meisels (1991), monitoring of individual children should be considered an important aspect of early intervention services. They propose defining early intervention as "a continuum of individualized services" (p. 22) and suggest that eligibility criteria for such services be based on individualized assessments, rather than arbitrary categorical distinctions. It should be assumed that an important part of an *individualized* assessment would focus on the physical environment of the child and would include a concern for possible environmental assaults. While all children and families should participate in screening on multiple occasions while the child is young (Kochanek & Buka, 1991), it is critically important that children exposed to environmental assaults participate in such screenings.

### Further suggestions for prevention

There follow some specific steps that might be taken toward actualizing recommended practices relating to prevention.

- Differentiate professional roles and skills by level of prevention and associated child and family interventions.
- Include information about environmental assaults in preservice and inservice programs for professionals involved in early intervention and early childhood special education services.
- Develop and utilize home and neighborhood inventories designed to identify possible environmental hazards for young children.
- Organize educational and advocacy training programs for parents living in neighborhoods with higher-than-average environmental health problems.
- Increase public awareness of environmental assault and environmental justice issues and advocate community mobilization to address these issues.

- Promote and increase comprehensive access to health screenings.
- Assist families in accessing key public and private health and social service programs.

## Impact of a disability on the home and school environment

Disabilities affect not only individuals with special needs, but others who interact with them as well. Major impacts are felt by other people in both the home and school environment.

### Impact in the home

A recent headline in a community newspaper read as follows: "Parents give up child with genetic disorder" (*The Blade*, 1997). The child referred to is Kyle, a 6-year-old boy suffering from Fragile X syndrome, a common form of hereditary mental retardation. According to the article, Kyle's parents gave temporary custody of their son to the county children services agency, because they found that Kyle's genetic disorder made it impossible to control his temper.

While the action taken by Kyle's parents represents a more extreme response to dealing with a child with a disability than that taken by most parents, frustration and feelings of not knowing what to do are not unusual for parents of children with behavior disorders and other types of special needs. From the moment a disability is manifested and/or identified, parenting does become more complex and difficult. Yet it would be incorrect to assume, just because Kyle's parents found it impossible to deal with his special needs, that all or most parents of children with disabilities are somehow unable to cope.

Research on families of children with disabilities conducted prior to the 1990s suggested that such families had an increased risk of family dysfunction. Parent education and involvement programs were then developed with this assumption in mind. Family needs assessments, for example, were often designed to identify the families' weaknesses. It was also not unusual for early interventionists to assume that families were having trouble coping and that, because of this, it would be better to keep the child in a full-day versus half-day program. The reasoning was that, due to the way the families were "handling the situation," time with the parents was not in the best interests of the child.

Recent research, however, focuses less on "the pathology of deficiency" and more on strengths and resources available to families of children with disabilities. Findings from this research suggest that the psychosocial functioning of families of children with disabilities is more like that of families of children without disabilities than it is different from them

(Howard *et al.*, 1997). This line of research is based on the premise that all families experience needs and stressors, but that they also have unique ways of coping with stress in their lives. Some families require the assistance of outside agencies to deal with this stress and meet some of their needs; others do not. Having a child with a disability, however, is not considered to be the determining factor in whether or not the family needs special assistance for coping with the challenges of daily living. In fact, as many parents have indicated, one of the things they want interventionists to keep in mind is that having a child with a disability does not make them "special, unusual, dysfunctional, or in any way homogeneous" (Howard *et al.*, 1997, p. 318).

It is true that, in addition to the basic needs of all families (e.g., financial stability, adequate housing, safe neighborhoods, food and clothing, health care, etc.), certain stressors may be more prominent in families of children with disabilities. While such stressors do not make the families deficient, weak, or dysfunctional, they may call for a greater amount of family "hardiness" (Failla & Jones, 1991). Howard *et al.* (1997) define hardiness in relation to the following three dimensions:

- a sense of control or the ability to influence events rather than being controlled by them;
- a commitment to becoming actively involved in events and viewing them as meaningful;
- recognition of life changes as opportunities for growth and development, and not as a burden.

Life is different, not dysfunctional, when a family has a child with a disability. One area of difference often experienced early in the child's life relates to parent–child interaction. The first minutes and hours of life are critical to the bonding process. A risk or disabling condition that prevents the parents from interacting with their newborn child can get in the way of such bonding. In response to this concern, nurseries and neonatal intensive care units are now allowing parents more opportunities to hold, touch, and observe their newborn children.

A possible adverse response to this research, however, could be an increase in parental anxiety and negative emotions already associated with the prospects of parenting a child with special needs (Hanson, 1996). A healthier response, in terms of parent–child interaction, would focus on a wide range of individual variation in meeting a child's psychological requirements. "Once mothers can appreciate this, that the neonate separated from his mother is not permanently damaged . . . that the child whose signals are not always easy to understand is not doomed to an unhealthy parent attachment . . . they can perhaps relax and actually become better mothers" (Chess & Thomas, 1982, p. 221).

This does not mean that early attachments are not important. As indicated in Chapter 5, early attachments are linked to the child's social/emotional development and the formation of subsequent relationships (Ainsworth, 1973; Bowlby, 1982). Parents and interventionists need to appreciate this importance and focus on enhancing the parent–child interactions. Infants born at risk often demonstrate behavioral difficulties that make engagement in social interactions especially challenging. Awareness of these difficulties can help adults become better observers and interpreters of the child's interactional cues and more effective in establishing a mutually rewarding relationship.

The behavioral difficulties often experienced by infants born at-risk or disabled tend to be in the areas of responsivity, irritability, motor, feeding, and visual responses. These difficulties tend to exert a powerful negative influence on the dynamics of parent–infant interactions. The infant's physical characteristics can also play a role in the way parents relate to their child. Muscle tone, posture, and medical fragility, for example, can affect the way the mother handles and positions the child. Even as the child grows older, the child's disability can continue to influence parents to be anxious and overly protective. They may find themselves restricting their child's independence and explorations.

Young children with disabilities are often less active and responsive than their typically developing peers. They also tend to provide fewer or different interactional cues, making them less competent interactive partners. In adjusting to these interactional differences, parents of children with disabilities tend to be more directive (i.e., use more commands) and less interactive than may typically occur with non-disabled children (Hanson, 1996).

It is not only the presence of a handicapping condition that should be considered when analyzing parent–child interactions. Other characteristics of young children that affect the parent–child interactional process include sex, birth order, temperament, and age. In working with parents, interventionists should thus consider the dynamics of the whole situation versus being specifically focused on the handicapping condition. Interventionists are probably most helpful to parents when they support them in their role (versus "taking over" for them) and provide assistance to them in reading, understanding, and responding to their child's cues.

### Impact on the school environment

Young children with disabilities require individualized educational experiences to promote attainment of their unique potential. Individualized experiences, however, need not be provided in a separate classroom or school setting. Most young children with special educational needs can be served in the regular classroom, as long as special supports are provided as needed. Such supports may include adaptive equipment, a teaching assistant, and the involvement of specialists (e.g., special educator, speech/language pathologist, occupational and/or physical therapists, etc.).

Having a child in the classroom with SEN places additional responsibilities on the teacher and special challenges for all involved, including intervention specialists, administrators, support staff, and even peers. Individual adaptations often have to be made in the areas of curriculum, materials, space, instruction, and expectations. In addition to issues of accessibility which need to be addressed, other areas of concern include social acceptance, health and safety, the increased need for one-to-one assistance, individualized educational goals and objectives, and ongoing assessment. The following case study illustrates how these added responsibilities and challenges might impact on an educational program.

---

## Case study – Ronnie

### Background information

Ronnie was diagnosed soon after birth as having fetal alcohol syndrome (FAS) and cerebral palsy. His mother, Cheryl, who was 17 at the time, had consumed alcohol several times a week during her pregnancy. Cheryl was unmarried, had dropped out of school, and had no permanent living arrangements. She was not interested in keeping her baby. Ronnie's father, Larry, however, felt that the baby should not be given up for adoption. As Larry was not able to care for the child, Ronnie was placed in a foster home upon his dismissal from the hospital. Ronnie was still living in this same foster home when he entered his first year (Reception year) of school.

Ronnie was small for his age, unable to walk independently or sit unsupported, and seemed to be functioning cognitively about two years behind his age-mates. Additionally, Ronnie would often strike out at the other children when they were "too close" to him and threw around his toys and other materials when he was angry or frustrated.

Mrs. Hyman, the Reception year teacher, had been the school district's "Teacher of the Year" two years previously. Her award was based on her creative use of literature and the arts in working with young children. While she had had children with SEN in her class before, none were as behaviorally challenged as Ronnie. Ronnie's inattentiveness and distractibility were major obstacles to his participation in many of the group activities that Mrs. Hyman had always found quite successful, even with children with varying abilities.

The first challenge faced by the school at the time of Ronnie's enrollment was physical accessibility. A wheelchair-accessible bus had to be re-routed to provide transportation for Ronnie to and from school. A ramp had to be installed at one of the school entrances and the learning centers in the classroom rearranged to accommodate Ronnie's wheelchair. Several pieces of adaptive equipment were ordered, including a "corner chair" and "safety swing," to provide support for Ronnie during both indoor and outdoor activities.

One of the most frustrating situations for Mrs. Hyman was having to deal with Ronnie's emotional outbursts during the day. Not only did these outbursts disrupt group activities, they were also distressing for the other children. Some children were fearful and cried when Ronnie screamed at them or hit them. Most of the children avoided being near him.

Mrs. Hyman also found it difficult to attend to Ronnie's many physical needs. Ronnie needed special assistance during lunch and snacks, as attempts to eat on his own always resulted in spills and he sometimes threw food and eating utensils around. Ronnie needed one-on-one assistance when going to the bathroom, when being transferred to or from his wheelchair or other seating arrangements, when putting on a sweater or coat, or when engaged in almost any other self-help task. Mrs. Hyman tried to balance large group activities with individual assistance. When leading a group activity in which Ronnie seldom participated, Mrs. Hyman would tell Ronnie that he would have to wait for assistance until she was ready to help him. Ronnie usually responded by screaming, throwing things if he could, and tearing at his clothes.

### Discussion

While physical adaptations were made to accommodate Ronnie's special needs, sufficient social and instructional adaptations were not provided. Additionally, Mrs. Hyman approached the challenge more as a one-person task, versus turning to others for support and assistance. While the physical therapist, occupational therapist, and speech/language specialist each worked with Ronnie for 40 minutes per week, they did so in isolation from each other and in a therapy setting away from the regular classroom. A considerable amount of time each session was devoted to trying to get Ronnie to attend to the planned activities. After three months into the school year, Ronnie was showing very little progress toward his physical and occupational goals and no improvement in his use of language, social interaction skills, and ability to attend to tasks. The other children still avoided Ronnie; his outbursts continued on a frequent basis, and he showed little interest in group activities of any kind. Mrs. Hyman and Ronnie's foster mother began talking about moving Ronnie to a more restrictive classroom – i.e., a classroom serving only children with special behavioral problems. They felt that since Ronnie wasn't participating in group activities nor interacting with the other children anyway, he would benefit just as much from a setting serving only children with SEN.

A transdisciplinary intervention approach might have led to a different and more positive outcome for Ronnie. Members of a transdisciplinary team might have coordinated their efforts toward success in the classroom versus the accomplishment of isolated skills. Intervention therapies might have been provided in the classroom and within the context of the instructional activities. This support in the classroom might have provided the one-to-one attention Ronnie needed to participate successfully in various activities. Recognizing that full participation in some of the group activities was not realistic at this point, "partial participation" could have been the goal toward which the team worked. Additionally, peers in the classroom could have been coached on how to approach Ronnie as a potential friend. Instead of being either "too close" and upsetting Ronnie or avoiding him altogether, peers might have been coached to wave to him during a game, offer him a cookie at snack time, and say hello to him when he arrived.

While costly, the physical adaptations for a child with SEN are often the easiest type of adaptations to make. Social and instructional adaptations can be more complex and require more planning and team involvement. Without the social and instructional adaptations, however, the physical adaptations that are made may serve little purpose in achieving a successful mainstreaming experience.

# Part III

# FOCUS ON THE TEAM

Meeting the needs of young children with disabilities requires a community, versus single discipline, effort. It requires comprehensive and coordinated services that are possible only through an attitude and practice of teaming at both the interdisciplinary and interagency level.

Some of the special challenges that need to be addressed by the intervention team include appropriate assessment of young children, individualized programming in inclusive early years classrooms, coordination of services, monitoring child progress, and program evaluation. Some of these challenges are addressed in this section of the book, along with some discussion as to what constitutes an effective team and different models from which teams can operate. First, however, there is a brief discussion of children's rights and the need for a community to work together as a team to protect these rights. At all levels of teaming, parents are considered equal partners in the process of planning, implementing, and evaluating services for their young children.

# 7

# "IT TAKES A VILLAGE"

In 1996, Hillary Rodham Clinton, the First Lady of the United States, wrote a book entitled *It Takes a Village*, in which she addressed the need for community involvement in assuring children a safe and healthy place in which to live and grow. She said she chose the old African proverb, "It Takes a Village," as the title of her book "because it offers a timeless reminder that children will thrive only if their families thrive and if the whole of society cares enough to provide for them" (Clinton, 1996, p. 12). While Mrs. Clinton stresses the fact that "parents bear the first and primary responsibility for their sons and daughters," she also notes that "children exist in the world as well as in the family" (p. 11).

This chapter is also titled "It Takes a Village," in recognition of the fact that the needs of young children with disabilities are complex and multifaceted and that meeting these needs requires the support and involvement of a community of people. Different disciplines and different agencies must come together to form a cooperative team if the best interests of children are to be protected.

## Children's rights

All children require special attention. Whether or not they are disabled or handicapped, they are certainly vulnerable. An understanding of this vulnerability and the need for special attention was first brought to the public's awareness in 1946 with the founding of UNICEF (United Nations International Children's Emergency Fund) after World War II, when there was a concern that children would not be adequately protected in the war relief effort. At the time, the concept that children required special attention was considered revolutionary (UNICEF, 1997).

At the end of the postwar reconstruction period, UNICEF's initial relief mandate was enlarged to include the survival and development of children. Recently, this mandate has changed dramatically once again. "The idea that children have special needs has given way to the conviction that children have rights, the same full spectrum of rights as adults: civil and political, social, cultural and economic" (UNICEF, 1997, p. 9).

The conviction that children have rights was formalized as the Convention on the Rights of the Child and adopted by the United Nations General Assembly on 2 September 1990. The adoption of this Convention by countries across the world suggests that "a *global* consensus about the meaning of childhood is emerging" (Garbarino, 1997, p. 15). Childhood, as proclaimed in this document, "is a protected niche in the social environment, a special time and place in the human life cycle, *having a special claim on the community*" (Garbarino, 1997, p. 15, emphasis added). The Convention clearly indicates that children have a right to be cared for, and that, while parents usually want to provide such care, they are not always able to do so without some support and assistance. In such cases, as outlined in the United Nations (UN) Convention, "society should pick up the tab" (Garbarino, 1997, p. 15).

As of September 1996, all of the UN countries except the Cook Islands, Oman, Somalia, Switzerland, the United Arab Emirates, and the United States have ratified the Convention, making it the most widely ratified human rights treaty in history. Ratifying the Convention obligates a country to undertake all appropriate measures to assist parents and other responsible parties in fulfilling their obligation to children, as described in the Convention.

The rights of children outlined in the Convention are comprehensive and include: (1) the right to survive and develop to their full potential; (2) the right to the highest attainable standard of health care; (3) the right to express views and receive information; and (4) the right to protection from all forms of sexual exploitation and sexual abuse. These rights also include the right to play (Article 31) and "the right of a physically or mentally disabled child to special care and assistance that will enable him or her to enjoy a full and decent life in conditions that ensure dignity and promote self-reliance" (Article 23). While the Convention recognizes that not every country has the resources necessary to ensure all economic, social, and cultural rights immediately, it does commit all countries involved to make those rights a priority and to ensure those rights are implemented to the maximum extent of available resources.

A Committee on the Rights of the Child has been established to monitor the process of implementing the Convention. Governments are required to report to the Committee within two years of ratification and every five years thereafter, outlining the steps taken toward protecting the rights of children. In addition to submitting their official reports, some countries have chosen to submit alternative reports as well, as a way of adding depth, detail, and perspective. The *UK Agenda for Children*, produced by the Children's Rights Development Unit, represents one such alternative report. Inspired by the Convention's directive to let the views of children be heard and make the Convention provisions widely known to adults and children alike, this report includes the input of children. There follow several examples of children's voices expressed in this report:

- "We need more bridges over the road so we can get to the park" (8-year-old from Bristol).
- "Parents shouldn't have the right to hit children. It just makes children grow up to be violent" (13-year-old from Lincolnshire).
- "Kids can't play where I live; needles everywhere, stolen cars, no one cares" (14-year-old from Manchester).

(UNICEF, 1997, p. 10)

The process of implementing the Convention is still in its infancy, but this international treaty has already started to make an impact. All around the world, lawyers, police officials, judges, teachers, and caregivers are being trained in the principles and application of the Convention. Individual countries have initiated important changes, such as the demobilization of child soldiers in Sierra Leone. Other major initiatives relating to the Convention include the World Congress against Commercial Sexual Exploitation of Children (Stockholm, 1996) and the International Conference on Child Labor (Oslo, 1997). While such initiatives are reason to celebrate, much remains to be done. More than 12.5 million children under age 5 in developing countries die each year, 9 million of them from causes for which inexpensive solutions and measures such as immunization and antibiotics have been routinely applied in the industrialized world for fifty years (UNICEF, 1997). As discussed in Chapter 6, there are many other social and environmental conditions which put young children at risk. These conditions are often associated with complex and difficult situations which can be remedied only through a concerted team approach in communities across the country.

## Ecological model for education and development

As stated by Mrs. Clinton and as outlined in the Convention on the Rights of the Child, children and families do not live in isolation. They live within a larger unit called a community. There are various levels of community affecting young children. These range from the community of the child's own family, to the local and state community, and finally to the global community extending across different countries of the world. The rights of young children need to be addressed and protected within each level of community.

Historically, intervention services for young children with disabilities focused primarily on the child with special needs, without much consideration as to the communities to which he or she belonged. Early intervention professionals spent most of their time assessing young children and planning instructional activities to enhance their development. While this child-focused approach will always be a part of early intervention, recent understandings add a broader perspective to the

125

factors that influence children's growth and development. Understandings based on the influence of one's community and systems theory have contributed significantly to this broader perspective.

According to the systems theory perspective, individuals, families, organizations, and agencies are viewed not as separate units, but as components of an "organized whole." This "whole" is comprised of interrelated and interdependent components. If one component experiences change, the whole system changes. If one component is weak or in trouble, the whole system is weak and in trouble. If a child has a disability, his or her entire family is affected, and the "whole system" (i.e., the community) needs to be involved in providing the support and resources necessary for maximizing the child's growth and development.

An understanding of systems theory has led to the development of an ecological model for education and development. According to this model, a child's ecological environment is "a nested arrangement of structures" (Bronfenbrenner, 1979), where each level is contained within the next level. Bronfenbrenner identified four levels of the environment: microsystem, mesosystem, exosystem, and macrosystem. The microsystem is the setting in which the child spends most of his or her time and usually includes the child's home, the homes of other relatives and friends, and child care centers or family day care homes. For some children with special needs, the hospital or other institutional settings may also be included in their microsystem. The mesosystem consists of relationships among the microsystem components of which the child is a part at a particular point in his or her life. For a young child with special needs, the mesosystem often includes relationships between parent and teacher(s), therapist(s), and physician(s), as well as professional-to-professional relationships. The exosystem consists of such societal structures as public and private service agencies, advocacy groups, and churches. The macrosystem consists of the cultural and legislative contexts in which the three other levels of the child's ecological environment operate. Such contexts include societal attitudes and values, court rulings, and governmental and agency regulations. From a systems theory perspective, it would be of minimal use to plan intervention strategies without consideration of the dynamics at each level of the child's ecological environment (i.e., microsystem, mesosystem, exosystem, and macrosystem). Likewise, from a systems theory perspective, co-ordination of efforts within and across the different levels of the ecological structure represents a more effective intervention strategy than working in isolation from each other.

## Interdisciplinary/interagency teaming

Comprehensive services for young children with special needs are provided by a team of professionals representing a variety of disciplines (e.g., education, speech/language therapy, physical therapy, etc.) and agencies (e.g., education, health, social service, etc.). Interdisciplinary teaming (i.e., teaming across disciplines) occurs at two different, but overlapping, levels. The first level involves parents and professionals directly concerned with planning, implementing, and evaluating a child's program. This level will be referred to as "collaborative teaming." The second level involves multiple agencies working together to provide coordinated and comprehensive services for young children with special needs and their families. This level will be referred to as "community collaboration." These two levels are interconnected and interdependent, in that success in achieving targeted goals at one level depends on collaboration and successful teaming at the other level.

### *Collaborative teaming*

Collaborative teaming involves professionals from varying disciplines and parents agreeing to work together to achieve common goals. A primary purpose of collaborative teaming is the coordination and interpretation of information from various disciplines and parents and/or other caregivers. A second purpose is to be mutually accountable for planning, implementing, and monitoring of strategies to achieve desired goals. Collaborative teaming, when done effectively, represents a more efficient and ecologically valid service delivery model than individuals working alone (Howard *et al.*, 1997).

Professionals involved in collaborative teaming for young children with special educational needs often include medical personnel, physical and occupational therapists, speech/language pathologists, educators, and school psychologists. While each of these professionals has a special part to play in providing necessary services to young children with SEN, some overlap exists in the mission and roles of the various disciplines. Additionally, the effectiveness of services from any one discipline is usually enhanced when professionals from different disciplines coordinate their efforts and work toward common goals. As an understanding of discipline-specific roles is often a first step toward successful collaboration, a brief description of various disciplines often involved in direct services to young children with SEN is presented in Box 7.1.

Collaborative consultation is often an important part of collaborative teaming. Collaborative consultation represents one type of joint activity that has been used successfully to foster collaboration among staff from various disciplines. Consultation entails the giving and receiving of

*Box 7.1* Discipline-specific roles

---

**Discipline and major role(s)**

Medical personnel
- Diagnose and treat medical illnesses
- Promote optimal health and well-being

Occupational therapy
- Assess and monitor development and functional performance in relation to purposeful activities (e.g., play and self-help skills)
- Develop and implement interventions to enhance functional performance in purposeful activities

Physical therapy
- Assess motor development needs of the child
- Develop and implement interventions to enhance performance in motor-related activities
- Assess need for adaptive equipment and secure such equipment as necessary

Speech/language pathologist
- Assess language and communicative competence of the child
- Develop and implement interventions to enhance speech, language, and communicative competence

Educator/teacher
- Plan and implement appropriate social, emotional, academic, and behavioral interventions in consultation with the rest of the intervention team
- Monitor child progress
- Share information with the parents and involve them in the educational program
- Work with the therapists on the team to incorporate therapy activities within the context of daily activities

School psychologist
- Assess psychological/behavioral characteristics of children
- Assist in planning appropriate social, emotional, academic, and behavioral interventions

---

information between two or more people for the purpose of (1) resolving a need, issue, or problem; (2) improving the understanding that one or both individuals have of the issue at hand; and (3) improving the ability of the individuals involved to respond effectively to similar problems in the future (Bruder, 1994).

Collaborative consultation is often used to provide both direct and indirect services to a child with special educational needs. Direct services are provided when the consultant works directly with the child. This may be to assess the child and/or to provide instruction in a particular area of concern (e.g., reading, writing, etc.). Indirect services are provided when the consultant works with the teacher and/or parents versus directly with the child. Indirect consultation services are designed to enhance the knowledge and improve the skills of the direct service providers (i.e., teachers and parents) in relation to meeting the child's special needs. For example, an occupational therapist provides indirect services when he consults with a teacher on how to position a child at the computer in a way that will provide maximum support for the child with balance and coordination problems. In this example, the occupational therapist is providing indirect service to the child by instructing the teacher on appropriate adaptations.

Indirect consultation can be effective in meeting the needs of children with SEN. In fact, consulting models of indirect service delivery in special education have proven to be as effective as direct services provided in therapeutic settings (Bruder, 1994). Additionally, teachers who worked with consultants demonstrated positive changes in their instructional techniques for working with children with SEN (Bruder, 1994). The positive outcomes of collaborative consultation suggest that it will "become an increasingly prominent method of service delivery for early childhood special educators and related-service personnel" (Bruder, 1994, p. 58).

### Community collaboration

Services for young children with disabilities and their families must be organized in a coherent and coordinated manner if they are to be effective in safeguarding the rights and meeting the special needs of the children involved. Sometimes, this coordination can be quite difficult, due to the fact that one family may be receiving services from multiple agencies. The Department for Education (DFE, 1994), in recognizing this need, calls for "close cooperation between schools, LEAs, the health services and the social services departments of local authorities" (p. 15). The Children Act 1989 and the Education Act 1993 also call for such interagency cooperation. Related statements from each of these Acts are presented in Box 7.2.

The cooperation required among different agencies serving young children and their families must include integration and coordination of services. Without such integration and coordination, it can be very difficult and frustrating for parents seeking services to find the right service at the right time. Without integration and coordination, parents often find that they have to learn about services in a piecemeal fashion; that it is difficult to access services due to confusing eligibility criteria and participation requirements, and that they have to spend hours completing application and intake forms (Hanson & Lynch, 1995).

In many communities, parents are asked to complete detailed forms for each agency from which they may be receiving services. In addition to

*Box 7.2* Mandates for interagency cooperation

District health authorities, LEAs, grant maintained schools and City Technology Colleges must comply with a request from a social services department for assistance in providing services for children in need, so long as the request is compatible with their duties and does not unduly prejudice the discharge of any of their functions.

(Children Act 1989, section 27)

Social services departments . . . and district health authorities, subject to the reasonableness of the request in the light of available resources, must comply with a request for help from an LEA in connection with children with special educational needs, unless they consider that the help is not necessary for the exercise of the LEA's functions.

(Education Act 1993, section 166)

asking for information about the child's history and developmental status, many agencies also ask questions about the parents' health, education, employment, family routines, and style of interacting. They may even ask for information about the family's financial resources.

After several different agencies have asked for the same or similar information, it is easy to understand how some families become quite frustrated with this time-consuming and intrusive process. Community collaboration, or collaboration across agencies, can reduce this duplication and make the process of accessing services easier and friendlier for the families involved. One way to do this is to adopt a common intake form (i.e., the same form used by multiple agencies). After a family completes this form for one agency, it can then be shared with other agencies as well. Of course, parent permission for the sharing of such information is a necessity.

The Department for Education in the *Code of Practice on the Identification and Assessment of Special Educational Needs* (DFE, 1994) discusses the need for working in partnership with the health services, social services, the education welfare service and other relevant local and national voluntary organisations. The *Code* specifies that when schools first suspect a medical problem they should, after obtaining the consent of the child's parents, consult the school doctor or the child's general practitioner. If a medical problem is confirmed, the doctor consulted should in turn notify the medical officer who is designated by the district health authority (DHA) to work with the local educational authority on behalf of children with special educational needs. The role of the general practitioner in serving children with SEN is discussed in the *Code* (DFE, 1994, p. 17), as follows:

> The role of the general practitioner will largely depend on whether he or she has provided the medical input to the programme of

pre-school child health surveillance which is delivered at child health clinics and, increasingly, within GP practices. A GP who has accepted a child for child health surveillance will be best equipped to provide an initial medical report for children up to age five. Elsewhere clinical medical officers, who usually work in clinics and in the school health service, and health visitors and school nurses may be capable of providing fuller information.

Additionally, as specified in the *Code* (DFE, 1994, p. 17), the role of the GP or other health provider includes the following duties:

- inform LEAs of children who they think may have special educational needs;
- provide medical advice to LEAs for the assessment of children within the prescribed time limits;
- consider, with LEAs and with regard to available resources, the health services' contribution to the non-educational provision to be specified in a statement [of special educational needs].

The *Code* (DFE, 1994, p. 17) also specifies that the designated medical officer should:

- ensure that all schools have a contact (usually the school doctor) for seeking medical advice on children who may have special educational needs;
- provide a resource to other health service staff – for example, GPs and therapists – who require assistance in preparing reports on the medical history and health needs of children for schools and LEAs;
- coordinate the health services' advice for a statutory assessment and, frequently, participate in multi-agency meetings on assessments and making statements [of special educational needs];
- coordinate the provision to be made by the health services for a child with special educational needs when, as may be the case with therapy and nursing services, either a DHA or GP fund holder may be responsible for the purchasing of these services.

As many children with SEN experience social and emotional problems, it is important for schools to encourage children to discuss their concerns with a relevant professional, such as an educational psychologist, a religious minister, an education welfare officer, or other social service professional. In the UK, social services departments are required to designate an officer or officers who are responsible for working with schools on behalf of children with SEN (DFE, 1994). Social services are especially needed in situations where a child has experienced trauma, such as homelessness, abuse, or neglect.

Schools should also work in close partnership with the providers of other special educational needs support services. Such services, as listed in the *Code* (DFE, 1994), include specialist teachers of children with hearing, visual, and speech/language impairments, teachers in more general learning and behaviour support services, educational psychologists, and advisers or teachers with a knowledge of information technology for children with SEN.

If services for young children with special needs are not organized in a coherent manner, the coordination of services to meet the needs of an individual family and the transition of the child from one intervention program to another can become major problems. Additionally, the family might be faced with incomplete, fragmented, and even conflicting information about their child's disability and ways to facilitate his or her development. For example, an occupational therapist working with a 6-year-old who has hand control difficulties may suggest that the parents use mealtimes to stress independent use of eating utensils. A physician treating this same child, however, may be more concerned about the child's tendency to be undernourished and suggest that the parents make mealtimes as relaxing and enjoyable as possible. A third opinion might be presented by the child's teacher who feels that mealtimes offer the best opportunity for the child to learn social and communication skills. The parents, in this case, may feel frustrated and confused as to how to proceed in meeting their child's needs.

In addition to coordination across agencies within a community, coordination must also occur across levels of government, with consistency assured between policies developed at state and local levels. While the complexity of government and the diversity of communities suggest that some inconsistencies and contradictions are inevitable, they need not be extreme. Questions proposed by the European Commission Childcare Network (no date) that might be used in studying the integration and coordination of services across differing policy-making units include the following:

- What contradictions about policies and priorities exist between departments at a national level?
- What contradictions about policies and priorities exist between departments at the regional or local level?
- How do national and local policies relate to one another?
- What contradictions exist within departments (such as education) about the priority given to services to young children?
- What contradictions exist between the aims and objectives of services at a local level?
- What strategies exist to address these contradictions?
- How do services for young children link up with systems of health care?

- How do fiscal policies affect families with young children?
- How do employment policies relate to families with young children?
- How do environmental policies relate to the needs of young children?

The European Commission Childcare Network is an interagency and interdisciplinary group concerned with the protection of the rights and well-being of children. This group, established in 1986, focuses primarily on child care issues. From its beginning, the Network has emphasized that child care services must be of good quality as well as sufficient in number.

As outlined by the European Commission Childcare Network, high-quality services for young children provide the opportunity for children to experience the following:

- a healthy life
- spontaneous expression
- esteem as an individual
- dignity and autonomy
- self-confidence and zest in learning
- a stable learning and caring environment
- sociability, friendship, and cooperation with others
- equal opportunities irrespective of gender, race, and disability
- cultural diversity
- support as part of a family and a community
- happiness

If a community can ensure that each of these opportunities is available for young children and their families, chances are that the community has a healthy network of comprehensive services. Once these opportunities are in place, the next challenge is to see that they are integrated and coordinated in a consumer-friendly format. Community collaboration is the key to achieving the necessary integration and coordination of services.

Community collaboration occurs when two or more programs or agencies establish an ongoing working relationship to achieve common goals. A truly collaborative relationship goes beyond cooperation and coordination in that it involves a greater commitment of time and resources than that which cooperation and coordination alone would require (Bruder, 1994). Interagency team models based on cooperation and coordination allow separate agencies and staff to maintain their own autonomy as well as their own philosophy and goals. There are serious limitations to this approach. In fact, "differing philosophies" and "distinct goals" have been identified as common barriers to interagency collaboration (Bruder, 1994).

## Gaps, overlaps, and other concerns

Without cooperation and collaboration, gaps and overlaps in services for young children with special needs often occur. A gap occurs when a service that is needed is not available in a given community. Quality child care for young children with special needs represents a gap in some communities. A 4-year-old child who is blind may attend a school-based program from 9 a.m. to 3 p.m. each day. Because his parents work until 5 p.m., they need after-school care for their son as well. They also need child care during school holidays and summer breaks. They find, after numerous phone calls, that the child care programs in their community do not accept children with disabilities. The parents respond to the situation by trying to "take turns" with child care responsibilities – either by taking time off work or finding neighbors and/or extended family members to fill in for them. Obviously, this gap in needed services puts a great deal of strain on the parents and can be a source of emotional stress for the child.

Overlaps in services can also be a concern. Overlaps occur when the same services are provided through multiple agencies in communities where the need or demand for the services fail to warrant such duplication. Overlaps in such cases can put an unnecessary strain on the financial resources of the community and can lead to unhealthy competition for clients and qualified personnel. An overlap in services might occur in a community if the schools decide to establish assisted-living arrangements for young adults with autism when such services are already being provided through a mental health agency.

Parents of young children with special needs have identified transitions from one program to another as times of particular stress for their families (Haines *et al.*, 1988). The nature of the difficulties involved during transitions suggest that cooperation and collaboration across providers and agencies are especially needed at this time. Educators and researchers have begun to address the issues of transition for children with special needs and their families and to develop models for easing the process. Further discussion about the transition process is presented in Chapter 10.

## Team models

Members of a team can work together in several different ways. Three basic models have been identified for the way early intervention teams might work together. These three models are: multidisciplinary; inter-disciplinary, and transdisciplinary. In a multidisciplinary team, members work independently within their own disciplines. They each provide assessment and direct services to a child and then meet as a group to share assessment findings and progress reports. With this model, there is little coordination of efforts. In an interdisciplinary team, members often conduct their assessments and plan goals together, but provide direct services independently of each other. In a transdisciplinary model, professionals share roles and may even combine their assessment and treatment tasks, so that any one member may be performing responsibilities and tasks usually associated with a discipline other than his or her own. There follows an example of how the role of Lonnie, a speech/language pathologist, might differ according to the team model being implemented.

- When working within the multidisciplinary model, Lonnie contacts the Year 1 teacher to schedule a time when she can conduct an assessment of a child's communication skills. She then conducts the assessment in her speech therapy room, tabulates the results, and shares a report at a "staffing" for the child. Lonnie develops and implements a speech/language intervention plan for the child, which involves individual therapy on a schedule of 30 minutes twice a week. At the next staffing three months later, Lonnie shares a report on the child's progress as she sees it in her therapy sessions.
- When working within the interdisciplinary model, Lonnie and the classroom teacher observe the school psychologist as she conducts an assessment of a child's cognitive skills. During the assessment, Lonnie records language samples and information about the child's speech sounds and language usage. In this way, Lonnie is able to complete a large part of her speech/language assessment without duplicating the testing in a separate session. Lonnie also talks with the school psychologist and the classroom teacher about how they might combine intervention goals and activities across domains or areas of instruction.
- When working within the transdisciplinary model, Lonnie meets with the classroom teacher to discuss how they might assess a child's pragmatic language skills within the context of the regular classroom activities. Lonnie also works with the teacher on how to make her (i.e., the teacher's) lessons more language focused, with special attention on how to address the speech and language goals of the target child and other children with SEN within the context of the classroom.

The team model used in a particular situation depends on the administrative policy of the school and service agencies involved. It also depends on the philosophical orientation, professional expertise, and cohesiveness of the professionals serving a particular child. Regardless of which model the intervention team follows or represents, collaboration among team members with information sharing and consensus decision making is critical for quality intervention services (McLean & Odom, 1996).

## Building and maintaining effective teams

### *Meaning of team*

While "team" can be defined as a noun (i.e., a group of people working or acting together), it can also be defined as a verb (i.e., to join forces). The most effective teams are the ones that focus on the verb-related aspects of teaming. They view themselves as a team in relation to what they *do* (i.e., they team; they work together) versus something they *are* (i.e., a group by association). They recognize that "teams do not naturally fall together; groups can, but teams cannot" (Howard *et al.*, 1997, p. 415).

Developing effective interdisciplinary and interagency service delivery teams is a complex and challenging task. Philosophical, professional, interpersonal, and administrative issues often hinder the process. A listing of some of the most common barriers to collaboration in early intervention services are presented in Box 7.3. Some typical Western culture perspectives are also in conflict with effective team behaviors. Competitiveness, for example, can serve as a major barrier to effective teaming. It has been suggested that early childhood professionals could benefit from specific instruction on how to move away from competitive work and toward collaborative efforts, if they are to be effective members of an interdisciplinary team (Kagan, 1991).

*Box 7.3* Common barriers to collaboration in early intervention

- staff, time, and budget limitations
- poor communication skills
- competitiveness
- narrow or self-serving interests
- lack of incentive
- lack of training and skill in coordinating efforts
- preoccupation with administrative structure rather than the function of the agency
- general resistance to change
- lack of political awareness and other political issues
- turf issues and territoriality
- lack of information about other agencies' mission and function
- haphazard team process
- lack of planning
- lack of monitoring of the collaborative process
- distance and other related logistical concerns
- questionable administrative support
- discipline-specific jargon and perspectives

## Strategies to enhance collaboration

There are steps that can be taken to minimize the barriers to interdisciplinary and interagency collaboration. The following five strategies, focusing primarily on interagency collaboration, have been suggested by Hanson and Lynch (1995).

- Develop new ways to meet community needs. Rather than getting trapped in bureaucracies or current administrative structures, communities would do well to find new ways to deal with identified needs. Communities might start by: (1) conducting a community needs assessment to determine how the community has changed over time; (2) helping agencies or groups write small grants to fund new projects, and (3) using faculty and students at nearby colleges to solve problems in new and creative ways.
- Increase community awareness about the issues and needs relating to young children who are at risk or disabled. Networking to increase awareness can facilitate collaboration. Forums for networking could include a series of meetings where professionals from different agencies get together to discuss current issues and practices, or be as simple as periodically getting together for lunch.
- Be responsive to people and agencies throughout the change process. "Being responsive," in the context of teaming, means about the same as it does in the context of interpersonal relationships. In fact, "many of the behaviors that people view as responsive are simply good manners" (Hanson & Lynch, 1995, p. 284). Examples of being responsive include acknowledging people's and agencies' accomplishments and following through in a timely manner on commitments. An expression of congratulations through telephone calls, written notes, and public recognition can do much to foster collaborative relationships, as can the willingness to share responsibilities on tasks to be completed.
- Acknowledge and respect turf and territorial issues while working to decrease them. Territorial issues usually reflect what has occurred in the past and "the rules" (spoken and unspoken) which tend to govern the present. While members of interagency teams should be aware of these territorial issues, they can keep such issues from becoming barriers to collaboration by focusing on a common vision for the future.
- Maintain frequent, open communications. A breakdown in communication is one of the most common barriers to effective teaming. It is important, therefore, for interagency teams to seek out ways to keep the lines of communication open. At times, outside group facilitators can be helpful in bringing groups together and establishing

procedures for ongoing communication. Regularly scheduled meeting times, with a commitment from all involved to participate on a regular basis, can also be critical to establishing and maintaining effective interagency communication. The following statement from the Department for Education (DFE, 1994) in the *Code of Practice* (p. 16) offers strong support for such meetings:

In order to achieve full collaboration at both school and local authority level, representatives of LEAs, social services departments and the health services may choose to meet on a reasonably regular basis to plan and coordinate activity. Such arrangements will vary according to local circumstances, but the principles of partnership and close working relationships between agencies, supported by meetings to discuss both strategic and operational issues, will have general application.

There is a considerable amount of literature on the team-building and team-functioning process, much of which can be found in publications developed for the business community and/or business education purposes. Many of the specific team-building strategies that are used in business can also be used to build and maintain early intervention teams. Some such strategies include the following:

- Establish regular meeting times with all staff involved. Staff should make participation in these meetings a priority.
- Clarify roles and responsibilities for all members of the team.
- Establish and maintain ongoing communication mechanisms among everyone involved. Such mechanisms should include oral and written communications.
- Establish a shared system of decision making and accountability. Each member of the team should understand and be committed to an organizational structure that includes such components as leadership selection, role assignments, agendas, and individual and group evaluation.

For professionals and agencies serving young children with disabilities, the following suggestions are also offered:

- Each member of the team should become familiar with the special education and related service personnel available to children with special educational needs. Not only should team members be familiar with the special services and service personnel within their own agency, but they should also have familiarity with such services and service personnel in other community agencies.
- Philosophies or mission statements regarding collaborative teaming

should be developed and adopted at the state level, at the regional level, in local or smaller communities, and even within a particular service agency (e.g., school, hospital, specialized clinic, etc.). Individual teams should establish their own philosophy or mission statement, and, once this is in place, all other decisions (personal and team) should be measured against the intent of this statement.

- Specific strategies for accomplishing goals should be discussed and agreed upon. Because members of an intervention team come from not only various disciplines, but also various professional training backgrounds, they are often guided by differing theories, methods, and models. Finding common ground on a method or approach to intervention can be a challenge. Advance planning regarding specific strategies to be used is important to ensure instruction that is intentional and sufficiently intensive to meet individual learner needs.

- Establish and maintain meaningful connections with the community. Working on joint projects can often serve as a vehicle for bringing individuals and groups together in a meaningful way. Examples of joint projects that some communities have initiated for young children and their families include: (1) offering developmental and health screenings in public areas, such as shopping malls and community fairs; (2) organizing information forums addressing issues relevant to new parents, such as health and safety, age-appropriate toys, behavior management, etc., and (3) developing community playgrounds, after-school child care programs, and summer recreation opportunities.

- Respect the contributions of all team members, recognizing that each individual and discipline contributes unique insights and skills to program planning and implementation. No one discipline or individual should be viewed as "more right" or "more of an expert" than any other discipline or individual. The sharing of multiple perspectives and the merging of skills and differing knowledge bases should be valued by all members of the team.

- Assure that all members of the team are familiar with each child's individualized objectives. It is important to recognize that neither teachers nor specialists "own" particular objectives. Instead, all team members share responsibility for the total educational program for individual children.

## Case study – Terry

### Background information

Due to a serious health condition, 7-year-old Terry is scheduled for a variety of medical tests and treatments on Tuesdays and Thursdays after school. Terry usually gets less sleep on the nights of the treatment, due to the travel time and other scheduling complications involved, as well as her physical and emotional re-action to the treatment. The mornings following the treatment are also hard for Terry – she does not want to get up and usually refuses to eat breakfast. A physical therapist, who has been working with Terry at school, sees her early every Friday morning for 45 minutes. Since the medical tests and treatments have started, Terry has been uncooperative and whiny during her physical therapy sessions. The classroom teacher and the physical therapist make arrangements for a behavioral specialist to come in to observe Terry during these sessions. A behavioral management plan (based on rewards and penalties) is developed and scheduled to begin the following week.

### Discussion

Terry's uncooperative behavior during her physical therapy sessions may be due to "treatment overload." Involving a behavioral specialist and adding another treatment (i.e., "behavior therapy") could easily result in more stress and discomfort for Terry, as well as her parents. While the behavior management techniques may modify her behavior over the short term, they will probably not alleviate her stress.

A team approach to the concern might have led to an entirely different plan of action. If members of the intervention team (i.e., teacher, medical personnel, physical therapist, and parents) had first met to discuss the situation, they may have been able to adjust Terry's schedule in a way that would be less stressful for her. The physical therapist, for example, might have been able to work with Terry on another day or at a later time on Friday. Terry's parents might have been able to rearrange things at home to make it possible for Terry to go to bed earlier on Thursday and perhaps make it a more soothing time for her. Terry's teacher might have been able to give Terry more rest time and reassurance. Additionally, the physical therapist, the classroom teacher, and the parents might have developed a plan for incorporating more of Terry's physical therapy activities into the classroom and home routines, perhaps resulting in less need for intensive therapy in an isolated setting. This arrangement would probably be a lot less stressful for Terry and more conducive to positive emotional and behavioral development.

# 8

# PARTNERSHIP WITH FAMILIES

## Rationale for a family-centered approach

Early childhood education has a history of being committed to parent involvement and family support. Thus it should not be surprising that parent education and involvement are also integral to services for young children with disabilities. Unfortunately, this family-focused approach has been relatively slow to develop in the field of early intervention/early childhood special education. Historically, the focus in programs serving young children with disabilities has been on the child and his or her areas of deficit. Even programs serving children at risk due to poverty have tended to focus more on enrichment for the child versus services for the family.

The trend in recent years, however, is to view the child within the context of the family and to consider working with families to be an essential aspect of early intervention (Topping & Wolfendale, 1985; Wolfendale, 1997). Factors contributing to this more family-centered approach include research findings, shifting philosophical and theoretical assumptions, and parental dissatisfaction with traditional parent–professional relationships (Bailey, 1994).

A family-centered approach to serving young children with special educational needs is based on the understanding that parents are the managers or decision makers for their children and that the role of professionals is to provide guidance and assistance to the parents in this process. The earlier approaches sometimes viewed parents as incompetent, dysfunctional, or irrelevant and viewed professionals as the experts and leaders of the intervention team. Parents were often relegated to passive roles in the intervention process – e.g., receivers of information, implementers of activities developed by the therapists, and supporters of school-sponsored initiatives, such as fund raising, holiday parties, etc.

A family-centered approach, in contrast, views parents as equal-status partners in planning, implementing, and evaluating intervention services for their children (Vincent & McLean, 1996). This approach recognizes the importance of enabling parents to become long-term advocates for their children and provides them with the necessary information and skills to be confident and competent in this role (Howard *et al.*, 1997). A family-centered approach goes beyond "helping" families to "enabling and empowering" them, so that they need not be dependent upon professionals for decisions regarding the education, care, and future of their children (Bailey, 1994).

As evident from the following excerpts, the national (UK) *Code of Practice on the Identification and Assessment of Special Educational Needs* (DFE, 1994, pp. 12–13) addresses the importance of partnership with parents:

> The relationship between parents of children with special educational needs and the school which their child is attending has a crucial bearing on the child's educational progress and the effectiveness of any school-based action.

> Children's progress will be diminished if their parents are not seen as partners in the educational process with unique knowledge and information to impart.

> If a child has a behavioural difficulty or is following a developmental activity of any kind which requires a structured approach in school, reinforcement at home by parents will be crucial.

> Professional help can seldom be wholly effective unless it builds upon parents' capacity to be involved and unless parents consider that professionals take account of what they say and treat their views and anxieties as intrinsically important.

The recent early intervention and early childhood education literature also indicates that the impact of educational programming is likely to be "more profound and lasting if the whole family . . . is involved" (Nickse, 1990, p. 3). Because the family often consists of more than the parent–child dyad, a number of family involvement programs have initiated ways to involve siblings, grandparents, and other individuals within or close to the family unit. Such programs reflect an understanding of systems theory and the influence of one's community on child growth and development. This ecologically based approach to family services views "the family from its center (the child) through the family system (a circle around the child) to the community (a circle around the family)" (Howard *et al.*, 1997, p. 330).

As indicated in Chapter 6, having a child with a disability places unique demands and stressors on a family. The presence of such demands and stressors, however, does not make the family dysfunctional, heroic, or incompetent; nor does it make all families with children with disabilities alike. Accordingly, parent education and involvement programs should reflect understanding and respect for diversity across families and should provide options for when, how, and to what extent parents wish to be involved with their child's educational program.

## Options for families

Partnerships between parents and professionals can focus on an individual child and his or her family and/or on issues related to the educational/intervention program as a whole. While many families may not choose to be involved at the systems level of decision making (i.e., with issues affecting the program as a whole), professionals and agencies should be prepared to build such collaborative partnerships with the families who are interested (Vincent & McLean, 1996). Professionals should encourage systems-level involvement and offer more options at this level than just inviting parents to serve on a formal board or committee. Other options for systems-level involvement might include: (1) assisting in planning and conducting orientations for parents and staff new to the program, and (2) reviewing written materials and other publicity about the program.

Family involvement at the level of the individual child and his or her family is often categorized into two broad types: educational enhancement and family support. A third type, however, should also be carefully considered. This type directly involves parents in the assessment, educational planning, and monitoring process, as these relate to their child's educational program. Following is a brief discussion of each of these three types of family involvement.

### *Educational enhancement*

Generally, the goal of educational enhancement activities is to help parents improve their parenting skills and become more effective in fostering their child's development. As such, educational enhancement programs designed for groups of parents may be devoted to such specific concerns as helping parents become more effective communication partners, managing child behavior, and fostering family literacy. At times, educational enhancement programs are conducted with individual families versus groups of parents. For children with special needs, such programs often focus on therapeutic activities (designed by specialists) that parents can do at home.

### *Family support*

The second type of family involvement – that of family support – is designed to provide support to the family in raising a child with a disability. This type of family involvement programming developed in response to a concern for the special demands and stressors experienced by parents of children with disabilities. Family support programs tend to focus on: (1) parent-to-parent interactions for mutual support, (2) personal reflections, and (3) assistance in learning about and accessing family support services in the community, such as respite care, resource-and-referral programs, and recreational opportunities for children with disabilities (e.g., summer camps, etc.).

Various sections in the *Code of Practice* address the need for family support activities. Following is one example (DFE, 1994, p. 13):

> Many parents can become discouraged by their child's continuing difficulties at home and at school, and feel themselves to be inadequate in dealing with the difficulty. The governing body, head teacher and the SEN coordinator should consider how the school can support such parents.

### *Parent involvement in assessment, planning, and monitoring*

As articulated in Chapter 7, a team approach to intervention is essential for serving young children with special needs. Parents should be considered an integral component of this team. The *Code* (DFE, 1994) specifies that schools should "utilise parents' own distinctive knowledge and skills" and their "understanding of how best to help their child" (p. 13). The *Code* also states (pp. 12–13):

> School-based arrangements should ensure that assessment reflects a sound and comprehensive knowledge of a child and his or her responses to a variety of carefully planned and recorded actions which take account of the wishes, feelings and knowledge of parents.

While the above excerpt from the *Code* addresses parent involvement during the assessment phase of intervention, the *Code* also makes it clear that there should be close consultation and partnership with the child's parents throughout all of the school-based stages, which involve the "continuous and systematic cycle of planning, action and review within the school to enable the child with special educational needs to learn and progress" (p. 21). At no part of the process, then, should parents be excluded. Not only should parents be informed all along the way, but the expression of their wishes, feelings, and knowledge should be encouraged, respected, and responded to.

Many parents may need assistance in learning how to be meaningfully involved throughout the assessment, planning, and monitoring process as these relate to their child's educational program. They may also need information, advice, and encouragement on how to be effective advocates for their child. Professionals can help parents by sharing with them some basic understandings about what it means to be an advocate. A listing of some of these basic understandings is presented in Box 8.1. As some parents may feel intimidated when talking with a team of professionals, some suggestions for making them feel more comfortable are presented in Box 8.2.

*Box 8.1* Characteristics of an effective advocate

- An advocate communicates effectively and is assertive.
- An advocate believes that he/she is an equal partner in planning and evaluating services for a child.
- An advocate is not afraid to ask questions.
- An advocate communicates effectively by documenting in written form and by keeping good records.
- An advocate is involved in the education process of his/her child.

*Source*: Adapted from the Family Collaboration module developed by Project PREPARE, Columbus, OH (USA): Ohio Department of Education.

### The option of non-involvement

Some parents may decide not to be involved with their child's program at all. This choice should be allowed and respected (Howard *et al.*, 1997). An important concept to keep in mind is that not being involved with their child's program does not mean that the parents are not involved with their child. Parents can be emotionally close to and interactive with their child and still choose not to participate in school-related functions. Parents may have needs and priorities not shared by professionals on the intervention team. Parents should not be made to feel uncomfortable or guilty about this. As specified in the *Code* (DFE, 1994), "schools should not interpret a failure to participate as indicating a lack of interest or willingness" (p. 13).

### Family assessment and parent involvement

Further discussion presented in the *Code* offers guidance on how to encourage parent involvement (p. 13):

*Box 8.2* Communicating with professionals – some suggestions for parents

1 Before each meeting or contact with a professional, remind yourself that you are an important part of the intervention team and that you have a right to be involved.

2 Prepare for meetings by planning in advance the important points you want to make. A written list may be helpful.

3 Feel free to take someone with you. Another person might take notes, help you make a point, and provide support.

4 When you don't understand something, ask questions.

5 Communicate assertively, rather than passively or aggressively.
   • An assertive person clearly states his or her point of view, while being open to what others have to say.
   • A passive person discounts his or her own ideas and needs, while deferring to the other person.
   • An aggressive person discounts the ideas and needs of others. Assertiveness can be expressed both verbally and nonverbally. Nonverbally, assertiveness can be expressed by taking notes and looking at people when you talk to them. Verbally, assertiveness can be expressed by clearly stating your needs and ideas. The ideas following are several examples of assertive statements: "I see the situation differently." "I would like to make a point." "I have a question."

6 When you have a complaint, discuss it first with the person most directly involved. If the problem still goes unaddressed, take your complaint to the next level (e.g., supervisor, administrator, etc.).

7 In addition to expressing concerns, it is also important to share compliments and to show appreciation for what goes right.

*Source*: Adapted from the Family Collaboration module developed by Project PREPARE, Columbus, OH (USA): Ohio Department of Education.

Parents may feel they are being blamed for their child's difficulties when the school first raises questions with them. Nonetheless, schools should make every effort to encourage parents to recognise that they have responsibilities toward their child, and that the most effective provision will be made when they are open and confident in working in partnership with the school and with professionals.

"Every effort" to encourage parent involvement includes offering options that are individualized to reflect each family's own culture and unique set of strengths, values, skills, expectations, and service needs (Bailey, 1994). A prerequisite to developing such individualized options is an understanding of the family's unique characteristics. Both formal and informal family assessment procedures might be used to arrive at this understanding. Professionals should take great care, however, in conducting any type of family assessment to safeguard the family's privacy and to avoid unwelcome intrusions. A variety of family assessment instruments have been developed to identify individual family profiles. Many of these instruments, however, have been used inappropriately. The original intent of some such instruments was for research purposes rather than for general use in intervention programs. The inappropriate use of family assessment instruments can be intrusive and offensive for the families involved, resulting in less rather than greater family involvement. Inappropriate use of such instruments tends to tear down rather than build up healthy partnerships between professionals and parents.

A family assessment should be an interactive process involving parents and professionals, rather than an activity conducted by the professional(s) on the family. This assessment should focus on family strengths as well as needs. Consideration of the following definitions developed by Bailey (1991, p. 27) may be helpful in conducting family assessments and developing family involvement programs that reflect a family-centered approach:

- *Family assessment*: the ongoing and interactive process by which professionals gather information in order to determine family priorities for goals and services.
- *Family need*: a family's expressed desire for services to be obtained or outcomes to be achieved.
- *Family strength*: the family's perception of resources that are at its disposal which could be used to meet family needs.

The definition of "parent" as outlined in the *Code of Practice on the Identification and Assessment of Special Educational Needs* (DFE, 1994, p. 128) should also be considered. In addition to the child's birth parents (i.e., natural parents), "parent" in relation to a child includes any person:

- who is not a natural parent of the child but who has parental responsibility for him or her, or
- who has care of the child.

The *Code* specifies that the school "should know in each instance who should be regarded as a parent of a particular child and who should therefore be consulted regarding the child's progress" (p. 13). Also noted in the *Code* is the fact "it is often the case that adults in more than one household qualify as parents" and that "all those with parental responsibility for a child have rights and responsibilities towards the child" (p. 13). The school, then, "should endeavour to keep records of all those with parental responsibility and involve them as much as possible in the child's education" (p. 13).

## Strategies for working with families

Preservice programs for early childhood special educators have tended to focus on child development, child learning, and intervention techniques and have not addressed team-building, collaboration, or partnership skills. In fact, lack of training has been identified as one of the most salient factors impeding a family-centered approach to serving children with special needs (Bailey, 1994). One research study found that the typical student in special education, physical therapy, occupational therapy, and speech/language pathology received only a few hours of training in working with families (Bailey *et al.*, 1990). Thus professionals committed to working with families as partners in the intervention process often face the question of *how* to implement a family-focused intervention program. It is hoped that the following suggested guidelines and related discussion will be helpful to professionals in moving toward a more family-focused approach to early intervention.

- Make family support a primary goal of any early intervention activity. According to Bailey (1994), "any child care provider, early child-hood teacher, special education teacher, therapist, physician, or any other professional working with young children with disabilities must recognize and assume this important professional role" (p. 27). Professionals involved in direct service to the child and family, however, cannot institute a family-focused program alone. Therefore, administrative supports and resources (e.g., adequate time and sufficient staff) must also be provided.
- Expand the traditional concept of successful parent involvement. Instead of defining and evaluating parent involvement *for* families, professionals should enable the parents to *self-define* family partici-pation in ways that are meaningful to them. Parents should be able to determine what would be helpful to them, and professionals should support the parents' decisions about how they wish to be involved with their child's program. This approach is different from the traditional concept of "professionals as experts." It requires pro-fessionals "to shift from involving families in the approval of professionally determined intervention plans to involving families as partners throughout the entire assessment and intervention process" (Vincent & McLean, 1996, p. 67).
- Encourage and support the family's dreams and visions for the future. As expressed by a parent of a child with special needs, professionals should allow parents to feel hope (Fialka, 1994). Without hope, she

149

says, it can be difficult for parents to face the demands of the present, even in such routine concerns as getting to their next appointment, or helping their child with reading or math homework. Dreams and visions for the future can also help parents make decisions in relation to life span planning (e.g., what skills are necessary for my child to make friends, function independently, etc.).

- Work with the family in identifying their resources, priorities, and concerns. Too often, family involvement programs have been designed around family needs or deficits, *as perceived by the professionals*. Recommended practices in early intervention/early childhood special education, however, indicate that the *family's perspective* on what they need must be an essential consideration in the design of family involvement programs. "A professional cannot make an 'objective' assessment of family needs without considering how the family members view their needs" (Bailey, 1994, p. 34). Additionally, a "resource" made available to a family is likely to be helpful to them only if they perceive it to be helpful. Thus, families should be involved in identifying their own resources and strengths and assisted in capitalizing on them.

- Identify the family's preferred method of maintaining healthy home–school communications. Many parents prefer informal versus formal avenues of communication (Mandell & Johnson, 1985). Parents have indicated, for example, that they find frequent short conversations (either face-to-face or via phone) with professionals just as meaningful as scheduled parent/teacher conferences, parent meetings at school, or home visits. Parents have also indicated that they learn as much about instructional and/or therapeutic techniques to use with their child by watching teachers and therapists as attending informational meetings about such techniques. Some parents prefer short written notes about their child's performance, while others prefer phone or face-to-face communications (Mandell & Johnson, 1985).

Of particular note is the importance of being aware of parents' oral and written language status. Do the parents speak English or Welsh? Can they read, and, if so, at what level? These concerns are addressed in the *Code of Practice on the Identification and Assessment of Special Educational Needs* (DFE, 1994), along with some suggestions for dealing with such concerns (p. 13):

> Some parents may have problems in understanding written information and communicating with schools because of literacy difficulties or if English or Welsh is not their first language. The school should consider how best to involve such parents, and whether to make written information available in the main languages of the local community, using

the resources of relevant community-based organisations. In some instances taped or videotaped information packs may be helpful, particularly in illustrating the type of provision and support which is available, and how parents may help their children at home.

Presented in the *Code* (DFE, 1994) are specific guidelines for a school's arrangement for parents of children with special educational needs. These arrangements, as presented in Box 8.3, address concerns in the areas of information, partnership, and access for parents.

*Box 8.3* A school's arrangements for parents of children with special educational needs

---

Information
- on the school's SEN policy
- on the support available for children with special educational needs within the school and LEA
- on parents' involvement in decision making, emphasising the importance of their contribution
- on services such as those provided by the local authority for children 'in need'
- on local and national voluntary organisations which might provide information, advice or counselling

Partnership
- arrangements for recording and acting upon parental concerns
- procedures for involving parents when a concern is first expressed within the school
- arrangements for incorporating parents' views in assessment and subsequent reviews

Access for parents
- information in a range of community languages
- information on tape for parents who may have literacy or communication difficulties
- a parents' room or other arrangements in the school to help parents feel confident and comfortable

---

*Source*: DFE (1994, p. 14). Crown copyright is reproduced with the permission of the Controller of Her Majesty's Stationery Office.

## Even Start – one example of a family-centered program

Even Start is a federally funded program developed in the United States in 1988 to enhance family literacy. As outlined in the Public Law statement which authorized the program (P.L. 100–297, Sec. 1051), the purpose of Even Start is to "improve the educational opportunities of the

Nation's children and adults by integrating early childhood education and adult education for parents into a unified program." Families eligible to participate in Even Start are those families with educationally disadvantaged adults (i.e., those without a high school diploma) who reside in a low-income neighborhood and who have young children between the ages of 1 and 7. The parents' low level of literacy and low-income status place their young children at risk of developmental delays and other special educational needs.

Even Start is based on the premise that the problem of illiteracy is entrenched in the home and that that is where the solution needs to focus (Wilson & Aldridge, 1994). Parents and young children are viewed as a learning unit, and program activities provide shared literacy experiences designed to benefit both parents and their young children. Exploring books together at a public library is one example of a shared literacy experience. Families who participate in the Even Start program have access to three types of services: core services, support services, and special one-time events. Following is a discussion of each of these.

### Core services

The core services include the following:

- Adult basic education;
- Parent-child activities;
- Parent education/child development services;
- Early childhood education

The adult basic education component of Even Start is designed to improve the parents' basic educational skills, particularly in the area of literacy. The motivation of many parents to participate in this component of the program is to learn to read to their children. Initial literacy levels are sometimes so limited that parents are unable to read even a simple book to their child. As one of the major factors relating to how well children learn to read is having parents who read to them, this component of Even Start can have a profound influence on developing literacy skills in young children.

The parent–child component of Even Start consists of regularly scheduled sessions devoted to activities or projects in which parents and their children participate together. Many Even Start programs conduct these parent–child sessions in the home; others offer them in a center with a number of families participating at one time. Parent–child activities often focus on language development and literacy. Such activities include a variety of instructional games, as well as having parents and children reading or looking at books together.

The parent education/child development component of Even Start is designed to help parents become full partners in the education of their children. Through this component, parents learn basic facts about child growth and development and ways in which they can enhance their child's learning. A major emphasis of this component of Even Start is the fact that parents are the child's first and most influential teachers and that parent involvement in their child's educational program can make a significant difference in how well their child does in school. Figure 8.1 gives an example of the kinds of materials developed and used to encourage parents with low literacy skills to foster reading with their young children. This particular form is used as both a reminder and an "activity log" of specific activities that parents can do to help their children become better readers. Both symbols and words are used on this form to make the reading of it easier.

Early childhood education is the fourth core component of Even Start. Children between the ages of 1 through 7 participate in this part of the program. The purpose of the early childhood education component is to enhance child development and prepare children for success in school. Early childhood education services are usually provided in a group setting and include screening activities to help identify young children with special needs. Many of the early childhood education activities center around books and reading. Stories are read, picture books displayed, experience stories written, and literacy-related materials added to the learning centers. Such literacy-related materials often reflect what children may find in their own homes, such as telephone books, note pads, recipe books, church bulletins, advertising circulars, newspapers, and magazines.

### Support services

In addition to the four core services, Even Start provides an array of support services, which may include all or some of the following: transportation assistance, child care, meals and/or other nutritional assistance, health care, special care for family members who are disabled, mental health/family counseling, employment counseling, etc. Support services are provided as a means of helping families deal with some of the barriers which otherwise may prevent them from participating fully in any of the core services provided through Even Start.

### Special events

Information fairs highlighting a variety of community agencies and services, book or toy exchanges, and presentations or demonstrations on topics of interest to parents are examples of special events that might

| Since you last came to class how often | Number |
|---|---|
| ... did you read to your child? | |
| ... did your child share a book with you? | |
| ... did your child watch you read or write something? | |
| ... did your child draw or color? | |
| ... did you take a family outing (like going to a movie, a park, church, or the mall)? | |
| ... did you point out colors, shapes, or numbers, when playing, reading, or talking with your child? | |
| ... did you watch TV with your child? | |
| ... did you play a game, sing, or talk with your child? | |
| ... did you talk with your child about something fun during mealtime? | |
| ... did you go to the library with your child? | |
| ? | |

*Figure 8.1* Even Start activity log

be offered by an Even Start program. These special events are usually conducted at public libraries or other community settings, making them accessible not only to the families involved in the Even Start program, but to other families in the community as well.

## Participants and impact

In 1993, a study was done to evaluate the impact of Even Start on some of the families who participated in the Toledo (Ohio) Even Start program (Wilson & Aldridge, 1994). Data collection was done by way of interviews with twelve parents who had participated in the program with their young children. There follow some excerpts from these interviews, along with some background information about the participants.

Most of the families who participated in the Toledo Even Start program were from neighborhoods considered "most in need" of community services. Of the families participating in the Toledo Even Start program during the 1990–1991 academic year (September through May), 63% represented single parent families, 74% relied on government assistance as their primary source of financial support, 85% were unemployed, 79% did not have a high school diploma, and 57% of the young children did not have any other type of early childhood education experience. These percentages were similar for other years of the project as well.

Kim's story is typical of many of the Even Start parents. Kim was 28 years old when she first enrolled in the Toledo Even Start program. She is the single parent of four daughters, ranging in age from 6 to 9. Kim dropped out of school after completing the eight grade. She is unemployed and depends on government assistance as her sole source of income. One of her daughters, Andrea, has a speech/language impairment and attends special classes during the summer. Kim decided to participate in Even Start so that she would "be better at helping the kids with their homework."

Another single parent, Sharon, found out about Even Start when she tried to enroll her 4-year-old daughter, Tina, in Head Start, another federally funded program for economically disadvantaged young children. Her daughter's birthday missed the Head Start cut-off point by two days. A teacher in the Head Start program, however, told Sharon about Even Start. Sharon was surprised to find out that Even Start would be for both herself and her daughter but was glad that she could be involved. During her interview, Sharon indicated that she had learned a lot from Even Start, especially about reading and parenting. There follows an excerpt from this interview:

It helped a whole lot with my reading and reading to Tina. She enjoys me reading to her – the laughter and the excitement she

155

gets out of me reading to her now – because before the program with me reading to her I would just pick up the book and just read to her. Now we really get into the book, the excitement, and we do things from the book. If there's jumping or bouncing a ball or whatever, we get into it – [we] do some of the things that the book is doing. . . . It's more alive, you know; she really gets into it and loves it.

As the following excerpts indicate, other parents, too, talked about the positive impact which Even Start had on improving their literacy skills and helping with their children's education.

I learned vocabulary, better English, and math. Since I started the [Even Start] program, I read a lot. I enjoy books better and I read to my kids.

The class has helped me understand and comprehend more. We discuss how I can help Wendy in reading. I can also relate to my older children better. . . . My household seems more stable than it was.

I've been learning a whole lot of different things I really didn't understand or know. . . . How to get along with people you don't like . . . how to look up things in phone books, because see I don't know how to spell that good, and they teach you how to look up stuff in the dictionary and stuff, where I haven't opened up a dictionary in a long, long time. But I learned. I went and got me one. Got me a dictionary to look up certain words.

Several parents talked about how Even Start has bolstered their self-esteem and helped them to deal with their children's behavior. There follow two examples:

I always had a low esteem about myself, always thought I never was doing a lot. . . . But now since I've been to Even Start, it has really given me a better outlook on life. And also it has helped me how to deal with the children now coming up.

I learned to deal with my children's behavior without spanking or hollering. I've learned that these children have feelings just like we do, so we have to treat them the same way that we want to be treated. So that has helped me out a lot, a whole lot.

## Discussion

Even Start is both an adult education and early childhood education program. One of the unique features of this program is the unified approach to meeting the special educational needs of families at risk. This unified approach is evident in all the components of the program. While the unified approach is probably most evident in the parent–child sessions (where parents and children participate in regularly scheduled activities together), it is also incorporated in other aspects of the program. For example, in the adult education component (which fosters basic academic skills – e.g., reading, writing, math, etc.), the focus is on how parents can become more competent in helping their children with school-related tasks. It is based on the understanding that more academically competent parents tend to raise more academically competent children. Likewise, the parent education component focuses on parenting skills that foster child development and learning, while both the support services and the special events are designed to enhance family functioning. The Even Start program thus works with parents and young children as a learning unit. The curriculum and structure throughout the various components are based on the realization that enhancing one part of the unit enhances the other part as well, and that both are enhanced when the programming and focus are connected.

# 9

# CHILD FIND

"Child Find," in the context of this chapter, refers to the identification of children with special educational needs. Unless such children are identified and assessed, their special needs may not be understood nor attended to. The result may be the development of secondary handicaps and negative impacts on learning and development which may have been avoided if appropriate adaptations had been made. As emphasized in Chapter 1 and discussd in other sections of this book, children with disabilities are similar in many ways to their typically developing peers and should always be viewed as such. Yet an awareness and understanding of their special needs are also important for planning and implementing educational experiences which maximize their chances of success.

The following statement from the *Code of Practice on the Identification and Assessment of Special Educational Needs* (DFE, 1994, p. 10) speaks to the importance of early identification:

> The importance of early identification, assessment and provision for any child who may have special educational needs cannot be over-emphasized. The earlier action is taken, the more responsive the child is likely to be, and the more readily can intervention be made without undue disruption to the organisation of the school, including the delivery of the curriculum for that particular child. If a difficulty proves transient the child will subsequently be able to learn and progress normally. If the child's difficulties prove less responsive to provision made by the school, then an early start can be made in considering the additional provision that may be needed to support the child's progress.

Identifying children with special needs is often a complex and multi-faceted task. The challenge is even greater at the early childhood level, in that many of the screening and assessment tools and procedures used with older children are not appropriate when working with young children. This chapter gives an overview of the different aspects of Child

Find and a discussion of the special challenges involved in assessing young children. Presented first, however, is a clarification of the reasons for conducting different types of assessments.

## Meaning and purpose of assessment

The term "assessment", when used in relation to educational programming, may, in some people's minds, mean about the same as testing. In fact, the terms "assessment" and "testing" are sometimes used interchangeably by the general public. For example, a parent may say, "My child is having her hearing tested today," while the audiologist might refer to the process as an assessment of the child's hearing ability. The term "assessment" actually has a broader meaning than the term "testing". Assessment refers to the process of systematically gathering information about a child. Its primary purpose is to help professionals "really know" the child (Neisworth & Bagnato, 1996). Testing, which involves the use of specific instruments and/or procedures to gather information about a child, is often part of an assessment, but not the same as the total assessment process.

There are several different reasons for assessing young children. One, as already mentioned, is to screen them for developmental delays and disabilities. Other reasons for assessing children include: (1) determining whether they should be given a specific diagnosis (e.g., hearing impaired, visually impaired, attention deficit disorder, etc.); (2) deciding if they are eligible for special services (e.g., speech/language therapy, special education services, etc.); (3) planning their instructional programs; (4) determining their educational placements; (5) monitoring their progress; and (6) evaluating the effects of the early childhood services. It is important to note that the information gathered for one of these purposes (e.g., screening) may not be useful for another (e.g., planning instructional programs). Thus decisions about which procedures and tools to use for any type of assessment should be determined by the purpose of the assessment itself (Wolery, 1994a). Early childhood educators need to be clear as to why information on a child is being gathered and know which assessment strategies are appropriate for that purpose. Unless the purpose is clear and the strategies appropriate, assessments should not be done (NAEYC/NAECS/SDE, 1991). There follows a brief discussion of screening and diagnosis, as these two types of assessment are critical to the Child Find process. Other types of assessment are discussed in subsequent chapters.

## *Screening*

Screening refers to an assessment conducted to determine whether the child should receive further, more in-depth assessment. Screening results can indicate *possible* cause for concern, but cannot be used to confirm a disability or a specific diagnosis. Screening procedures are not appropriate for planning instructional programs nor should they be used for grouping children for instructional purposes. Some screening programs focus on the developmental status of a child; others on physical and health concerns and/or sensory functioning (i.e., sight and hearing).

Assessment strategies appropriate for screening include the use of specific screening instruments and systematic observation over time. Screening should not be done without the consent and involvement of the parents. Parent involvement often includes a parent questionnaire and/or interview, which can provide valuable data for the screening process. Box 9.1 gives an example of a parent questionnaire that might be used for screening purposes. As illustrated, this questionnaire is designed to be brief and open ended. At this point, there is no need to alarm the parents nor to subject them to a lengthy process.

*Box 9.1* Parent questionnaire for screening

---

1 Did you have any special concerns about your child when he or she was a baby? ____ no ____ yes. If yes, what type of concerns?

2 Were you happy about your child's progress during his or her first few years of life? ____ no ____ yes. If no, why not?

3 Did you receive any special advice or help for your child during his or her first few years of life? ____ no ____ yes. If yes, from whom?

4 Do you have any concerns about your child's health at this time? ____ no ____ yes. If yes, what kind?

5 Do you have any concerns about your child's learning? ____ no ____ yes. If yes, what kind?

6 Do you have any concerns about your child's behavior? ____ no ____ yes. If yes, what kind?

7 Do you have any concerns about your child's speech and language? ____ no ____ yes. If yes, what kind?

8 Do you have any other special worries or concerns about your child? ____ no ____ yes. If yes, what kind?

---

Children who are identified by screening efforts as *possibly* having special learning needs should be scheduled for further assessments without undue delay. Appropriate follow-up assessment procedures should include teacher and parent consultation, observation, and test-based assessments. Screening results relating to specific physical conditions (e.g., hearing, vision, or health concerns) may require referral to medical specialists. The primary purpose of this follow-up assessment is to thoroughly identify and describe the child's special needs and to develop appropriate interventions. It is important to remember that screening results cannot be used to positively identify a child as being handicapped or in need of specialized interventions; nor should screening results be used to exclude children from participating in a program or service. When sharing screening results with parents, professionals should take great care to emphasize the tentative nature of the screening decision.

Box 9.2 gives a number of problems and concerns related to the process of screening. These should be kept in mind when planning, implementing, and interpreting the screening process.

*Box 9.2* Screening-related problems and concerns

---

- Limiting screening activities to "tests," rather than incorporating a range of approaches
- Neglecting to involve parents before, during, and after the screening procedures
- Using a locally developed screening instrument that is of poor technical quality
- Using a screening facility or approach that is not comfortable for young children
- Using screening personnel who are not knowledgeable about young children and are unable to facilitate their best performance
- Interpreting screening data as diagnostic information for making educational placement and program planning decisions

---

*Source*: Adapted from Ohio Department of Education (1989).

## Diagnosis

Assessments used to determine a diagnosis indicate whether or not a child has a developmental delay or disability. Such assessments may also provide information about the nature and extent of the delay or disability. It is important to note that a medical diagnosis and a developmental/educational diagnosis, while related, are not the same. A medical diagnosis is conducted by physicians and other health care professionals. The presence of a medical diagnosis does not confirm a disability. For example, a medical diagnosis of recurrent otitis media (middle ear infection) does not necessarily mean that a child has or will have related language and learning disabilities. Although the medical condition places the child at greater risk of such problems, further diagnostic assessments are required to determine the presence of a disability.

Diagnostic assessments are conducted by a multidisciplinary team of individuals. This multidisciplinary model offers several advantages over a single-discipline approach. For example, it provides a way of checking information across several data sources and settings. Such validation can play a critical role in analyzing strengths and weaknesses needed to plan appropriate interventions.

Perhaps the best way to implement a multidisciplinary model is to utilize a core team with consistent membership. This core team should include three professional disciplines: school psychology, speech/ language therapy, and early childhood education. One member of the core team usually assumes the role of case coordinator and takes responsibility for compiling all the information pertaining to the child and serving as the primary contact for parents and other personnel involved with the child. The composition of the rest of the team and the assessment measures used vary in relation to the diagnosis being considered. For example, a physical therapist would be involved and make diagnoses in relation to gross motor concerns, while an audiologist would be involved and make diagnoses for a hearing impairment. It is important to note that early childhood personnel should also be involved in diagnostic assessments. The role of the early childhood educator is to provide relevant information about a child's performance across developmental domains to the other team members. Parents, too, should be considered an integral part of the assessment team. Their input is crucial for information about the early history of the child and the child's current level of functioning at home and within the family structure. Collecting this information is often by way of a parent questionnaire and/or interview. Box 9.3 gives the type of information often collected from the parents during the assessment process. As illustrated, this questionnaire is more in-depth than the parent questionnaire used for screening. The purpose here is to collect more comprehensive and detailed information about the child.

To receive special services through the schools, children must meet certain criteria. Diagnostic assessments confirming the presence of a disability often play an important role in determining such eligibility. The eligibility role of assessment is not without controversy. In fact, this role of assessment, sometimes referred to as "gate-keeping," probably provokes the greatest dispute in relation to diagnostic assessments (Neisworth & Bagnato, 1996).

The completion of assessment activities should be viewed as the beginning of important interventions for children. Without follow-up, screening and assessment are of little value. Follow-up should include communicating with parents, planning appropriate interventions, keeping

*Box 9.3* Parent questionnaire for assessment

---

### A  THE EARLY YEARS

1  What do you remember about the early years that might help?
2  What was he or she like as a young baby?
3  Were you happy about progress at the time?
4  When did you first feel things were not right?
5  What happened?
6  What advice or help did you receive – from whom?

### B  WHAT IS YOUR CHILD LIKE NOW?

1  **General health** – Eating and sleeping habits; general fitness, absences from school, minor ailments – coughs and colds. Serious illnesses/accidents – periods in hospital. Any medicine or special diet? General alertness – tiredness, signs of use of drugs – smoking, drinking, glue-sniffing.
2  **Physical skills** – Walking, running, climbing – riding a bike, football or other games, drawing pictures, writing, doing jigsaws, using construction kits, household gadgets, tools, sewing.
3  **Self-help** – Level of personal independence – dressing, etc.; making bed, washing clothes, keeping room tidy, coping with day-to-day routine; budgeting pocket money, general independence – getting out and about.
4  **Communication** – Level of speech, explains, describes events, people, conveys information (e.g., messages to and from school), joins in conversations; uses telephone.
5  **Playing and learning at home** – How . . . spends time, watching TV, reading for pleasure and information, hobbies, concentration, sharing.
6  **Activities outside** – Belonging to clubs, sporting activities, happy to go alone.
7  **Relationships** – With parents, brothers, and sisters; with friends; with other adults (friends and relations) at home generally, 'outside' generally.
    (a) Is . . . a loner?
8  **Behaviour at home** – Cooperates, shares, listens to and carries out requests, helps in the house, offers help, fits in with family routine and 'rules.' Moods good and bad, sulking – temper tantrums; demonstrative, affectionate.
9  **At school** – Relationships with other children and teachers; progress with reading, writing, numbers, other subjects and activities at school. How the school has helped/not helped your child. Have you been asked to help with school work – hearing child read – with what result?
    (a) Does . . . enjoy school?
    (b) What does . . . find easy or difficult?

### C  YOUR GENERAL VIEWS

1  What do you think your child's special educational needs are?
2  How do you think these can be best provided for?
3  How do you compare your child with others of the same age?
4  What is your child good at or what does he or she enjoy doing?
5  What does . . . worry about – is . . . aware of difficulties?
6  What are your worries, concerns?
7  Is there any other information you would like to give
    (a) about the family – major events that might have affected your child?
    (b) reports from other people?
8  With whom would you like more contact?
9  How do you think your child's needs affect the needs of the family as a whole?

---

*Source*: DFE, 1994, pp. 72–73. Crown copyright is reproduced with the permission of the Controller of Her Majesty's Stationery Office.

other professionals informed, and conducting periodic reviews. At times, assessment for diagnosis results in applying a diagnostic label to a child (e.g., deaf, autistic, mentally retarded, etc.). There are both concerns and advantages associated with labeling. Applying diagnostic labels to young children is a serious matter, whether these labels are special education categories or clinical terms (Leigh, 1983). At times, diagnostic labels may restrict opportunities available to children and/or result in bias, low expectations, and self-fulfilling prophecies.

Diagnostic labels, however, can also produce some positive results. They can "open the door" for children to receive appropriate intervention services and be helpful to parents in understanding their child's behavior. To emphasize the positive and minimize the negative aspects of labeling, the following suggested practices are offered:

- Avoid using labels indiscriminately to generate funds.
- Communicate clearly to parents the meaning of a label and the reasons why it applies to their child.
- Work from the premise that the diagnostic label *represents* the team's *current* judgment and, except in rare cases, should not be interpreted as being permanent.
- Review the use of a diagnostic label regularly and change it, as appropriate.

## Assessment strategies

Information about a child can be gathered in a variety of ways. To fulfill the needs of an assessment, however, such information should be gathered in a systematic way. For a valid assessment, it should also involve more than one tool and/or strategy. The goal of this multiple-data approach is to sample many different types of behavior in a variety of ways. There are a number of different information-gathering methods that might be used during the assessment process. These include testing, direct observation, interviews, anecdotal and running records, work samples, questionnaires, and rating scales completed by a professional or someone familiar with the child. Assessment strategies appropriate for diagnosis are presented in Box 9.4, along with a brief statement about the benefit(s) of each.

A combination of strategies tends to result in a more valid assessment of the child than any one strategy used in isolation. It should also be noted that there is often more than one way to use an assessment strategy, and, as indicated earlier, the purpose of the assessment should determine the tools and procedures to be used. At times, certain tools and methods used for one type of assessment can also be used for another purpose (e.g., tools and procedures used for program planning might also be used for

*Box 9.4* Assessment for diagnosis: sources of data

1 Parent interviews
   • provide critical information that only a parent may be able to provide
   • provide insights about the child within the family context

2 Parent questionnaires
   • complement information from direct assessment by providing a more comprehensive view of the child's behavior

3 Teacher interviews
   • contribute to a complete assessment by adding information about the child's classroom performance

4 Teacher checklists
   • quantify teachers' observations about a child

5 Work samples (e.g., art work, reading and/or math worksheets, etc.)
   • contribute to a complete assessment by adding information about the child's academic performance

6 Systematic observations
   • provide information about a child's behavior that may not be gained from other procedures (e.g., interactions with peers and adults, adaptability to differing situations, use of language, etc.)

7 Data from other professionals
   • contribute to a complete assessment by adding information about the child from other disciplines (e.g., physicians and therapists) and other child experiences (e.g., day care)

8 Structured testing
   • provides information about a child's knowledge and skills that may not be assessed through other means
   • provides information about a child's behavior in a structured context
   • provides information about a child's knowledge and skills in relation to age expectations and/or established criteria

monitoring child progress) (Neisworth & Bagnato, 1996). There follows a brief discussion of interviews, observations, and tests, as these three information-gathering formats represent the most commonly used assessment strategies at the early childhood level.

## Interviews

Interviews, as an assessment strategy, involve asking others who know the child well to provide information about how they perceive the child and his or her level of functioning. Interviews can be quite structured, with questions to be asked determined in advance. When interviews are a part of a formal assessment tool, the questions may have to be asked in a specific way and the interviewee given limited choices of specific responses. For example, a parent or teacher may be asked to describe a child's level of independence during mealtimes but be limited to one of the following three responses: "independent," "needs some help," "needs a great deal of help." Other interviews may be quite open ended, allowing for more detailed information and addressing a wider range of issues. In an open-ended interview, a parent or teacher may be asked, "How does Jimmy do at mealtimes? Could you talk about how well he does in trying to feed himself?"

There are, of course, a number of different interview formats that fall between the two examples presented above. The purpose of the assessment should determine the format used. If the interview is part of a screening to determine possible developmental delays, the more structured interview would usually be more appropriate. If the purpose of the interview is to determine the child's special interests or to "fill in the picture" of what he or she likes to do at home, the open-ended format would be more appropriate.

### *Observation*

Observation, when used for assessment, entails gathering information by watching and listening and then making a record of what is observed. There are a number of different observational systems that can be used for assessment purposes. One type consists of printed rating scales that the assessor completes during or after an observation. The following is an example of an item that might appear on such a scale: "Engages in simple make-believe activities." Other observational systems involve counting and/or timing specific child behaviors. Such systems can be as simple as recording the length of time a child stays with a chosen activity during learning center time. Observational systems can also be quite complex, such as recording not only the frequency and type of a child's disruptive outbursts during a specified period of time, but also the antecedents of such outbursts (i.e., events that happen before).

Observation, as an assessment tool, has rich potential. Observation can occur in the child's natural environments (e.g., classroom or home) and provide information about how a child usually functions. Observation can be used to gather information that may be difficult to obtain in other ways, such as how children interact with peers, how they respond to frustration, and how they play.

In spite of its rich potential, systematic observations seem to be used less frequently for assessment purposes than either interviews or testing. This is due perhaps to the complexity of the task and the skill required for analyzing and interpreting the data. Some noteworthy attempts have been made to provide an organizational framework for conducting on-going systematic observations in natural settings. The "arena assessment" represents one such system. With this approach, one member of the team interacts with a child in a play-based setting, while other members of the multidisciplinary team observe and record observations of the child. (More information about the arena approach is presented in a later section of this chapter.)

## *Testing*

Tests tend to be less useful than interviews and observation when working with young children, especially young children with disabilities. The following are some of the limitations associated with testing, as outlined by Wolery (1994a): (1) tests rarely include adaptations to accommodate to children's disabilities; (2) tests often contain items or sequences of items that are not instructionally relevant, and (3) tests are frequently administered in artificial situations rather than in natural contexts.

There are generally two broad types of tests: norm-referenced and criterion-referenced tests. Norm-referenced tests indicate how a child performs in comparison to the group on which the test was normed. These tests are often used for screening purposes and for making diagnoses related to special needs. Such tests, to be valid, must be administered according to the developers' specifications. Criterion-referenced tests indicate how a child performs in comparison to specific criteria for each item, and scores for each item are reported in relation to a specified level of performance or knowledge. Curriculum-referenced tests, a type of criterion-referenced test, compare children's performance to the objectives of a specified curriculum. Some tests address a specific area of child development, such as motor development or language development. Other tests focus on multiple aspects of child development and address all the major developmental domains (cognitive, motor, communication, social/emotional, adaptive, etc.). Many tests can be administered by early childhood personnel who are familiar with the tests; others must be administered only by specifically trained professionals, such as psychologists or speech/language pathologists.

Some type of structured testing is often included in assessment for screening and for diagnosis. Serious concerns associated with the use of structured testing for young children necessitate careful consideration when choosing which tools and procedures to use. While there are a number of variables to consider, including complexity and cost, the following variables warrant special consideration:

- reliability – Reliability refers to the degree to which test results can be trusted in relation to accuracy. Every test has some degree of error, with measures of young children's performance more susceptible to

167

error than those designed for older children and adults. A test that is characterized by too much error is unreliable and should not be used.

- validity – Validity refers to the degree to which an instrument measures what it is designed to measure. For example, a test of cognitive functioning that actually measures the child's cognitive skills rather than other skills is said to be valid. If a test of cognitive functioning relies heavily on a child's receptive and expressive language skills and the child is weak in these areas, the results may not be a true indicator of the child's cognitive abilities. A test lacking in respectable test validity may not provide a fair assessment of the child's true abilities and may thus be discriminatory against the child.

- standardization and norming – Assessment instruments should be critiqued in relation to the normative population used for standardization. It is important that the group on which the assessment instrument was normed matches the group on which the instrument is used, especially in relation to such factors as ethnic background, socioeconomic level, geographic region, age, and special needs. While some programs like to use locally developed instruments for screening, such instruments are rarely of adequate technical quality, due, in part, to problems with standardization and norming (Meisels, 1985).

- administration time – Structured testing situations are usually not a good match to the characteristics of young children. Thus administration time should be carefully considered when making choices about which assessment tools to use. Screening is designed to be a brief process and should usually require no more than 15 to 20 minutes for administration. Assessment for diagnosis may take a longer time to administer, but should not exceed the child's tolerance level. Child-friendly materials and procedures can minimize some of the concerns associated with a longer administration time.

- personnel – Some assessment instruments and procedures require a trained or certified individual to administer them. Others require the involvement of a team of individuals. Because both screening results and assessment for diagnosis should be as accurate as possible, anyone involved in the assessment process should be knowledgeable about young children and able to facilitate their best performance. They should also be aware of the purpose of the assessment and familiar with the instruments and procedures being used.

- appeal for children – Ideally, assessment activities should be pleasant for children, as they are more likely to demonstrate their best performance when they are comfortable and interested in the activities.

168

- setting – Some assessment instruments and procedures require a specific type of environment (e.g., a sound-proof room, a quiet place for parent interviews, individual workstations for children, etc.). Such requirements should be attended to, as should considerations relating to parent and child comfort and accessibility in terms of location and special needs (e.g., wheelchair accessibility, adaptive equipment available, etc.).
- cost – Screening and assessment instruments tend to vary considerably in cost. As there seems to be no direct relationship between price and quality (Ohio Department of Education, 1989), purchasers should take care not to equate the two. Some screening instruments have certain "hidden costs" that should be taken into consideration. These might include individual record forms, training requirements, or essential computer scoring.

### Multiple sources of information

Effective assessment requires the collection of information from multiple sources. In addition to using a combination of the assessment strategies outlined above (i.e., interviews, observation, and testing), it is critical that expressions of concern and information provided by parents be viewed as valuable assessment data. It is also important for schools to make full use of information passed to them when the child transfers from one classroom or program to another.

## Special issues and concerns

As indicated above, there are some special issues and concerns relating to the assessment of young children that go beyond the concerns associated with assessment of older children and adults. The following is a discussion of some of these issues and concerns.

### Intrusiveness

While assessment plays a pivotal role throughout the early intervention process, considerable debate and concern surrounds the process (Neisworth & Bagnato, 1996). Part of the debate centers around the "intrusiveness" of the assessment procedures. Assessment can be intrusive to the child, his or her family, and to the professionals involved. Some assessment procedures subject the child and his or her family to invasions of privacy, to inconvenient scheduling, and to assessment-related demands (or tasks) that threaten their feelings of confidence and trust. Assessment procedures can also be intrusive in terms of time constraints, experienced by both professionals and parents.

Neisworth and Bagnato (1996), in discussing assessment-related concerns, suggest that professionals involved in making assessment decisions should take care to gather, synthesize, and interpret enough information to serve the intended purposes of assessment while avoiding "over-assessment." They refer to "low stake" and "high stake" assessment decisions and suggest that the higher stake decisions should be based on greater sampling and include low inference measures. Deciding which of three acceptable goals for the child should be worked on first is an example they use of a "low stake" decision. Diagnosing the presence of mental retardation and determining eligibility for specialized treatment are examples they use of "high stake" decisions. It should be evident from these examples that "low stake" and "high stake" considerations relate to the potential social consequences of the assessment results.

To help professionals weigh "high stake" and "low stake" considerations, Neisworth and Bagnato (1996, pp. 25–26) offer the following implications for practices:

- Strive to obtain the best and closest descriptions of child status when decisions to be made are not trivial.
- Decisions that are not high stake need not be made with the same set of assessment materials, crew of professionals, and expenditures of times [as decisions that have high stake implications].
- The possible use of a given assessment instrument and approach should be pitted against alternative assessment or means to achieve similar outcomes, including no assessment.

### Appropriateness

It is generally not appropriate to use a "downward extrapolation of school-age practices" to test young children (Neisworth & Bagnato, 1996, p. 26). This is because assessment methods used with older children often do not match the developmental characteristics of younger children. This mismatch is especially evident when norm-referenced assessments are being used. "The expectations of most norm-referenced standardized assessments run counter to the realities of the behavior of young children" (Neisworth & Bagnato, 1996, p. 26). Some of the "realities of behavior" that get in the way of standardized testing include "the child's distractibility, lack of interest in the standard objects in the test kit, oppositional behavior and noncompliance, lack of endurance, persistence at other competing (more interesting) activities, and frustration with test tasks" (Neisworth & Bagnato, 1996, p. 26).

The process of early development represents another concern that needs to be considered in relation to appropriateness in assessing young children. Normal early development tends to be nonlinear and intermittent.

These characteristics make prediction and inferences related to assessment problematic (Neisworth & Bagnato, 1996). Transitional phases in early child development add to the concern. If a child is assessed during a transitional phase (i.e., a time characterized by emerging and fluctuating skills), conclusions about the child's current level of functioning may be either exaggerated or depressed. During the early childhood years, it is not unusual for children to exhibit a more advanced skill and then return to a former, less skilled performance. A skill that is "emerging" may be evidenced, or "previewed" a month or so before it becomes a part of the child's daily repertoire of skills. It is thus quite difficult to build an accurate picture of the child's current level of functioning, as this level may fluctuate from week to week or even day to day.

Uneven or nonparallel development, which is characteristic of very young children and children with disabilities, also causes a mismatch between the characteristics of young children and the demands of standardized assessments. With young children and children with disabilities, "parallel development across the interrelated and interactive developmental domains cannot be expected" (Neisworth & Bagnato, 1996, p. 27). Making decisions about a child's cognitive functioning based on his or her language skills illustrates the type of problem encountered with uneven or nonparallel development. A 4-year-old who is deaf, for example, will not be able to use age-appropriate language skills, even though his or her cognitive functioning may be at or above age expectations.

### Nondiscriminatory practices

Discrimination can enter into assessment practices in a number of ways. One way is through the disregard of a child's communication status when his or her first language is not English or Welsh. Lack of competence in English or Welsh must not be equated with learning difficulties. Nondiscriminatory assessment "takes into consideration children's ability in English, their stage of language acquisition, and whether they have been given the time and opportunity to develop proficiency in their native language as well as in English" (NAEYC & NAECS/SDE, 1991, pp. 32–33).

To be nondiscriminatory in assessment, care must also be taken to consider the child within the context of his home, culture, and community. If necessary, bilingual support staff, interpreters, and translators should be used to help the child and his or her parents to understand fully the assessment measures the school is taking. It is also important for assessment tools to be culturally neutral and useful for a range of ethnic groups. Additionally, when assessing children from minority ethnic groups, "schools should make use of any local sources of advice relevant to the ethnic group concerned" (DFE, 1994, p. 10).

Discrimination can also enter into assessment practices due to a child's disability or special needs. Some tests of cognitive functioning involve the manipulation of materials such as puzzle pieces or paper and pencil. In such instances, a child's inability to score well on a particular test item may be due to cerebral palsy or some other condition relating to poor muscle control rather than delayed cognitive functioning.

### Appropriate interpretation

Assessment data should never be viewed as the "total picture" of a child; nor should it be used to predict future performance. At best, assessment data – particularly in the case of young children – should be viewed as "a picture in time" of the child's performance. People perform differently at different times and under different circumstances – again, this is especially true in relation to young children. Appropriate interpretation of assessment data is further complicated by the fact that the expression of handicapping conditions and special educational needs may be very different in young children than in older children and that differentiating between a handicapping condition and inexperience can be difficult in young children (Rogers, 1986). Thus making predictions about a child's subsequent adjustment is not recommended.

## Approaches and recommendations

### Approaches

How professionals approach the assessment of children depends to a large extent on their general philosophy about how young children learn and develop. This, in turn, is usually a result of their professional training (Zirpoli, 1995). Historically, assessment of children for educational purposes has followed a medical model approach. The traditional medical model is characterized by various professionals conducting their assessments in isolation, with little communication among the professionals and caregivers involved. More recently, the educational assessment of children has been moving away from this medical model to a more collaborative approach.

In early childhood education and early childhood special education, this move has resulted in the development of an "arena approach" to assessment. With this approach, assessment is completed by one professional who acts as a facilitator, while other members of the team, including the parents, observe and record observations relevant to their discipline. The role of the facilitator in an arena assessment is to engage the child in activities that demonstrate the child's developmental strengths and weaknesses. Prior to the assessment, team members often meet and identify the facilitator behaviors they would like to see for their individual evaluations. This information helps the facilitator make decisions about the kind of activities and materials to introduce with the child.

An arena assessment is usually conducted in a creative play environment, where materials invite expression in all areas of development, including exploratory, manipulative, and problem-solving behaviors, emotional expression and language skills (Linder, 1990). Two or three children are often observed at one time, allowing for observations about child-to-child interactions. A play-based arena assessment is generally appropriate for all children who are developmentally functioning between 6 months and 6 years of age. It can be used effectively with children who are typically developing, those who are at-risk, and for children with disabilities (Linder, 1990).

Parents are involved in the arena assessment process prior to, during, and after the observation period. Before the observation, parents complete developmental checklists and/or participate in an interview to share information about their child's level of performance at home. During the observation, parents observe along with the professionals. At times, they may help facilitate their child's play. After the observation, parents are involved in the discussion of their child's performance and in planning an appropriate program for their child.

The arena assessment is generally receiving positive reports. "Professionals who use arena assessment indicate that it saves time, and that with training they can see what they need for their discipline-specific evaluations while also seeing the whole child" (Raver, 1991, p. 34). It has also been observed that "children who were previously deemed untestable played and interacted comfortably in the play-based [arena] assessment" (Linder, 1990, p. ix). Parents, too, have indicated that they prefer the multidisciplinary arena approach to separate (single discipline) assessments (Linder, 1990). The arena assessment approach, then, has advantages for the family, the child, and the team. A listing of some of these advantages is presented in Box 9.5.

## Recommendations

In response to the many concerns relating to traditional approaches to assessment with young children, a number of professional organizations, researchers, and practitioners have worked to develop recommendations regarding appropriate assessment practices. Such recommendations have been outlined in a number of publications, including a Position Paper developed by the National Association for the Education of Young Children and the National Association of Early Childhood Specialists in State Departments of Education (NAEYC & NAECS/SDE, 1991). The

*Box 9.5* Advantages of the arena approach to assessment

---

For the family
- Includes the family as fully functioning members of the team
- Avoids duplication of assessment questions and procedures addressed to or involving them
- Leads to a better understanding of specific skills that are being addressed
- Tends to be less stressful and intimidating for the parents

For the child
- Provides a more comfortable environment, in that the child's parents are present, the facilitator is a play partner versus an examiner, and the materials are fun and interesting
- Participates in one assessment session, versus several domain-specific or discipline-specific assessments
- Provides the opportunity to demonstrate strengths and functional skills in a natural context
- Provides information about a child's learning style, interests, and interaction patterns
- Allows flexibility in testing, thus avoiding assessment bias in relation to a child's disability
- Provides qualitative information about the child's functioning, not just quantitative (e.g., information about how a child performs a task, not just the number of tasks he or she can perform)

For the team
- Allows for immediate access to the skills and knowledge of their team mates
- Results in a comprehensive, integrated assessment of the child
- Provides the opportunity to share information based on simultaneous observations of the child, leading to easier consensus
- Expands the knowledge of all team members as they share information from the perspective of various disciplines
- Represents a less costly and less time-consuming process than traditional assessments

---

*Source*: Material adapted from Linder (1990) and Raver (1991).

following recommendations are based on this Position Paper. While the Position Paper addresses all aspects of assessment, the following selected recommendations relate primarily to the Child Find process (i.e., the identification of young children with special needs). Several of these recommendations have already been discussed and some overlap between them will be evident.

1    Child assessment should address all domains and aspects of child development. As a disability seldom affects only single areas of development, assessment should address all of the developmental domains.

2 Assessments should be conducted, as much as possible, in natural settings and through procedures that are familiar and meaningful to the child.

3 Assessments should utilize an array of different assessment techniques.

4 Assessment procedures should be sensitive to individual diversity including differences in styles and rates of responding, as well as in children's use of language.

5 Assessment procedures should avoid situations that threaten children's psychological safety or feelings of self-esteem. Children's usual behavior in natural situations can easily be assessed without causing children undue stress.

6 Assessments should focus on children's strengths and what they can do – not just their weaknesses or areas of deficits.

7 Assessment should be a collaborative process, involving parents and a multidisciplinary team of professionals.

8 The choice of which assessment tools and procedures to use should be given careful consideration. Some questions that might be used to guide the selection process are presented in Box 9.6.

*Box 9.6* Selecting assessment tools and procedures

1 Are the materials and procedures reliable and valid?
2 Are the materials and procedures child friendly?
3 How much training is required to administer the assessment?
4 What adaptations, if any, are provided to meet the needs of children with physical, sensory, or other impairments?
5 What role do parents have in administering this assessment?
6 What was the cultural orientation of the normative sample (if norm-referenced)? Were efforts made to provide norms on a separate sample or to include minority cultural groups in the sample? Are non-English forms available?

## Case study – Amanda

### Background information

Amanda is 4 years old and has been participating in a Reception year class for about three weeks. Her teacher, Ms. Lane, is concerned about Amanda's continued "shyness" and limited use of expressive language. Amanda rarely speaks to anyone except to answer direct questions, and then her responses usually consist of one- or two-word utterances. Many times, she responds with gestures instead of words and seems to avoid contact with others as much as possible. Ms. Lane called Amanda's parents to discuss her concerns. Mr. and Mrs. Smith, Amanda's parents, indicated that Amanda does not talk much at home either. She likes to watch television and usually plays by herself.

Ms. Lane talked to Mr. and Mrs. Smith about doing a screening with Amanda. She explained to them that she does not really know if Amanda will need special help, but that she is concerned about Amanda's speech, language, and social skills. Mr. and Mrs. Smith agreed to the screening and completed a questionnaire about Amanda's early child development and current functioning at home.

In addition to the parent questionnaire, other components of the screening process included an observation by the speech/language pathologist, a hearing acuity screening, and a developmental checklist completed by Ms. Lane. The speech/language pathologist found it very difficult to get Amanda to respond to any prompts or other screening activities. Amanda would not talk beyond giving a whispered "yes" or "no" to direct questions. For the hearing screening, Amanda would sometimes look toward a source of sound (e.g., a bell ringing) but would not raise her hand to show that she had heard the sound nor would she repeat words and sounds as she was requested to do. Ms. Lane had to score many items on the developmental checklist as "don't know" or "not observed," as Amanda's participation in classroom activities was quite limited, and direct prompts were usually ignored.

After reviewing all of the screening information, Ms. Lane asked Mr. and Mrs. Smith to meet with her at their earliest convenience. They came to school the following week. At this conference, Ms. Lane shared her observations and concerns with Amanda's parents and said that she would like further assessments done to determine whether or not Amanda might need special services. While reluctant, Mr. and Mrs. Smith did agree to follow-up assessments.

These assessments started three weeks later. First, the speech/language pathologist took Amanda with her to a therapy room to administer a communication assessment in both the receptive and expressive language domains. As she had done during the screening process, Amanda gave very limited responses to items on the assessment measure. Her score placed her at about a twenty-six-month level of functioning. The next assessment was conducted by the school psychologist in his office. This assessment focused on cognitive functioning. Again, Amanda responded with very little verbal interaction and minimal attempts to complete tasks as requested (e.g., draw a circle). The psychologist also concluded that Amanda was functioning somewhere between 24 and 26 months of age. Finally, an audiologist conducted an assessment of Amanda's hearing. She found her hearing to be normal. Using a norm-referenced test, Ms. Lane completed an assessment of Amanda in the areas of social/emotional, motor, and adaptive skill development. While her social/emotional score on this test was around the three-year level, scores in the motor and adaptive skill areas were closer to the four-year level. Reports from the family physician indicated that there were no health-related concerns at the time.

A "staffing" was held to compare assessment results and to develop a "combined report" that would then be shared with the parents. Attending the staffing were Ms. Lane, the school psychologist, the head teacher at the school, and the speech/language pathologist. The team decided that Amanda was developmentally delayed and needed special education services.

Ms. Lane scheduled another conference with Mr. and Mrs. Smith to share this report with them. They were quite upset with the team's finding, which were reported in age-equivalent terms (as indicated by the test scores). Mrs. Smith cried, while Mr. Smith argued. Both felt the team's report was not an adequate reflection of Amanda's skills. Their decision was to take Amanda out of school for now and "work with her" at home.

### Discussion

The Smiths had moved from France to England three months before Amanda started Reception year at school. In France, the family were living with a maternal grandmother who was Amanda's primary caregiver while both her parents worked. French was the primary language used in the home, as Amanda's grandmother spoke very little English. After Amanda's grandmother died suddenly, Mr. and Mrs. Smith decided to move to London where Mr. Smith's company had a second office. Mrs. Smith also had a sister living in London and looked forward to living closer to her. Amanda's parents enrolled her in the Reception year class, thinking that it would be a good way for Amanda to make friends and become more skilled in using English.

Amanda, however, was not doing well with the move to England. She missed her grandmother greatly and had had very little experience playing with other children. Amanda's response to the differences in language and customs, along with the trauma of losing her grandmother and moving to a new country, was to retreat within herself. These considerations were not addressed during the screening and assessment process. The procedures used were discriminatory against Amanda in that they failed to consider the context of her language, culture, home, and community. Had the process been conducted in a nondiscriminatory manner and with more involvement on the part of the parents, the outcome might have been quite different. Amanda might not have been labeled "developmentally delayed," and appropriate supports might have been identified to make her school experience more positive. Additionally, Mr. and Mrs. Smith might have felt themselves a valuable part of the intervention team and become actively involved in Amanda's educational program.

# 10

# PROGRAM AND COMMUNITY RESPONSES

## Common philosophy

A theme expressed in various ways throughout this book is the concept that professionals working with young children need a clear understanding of how young child learn and ways in which the characteristics of young children differ from those of older children. The first sentence in the Introduction of this book introduces this theme: "Young children learn through play and through interactions with people and objects in their environment." Understanding how young children learn and ways in which they differ from older children is critical to program planning both for children who are typically developing and for children with special needs.

To serve children well, it is important for service providers representing different disciplines and/or different agencies to work from a common understanding about young children. Within a program, this understanding is sometimes articulated in the form of a philosophy statement. Without a common philosophy, team efforts (both within and between different disciplines and agencies) can be seriously jeopardized.

A program philosophy might be viewed as the framework of a program. It provides information about the program's goals, priorities, and practices. A program philosophy can also provide guidelines for decision making and help to sensitize staff to key educational issues. Additionally, a written program philosophy tends to facilitate team building (especially if the staff and parents are included in the development of the philosophy), establish consistency in approaches and practices, and help identify unique characteristics of the program to other service agencies. Finally, a program philosophy can assist parents in making informed choices about programs for their children. While a common philosophy within a program is certainly desirable, a common philosophy across programs – while often difficult to achieve – is a vision that some communities are committed to as a means of providing more effective services to young children and their families.

A program philosophy should reflect sound practice, research, and theory related to young children and their unique characteristics. For inclusive programs (i.e., early childhood programs serving children with disabilities), the program philosophy should address the rationale for including young children with special needs. As such, it should address educational, exceptionality, and developmental issues. It should also include statements about the purposes of education, the nature of learning, and the nature of the learner. The following are some of the specific items that might be included in a program philosophy statement:

- a rationale for the inclusion of children with disabilities
- the role and involvement of families
- the curriculum model or approach used in the program
- the nature and composition of the educational team
- the value of play and peer interaction

Presented in Box 10.1 is a sample philosophy statement that would be appropriate for a program serving children with special needs in an inclusive setting.

*Box 10.1* Sample program philosophy

---

The Forest School program is designed to provide children of varying abilities with the following opportunities:

- to learn and grow to their maximum potential
- to feel safe and cared for by responsive and competent adults
- to play and learn in an environment that helps them understand that they are a valued part of a group
- to have their parents involved in their educational program to the extent possible and desired by each parent
- to play and work with their peers and teachers in situations that are appropriate to each child's needs and abilities
- to learn about their world in a way that allows for each child's differences and strengths to be recognized and valued.

---

## Common practices

In addition to having a common philosophy, it is also important for a team to agree on how to translate this philosophy into practice. Fortunately, clear guidelines for practice in the field of early childhood education have been developed and articulated in the form of developmentally appropriate practices (DAP) (Bredekamp & Copple, 1997) and in early childhood special education in the form of "recommended practices" (Odom & McLean, 1996). A discussion about DAP has already been presented in Chapter 2, along with some of the myths and concerns relating to the effectiveness of DAP with children with special needs. It is important for teachers and other team members to be aware of these myths and concerns and to know how to work from within a DAP approach. Without this understanding, young children and their families may be exposed to conflicting messages and practices as these relate to educational and/or therapeutic activities.

All team members should work from the understanding that the DAP approach is considered an appropriate framework in which intervention for children with special needs can be embedded. They should also know that, at times, the special needs of children with disabilities may necessitate adaptations and modifications of the DAP approach. While special adaptations and modifications (sometimes referred to as "exceptionality appropriate practices") will be addressed in greater detail in Chapter 12, the following discussion is designed to provide further clarification about embedding exceptionality appropriate practices within a DAP curriculum.

### DAP and children with disabilities

Developmentally appropriate practices (DAP) emerged out of a concern shared by many early childhood educators that programming for young children was moving toward a greater emphasis on academic performance and structure, or teacher directedness (Cook *et al.*, 1996). The DAP guidelines, which focus on expectations and learning environments that match the developmental levels of young children, were designed to counteract this trend. As discussed in Chapter 2, early childhood special education evolved from a different model – one that is more medical or therapeutic in nature. The early childhood special education model tends to focus on the identification of desired outcomes, which are specifically described skills or behaviors. Other foundations of early childhood special education include the following:

- accountability – that is, holding professionals accountable, or responsible, for ensuring that children with special needs are making steady progress toward their individualized goals and objectives;
- the belief that the development of a child with special needs can be accelerated or enhanced through careful program planning and direct instruction;
- a commitment to individualized instruction;
- an emphasis on parent–professional collaboration and family empowerment;
- a focus on transition planning and preparation for the next environment;
- an emphasis on interdisciplinary and interagency collaboration.

181

While most of these foundations are compatible with DAP, others may appear to be outside the realm of DAP principles. Because of a commitment to serve children with disabilities in the least restrictive environment (i.e., the most integrated or inclusive setting in which a child may function successfully), it becomes necessary to combine early childhood education and early childhood special education services in the same setting. Some reconciliation between the two approaches (i.e., early childhood education and early childhood special education) is beginning to evolve. This reconciliation reflects a transdisciplinary approach to teaming, where early childhood education incorporates early childhood special education practices, and early childhood special education incorporates early childhood practices. A growing number of professionals involved in the education of young children feel that eventually there should be no division between early childhood education and early childhood special education (Cook *et al.*, 1996). Efforts are currently underway to make this happen (Bredekamp, 1993; Wolery & Wilbers, 1994; Wolery *et al.*, 1992).

### *Activity-based intervention*

Activity-based intervention is designed to blend child development principles with exceptionality appropriate practices and other early intervention strategies. As developed by Bricker and Cripe (1992), this approach uses natural environments and events to foster specific goals for children with special needs. The activity-based intervention approach emphasizes child-initiated activities and social interaction but also allows for some highly structured approaches, which are typical of special education. Thus such strategies as behavior analysis and behavior modification might be used with the activity-based model, but are not used as the predominant teaching methodologies (Cook *et al.*, 1996).

Transdisciplinary play-based intervention (TPBI), a curriculum developed by Toni Linder (1993), reflects the activity-based orientation. The TPBI curriculum is based on the understanding that young children learn best through "playful" activities – i.e., activities that the children enjoy and freely participate in. Intervention using the TPBI approach is "comfortable, pleasurable, and easy to implement" (Linder, 1993, p. ix). The TPBI approach reflects recommended practices in early childhood special education, in that it is minimally intrusive and capitalizes on individual strengths. TPBI for an individual child begins with an understanding of his or her developmental skills, underlying developmental processes, learning style, and interaction patterns. This information, along with knowledge about the child's interests and the family's goals and vision for their child, is used to develop an individualized intervention plan. When developed according to the TPBI model, the resulting intervention plan reflects the interrelated nature of the child's abilities and disabilities.

Additional benefits of the TPBI model include its flexibility and transportability. TPBI and other versions of activity-based intervention can be incorporated into the child's routine at home and at school. It can also be transferred from home to infant and toddler or early childhood programs, and for the most part does not require special toys or other play materials. Additionally, the TPBI approach to intervention involves a transdisciplinary team that includes the parents. Each member of the team becomes familiar with the child's goals and developmental levels of all the domains and considers the whole child in planning instructional strategies, rather than focusing on the child's needs in a specific area.

(Further information about how to implement an activity-based intervention model is presented in greater detail in Chapters 11 and 12.)

## Common program

The *Code of Practice on the Identification and Assessment of Special Educational Needs* (DFE, 1994) outlines a number of "fundamental principles" that serve as a basis for the practices and regulations concerning the education of children with disabilities. One such principle is that "children with special education needs require the greatest possible access to a broad and balanced education, including the National Curriculum" (p. 2). A related principle specifies that "children with special educational needs ... should, where appropriate and taking into account the wishes of their parents, be educated alongside their peers in mainstream schools" (p. 2). As indicated in Chapter 2, a "common program," or a mainstream experience, also represents recommended practices as outlined in the early childhood special education literature (Odom & McLean, 1996).

### Definitions

There are several different terms often used to refer to the placement of children with disabilities in the same physical setting as children without disabilities. These terms include mainstreaming, least restrictive environment, integration, inclusion, and normalization. Using these terms interchangeably, which is sometimes done, tends to generate confusion. The following definitions are offered as an attempt to define them in relation to discrete practices.

- mainstreaming: the placement of a child with a disability in a program designed for children without disabilities. Mainstreaming is generally considered appropriate in situations where a child with a disability can participate in the regular program with the same chances of success as their non-disabled peers. In other words, their disability is not expected to affect their performance as compared to the majority of their peers. If an adaptation to a program must take place in order for the child to be successful, he or she will usually not be mainstreamed.

- least restrictive environment (LRE): the understanding that to the maximum extent appropriate, children with disabilities will be educated with children who are not disabled. LRE is also based on the understanding that special classes and separate schooling occur only when the nature or severity of the disabling condition is such that education in regular classes with the use of appropriate aids and services cannot be achieved satisfactorily. The least restrictive environment thus represents the most integrated or inclusive setting in which a child may function successfully.

- integration: the practice of bringing together different groups which have previously been segregated. In early intervention or early childhood special education, the term "integration" is used to refer to the practice of educating children with disabilities in specialized separate classrooms within a public school. This arrangement allows for a specialized program *and* the opportunity to see and interact with other children without disabilities. This arrangement, however, still separates the children with special needs into a group of their own. It highlights their differences and distances them from others (Howard *et al.*, 1997). Integration often allows for the participation of children with disabilities in regular classroom environments for nonacademic activities (e.g., recess, lunch, physical education, school assemblies, etc.). At times, it may also include participation in the regular classroom for part of the day (e.g., just for reading or speaking and listening activities). This arrangement usually gives the child with a disability a "visitor" status versus "full member" status.

- inclusion: the practice of including all children as full-time contributing members of a heterogeneous group of children. With inclusion, all students participate in all the regular daily routines of the classroom. These routines are modified to meet each child's individual goals and objectives. Additionally, each child has multiple opportunities during the day for naturally occurring positive interactions with typically developing children. The classroom teacher, with support from educational specialists, serves as the primary interventionist. Full inclusion stands out as different from mainstreaming and integration, in that it represents "not simply a child's placement, but has to do with the integrity of the placement. . . . Full inclusion occurs when a student with a disability becomes a full-time member of a program the child might attend if he or she did not have a disability, and the child is not removed for the delivery of educational, social, or related services" (Howard *et al.*, 1997, p. 7). Inclusion assumes that membership of the group should be "a given" versus something that is discussed and decided.

- normalization: refers to an approach (versus a placement) used by various providers which serve individuals with disabilities. This approach stresses that individuals with disabilities should experience patterns of life and conditions of everyday living which are as close as possible to the regular (i.e., normal) ways of life in their society.

### Four different approaches

There have been major changes in attitudes and practices over the past fifty years relating to educational programming for children with disabilities. These changes have been described in relation to the following four different approaches: the denial approach, the box approach, the permission approach, and the inclusion approach (Wilson, 1991).

The "denial approach" failed to recognize individual differences and operated from the belief that "one program should fit all." If a child was not succeeding in the regular classroom, this must mean that he or she is not trying hard enough. If a child was severely disabled and clearly not able to participate in the regular classroom in a meaningful way, he or she was denied access to educational programming. The parents could either choose to keep their child at home or place him or her in an institution that would take care of the child's physical needs. Educational needs were not even recognized, and children with special needs who grew up during the time of the denial approach rarely became a part of the mainstream of life.

The "box approach" focused on individual differences to the point of categorizing children as "regular education" or "special education" students. Each group was then assigned their own box (i.e., classroom). Children (and teachers) generally stayed in their own boxes throughout their educational experience. The message this approach gave to children with special needs was that "You're different and you don't belong with 'normal' children." This approach often resulted in poor self concepts, low expectations, and learned helplessness on the part of the children with special needs. For the typically developing children, this approach failed to foster an appreciation of diversity and led to misunderstandings about individual differences.

With the "permission approach," children with special needs were allowed to come into the regular classroom "if they were ready" or "if they passed the test." The message to the children with this approach was that "We hear you knocking, and we'll be nice enough to share our space with you, but only if you've learned the right skills. Can you communicate your needs and wants? Can you read and write? Can you work independently? Can you interact in a positive way with other children? Do you know all the right words?" Questions that were not asked included "Do we know how to read the communicative attempts of the child with special needs?" and "Do we really value diversity?" The permission approach often led to anxiety on the part of parents and pressure on the part of children with special educational needs. The children had to "get ready" or "prove themselves" in order to participate in the mainstream.

The "inclusion approach" is based on the understanding that everyone belongs and that it is inappropriate to design a standard program and expect it to "fit" every child. With the inclusion approach, the emphasis is on *fitting the program* to what the child needs. No one is excluded, and every child is valued as an individual. The focus of this approach is on finding ways for every child to participate and to be successful. It assumes that all children have the right to attend the same neighborhood schools and the same classrooms. It also assumes that children with disabilities can participate in the same extracurricular activities and community programs they would if they did not have a disability. The inclusion approach is driven by a vision of unity, of "being included." With this vision, inclusion becomes much more than a placement. It becomes a way of being.

### LRE controversy

Placing a child with a disability in the "least restrictive environment" (LRE) tends to mean different things for different people. While, for some, the least restrictive environment is equivalent to mainstreaming, others maintain that only full inclusion can provide a child with a "least restrictive" experience. Obviously, the concept of inclusion is not without controversy. To some, it represents no more than a current trend that will pass with time (Fuchs & Fuchs, 1994).

Strong justifications for full inclusion, especially in relation to young children, have been presented in the literature. There follow two of the arguments often used by proponents of full inclusion.

- When children with and without disabilities are educated together, they learn life-long lessons and skills necessary for positive relationships with each other. This argument is backed by research data which indicate that supported inclusion leads to a higher frequency of interactions and fosters the development of social and adaptive skills of children with disabilities (Hanline, 1993b). These findings apply to children with autism as well as children with other types of disabilities. Research data also indicate that when young children with disabilities attend inclusive programs, their peers are more accepting of them than of children with disabilities served in separate classrooms (Guralnick & Groom, 1988). The inclusion model is also more compatible with society's emphasis on pluralism.

- Young children with disabilities can achieve their highest potential only when they are provided with "normal" opportunities. This argument reflects a philosophy of normalization, which has been promoted in the field of special education since the late 1960s. According to this philosophy, "when persons are segregated, labeled, or treated in any way that sets them further apart for their differences, then their worth is devalued" (Howard et al., 1997, p. 8). It has been argued that the normalization principle should apply to all persons with special needs, regardless of their degree of disability. While normalization will not remove a person's disability or make them normal, "it does make possible a more normal and nonstigmatized life style" (Peterson, 1987, p. 338).

Some would say that the practice of "full inclusion" is not something that should have to be justified on any other premise than that it is the "right thing to do." As expressed by a father of a child with a disability, "Why must children 'prove' they are ready to be in regular classrooms? We do not ask that of any other members of our society" (Howard et al., 1997, p. 9).

Research on the topic of full inclusion is complex and, at times, arrives at conflicting conclusions. Some research, for example, indicates that, while children who are higher performing do better in inclusive settings, lower performing students tend to perform better in more segregated settings (Cole et al., 1991; Howard et al., 1997). And not all parents are in favor of inclusion. Some parents feel that separate schooling is necessary to protect children with disabilities from rejection by their typically developing peers.

Many agree that there is no one "right answer" to the question of what constitutes the least restrictive environment for young children with special needs and argue for placement decisions to be made on a case-by-case basis. Peterson (1987) proposed taking the following three important considerations into account when making such decisions:

- the extent to which the "intervention" increases the chances that the child will be developmentally more capable of functioning later in a less restrictive environment;
- the extent to which the setting is culturally compatible with the values and practices of the community or subculture of which the family is a part;

- the extent to which the setting is equipped to provide the forms of stimulation and care that are age-appropriate for the child and consistent with the child's special needs.

It should also be noted that normalized experiences can be provided even in a segregated setting. The physical setting is only one aspect of an intervention program. Other aspects include materials, staffing, schedule, and activities. Each of these aspects should be evaluated in relation to the principle of normalization. The following questions might be helpful in conducting such an evaluation (for either a segregated or inclusive setting):

- To what extent does the physical environment appear and function like the environments serving typically developing children? Considerations related to this question include physical appearance, program location, and name of the program. The physical environment should reflect a child-centered versus clinical orientation. As such, it should feature age-appropriate decorations and furnishings and should include a display of children's creations. Intervention services (e.g., therapy sessions) should share the same space or be located in close proximity to the regular education program. Adaptive equipment should be used and stored in ways that do not call attention to its presence, and children's privacy should be respected. Privacy is violated through such practices as posting individual child goals, data charts, and behavior plans. Privacy is also violated when there are no separate areas of the room for assisting individual children who may need to be diapered and dressed.

  The name of the program, too, should be chosen in relation to the normalization principle. Names such as "Sunshine School" and "Camp Cheerful" usually reflect a special education orientation, while names such as the "Gulf Coast School" and "Lake Rice Camp" reflect a regular education program.

- To what extent do materials and activities match those provided for typically developing children? A normalized program would offer activity centers (e.g., dramatic play area, art center, water and sand play, block area, etc.), a book area, an outdoor play area, and displays of children's work versus focusing primarily on therapeutic equipment and activities.

- To what extent do staffing roles and responsibilities reflect staffing patterns in programs serving typically developing children? While additional staff are often required to meet the needs of young children with disabilities, staff should not be assigned to work exclusively with an individual child. As one-on-one instruction is not the norm in regular education programs, it should not be the norm in programs serving children with disabilities. "Extra assistance should be used in a manner that is nonintrusive and normalized" (Noonan & McCormick, 1993, p. 340). If a child with SEN needs assistance in an activity (such as working at the computer), a staff member may be assigned to monitor and assist all the children involved in that activity. This staff member can provide special assistance to the child with SEN nonintrusively in several different ways: she can reinforce children who are using the computer correctly, call attention to the different ways children are using the computer, encourage children to watch and imitate more competent peers, and suggest cooperative learning activities.

Specialized staff (i.e., speech/language therapists, physical therapists, etc.) should also provide services in a nonintrusive and normalized way. Therapy sessions should be scheduled so as to interfere as little as possible with the typical schedule and activities of the classroom. In fact, recommended practices call for incorporating specialized therapies into the natural activities of the regular education program (Noonan & McCormick, 1993). This approach to therapy is sometimes referred to as "integrated therapy" and contrasts with the "pull-out" model in which children are removed from the classroom for their individual therapy sessions. The integrated therapy model has several major advantages. "In addition to being non-intrusive and normalizing, the integrated therapy approach ensures that specialized interventions are designed to be practical and immediately useful in natural settings" (Noonan & McCormick, 1993, p. 340).

### Concerns relating to inclusion

While the controversy about full inclusion continues, many young children with disabilities are being served in the regular classroom setting. It is therefore necessary for early childhood teachers to learn how to meet the needs of children with special educational needs within the context of the daily routine. They should see to it that the child with SEN is not only mainstreamed into the physical dimensions of an early childhood program, but in the instructional and social dimensions as well. Instructional inclusion means that, as much as possible, the activities in which the child with SEN participates should be the same as the activities in which the other children are participating. To make this a successful experience, the child with SEN will often require some special assistance and/or encouragement from both the classroom teacher and other members of the intervention team. It should be understood that unless an early childhood classroom can provide the appropriate services and

189

support for children with SEN, it cannot serve effectively as the least restrictive environment for them.

As the literature indicates, many of the proposed benefits of inclusion do not occur without purposeful and careful supports to promote them. Wolery and Wilbers (1994) offer the following examples:

- Many children with disabilities do not imitate their peers unless taught to do so.
- Many children with and without disabilities do not interact frequently unless supports are provided to encourage such exchanges.
- Acceptance and positive attitudes about children with disabilities do not necessarily result simply from integration. Adults' behaviors can substantially influence the way children think and feel.

Physical inclusion alone, then, does not guarantee that the proposed benefits will occur. While more specific information and ideas on how to foster inclusion *within the classroom* will be presented in Chapter 12, the following discussion addresses several barriers to successful inclusion that exist *at the community level*, and some suggestions for dealing with these barriers.

- *Barrier 1: Lack of adequate training in general and special early education.* General early education teachers often feel that they do not have the knowledge and skills necessary for working with children with special educational needs. Special early education teachers, on the other hand, often cite the lack of adequate preparation in early childhood development and consultation as barriers for them in effectively serving young children with SEN within the context of the regular classroom. The idea of joint training programs (i.e., for general and special early education teachers) has been suggested at both the preservice and inservice level of professional development as a positive step toward addressing this barrier. To make this happen, cooperation and collaboration are required, not only between training programs at universities, but also among different community agencies involved in providing direct and indirect services to young children with disabilities and their families.

- *Barrier 2: Lack of "related services" in many programs.* As discussed in previous chapters, young children with SEN and their families are often in need of services from a variety of disciplines and agencies. Many early education programs which include children with SEN do not employ – even on a part-time or consultant basis – members from disciplines directly related to the children's disability (such as physical therapy, speech/language therapy, and occupational therapy). Additionally, many early childhood programs are not in a position to address other critical family needs, such as housing assistance, education and employment opportunities, health and nutrition, family counseling, etc. Gaining access to and coordinating such services often become a major concern for families of young children with SEN. One positive step toward addressing this concern is the development of early childhood centers, which bring together a variety of services within one location. Both regular education and special education programs can be housed in these centers, along with therapists, social workers, and health-related programs. Parent education and support, and even staff development activities, are often offered as part of the programming of early childhood centers as well.

## Working in the early years classroom

There was a time when to be a teacher meant working as the single adult with a group of between fifteen and twenty-five children. It meant planning and directing large-group activities for the majority of the day. Such activities often involved rote responses and everyone being on the "same page at the same time." The teacher, as the director and assessor of learning, would periodically share progress reports with parents and keep individual "cumulative folders" up to date in the school office.

As children with disabilities were not expected to be able to "keep up" with the rest of the class, they were often served in separate classrooms with a "special educator" filling the role as teacher. There was usually little communication between the regular education and the special education programs within a school. Children from the two different programs usually had lunch separately, went on separate field trips, and had few opportunities to get to know each other.

Today, with an emphasis on the least restrictive environment for children with disabilities and a recognition of the value of transdisciplinary teaming, teachers are beginning to work as members of a team versus in isolation. While some teachers may still be the one adult in a room with a group of children for part of the day, it is becoming more and more common for several adults to be working in the same classroom at the same time. These other adults often include paraprofessionals, specialized staff (i.e., speech/language therapists, physical therapists, etc.), and parents. Recommended practices call for a coordination of the efforts of these other adults in the classroom rather than having each of them work in relative isolation from each other. The following discussion addresses such coordination.

## Working with paraprofessionals

To facilitate the inclusion of children with disabilities, some schools are introducing paraprofessionals into the classrooms. Because paraprofessionals do not usually have the same grounding in early childhood development or an understanding of young children with disabilities as the classroom teachers, initial and ongoing training and supervision are critical to their effectiveness as a member of the educational team. Much of this training and supervision becomes the responsibility of the classroom teacher.

## The professional development process

As previously stated, personnel working with young children with disabilities need information and skills from both early childhood education and early childhood special education. As such, their professional program should focus on both typical and atypical early childhood growth and development. Their professional development program should also address teaming and collaboration and reflect a family-centered orientation.

Ideally, preparation programs designed for personnel working with young children with disabilities should be interdisciplinary in nature. To be interdisciplinary is not the same as being multidisciplinary. Multidisciplinary programs are often "pieced together" by taking existing courses from various departments and listing them as program requirements or electives. For example, a student majoring in early childhood education may take a special education course from one department, a communication disorders course from another department, and the majority of his or her courses from the early childhood department. This program can be considered multidisciplinary, in that it incorporates courses from more than one discipline. The content across the various courses, however, may be fragmented and contradictory.

An interdisciplinary program, on the other hand, involves a greater degree of collaboration between disciplines. While the interdisciplinary curriculum is derived from several related disciplines, it is planned and implemented jointly. The result is a unified program versus a piecing together of existing courses. Interdisciplinary programs are usually developed, implemented, and evaluated by a team of faculty from different departments.

As preservice preparation can usually provide only entry level knowledge and skills for a profession, inservice programs are needed to continue the professional development process. Quality inservice programs are especially important for professionals serving young children with disabilities, as the field of early childhood special education is relatively new and evolving quickly. Inservice programs can serve as a vehicle for professionals to keep up to date in a changing field.

Changing practices in early childhood special education necessarily result in changing roles for personnel involved in the process. These personnel are not only the teachers, but other members of the team as well, including speech/language pathologists, physical therapists, school psychologists, supervisors, and others. To work together effectively, all members of the team should receive specific training in providing family-centered services, in collaborating as team members, and in providing consultant or direct services in inclusive settings (Miller & Stayton, 1996).

Recommended practices indicate that inservice programs should be based, in large part, on a "needs-based" approach – i.e., from the assessed needs of the participants. To be most meaningful and effective, the needs assessment should address competencies that are directly applicable to the individual's professional role. Needs-based inservice acknowledges the experiences of the participants and builds upon those experiences that are relevant to the learner's situation. Needs-based inservice also recognizes the learner's own goals as the primary incentive for participation.

One program, committed to a more unified approach to intervention, developed its own "self-rating scale" to evaluate individual performance in relation to program priorities. Staff from this program then used the results of this evaluation to identify specific areas for inservice. According to staff reports, this form of self-evaluation was far less intimidating and much more affirming than an evaluation based on a more "generic" scale and conducted by a program supervisor (Wilson, 1991). Staff also reported that another positive outcome of this process was the development of an inservice plan that was meaningful to them and which they felt confident would address their most immediate professional development needs.

## Transitions – linking programs

Children with disabilities are often faced with transitions from one setting, class, or program to another. Such transitions usually involve stress and anxiety for both the child and his or her family. Getting used to something new, leaving something familiar, not knowing what new expectations and challenges must be faced – these are some of the factors contributing to stress and anxiety during times of transitions.

While everyone must face transitions in their lives, for young children with disabilities and their families these transitions tend to be more frequent and more demanding. This is due, in part, to the fact that children with disabilities often require individualized services involving multiple disciplines and a variety of agencies. A child's need for these services and his or her eligibility to receive such services tend to fluctuate over time. Eligibility is sometimes determined by age; sometimes by type and extent of need. Such conditions vary over time, resulting in a need for a change in services.

For many children and their families, the first major transition is from home to school. In the UK, children are required to attend school between the ages of 5 and 16. They may start earlier or leave later, but this is optional. Box 10.2 gives some "dos" and "don'ts" that have been developed for parents to help prepare their child for a successful transition to school. Figure 10.1 is a humorous reminder that it is not unusual for the initial transition from home to school to bring some surprises for parents, children, and teachers.

*Box 10.2* Preparing children for school (a parent's guide)

| | |
|---|---|
| DO | Take children to see their new school before they start. |
| | Tell them how exciting school is and how much children like going. |
| | Make sure they are house-trained (can use the toilet, fasten their shoes, put on their coats, etc.) [For some children with disabilities, this may not be completely doable. The goal should be to help the child become as independent as possible in taking care of his or her self-help needs.] |
| DON'T | Threaten them with 'Just wait till you start school . . . they'll soon straighten you out.' |
| | Get over-anxious – even if you feel blind panic, control it! |
| | Overdo the bribes – 'When you come home there'll be a big bar of chocolate' – it just swaps school phobia for obesity, so stick to small, non-fattening treats. |

*Source*: Wragg (n.d.), with kind permission.

Similarly, it is not unusual for a child's transition from one program to another to generate some frustration, confusion, anxiety, and surpises. For children and families – and, to a certain extent, staff – transitions represent times of vulnerability and the potential for problems. While all the stress associated with transitions may not be avoidable, it can be minimized. Careful planning plays an important part in reducing problems during times of transitions. Planning can remove the arbitrary boundaries among agencies and programs and minimize the differences between settings and expectations (Noonan & McCormick, 1993).

Because transitions often involve the movement from one agency to another, interagency cooperation and coordination become critical to smooth transitions. Lack of coordination between agencies may place children and their families at risk of the loss of appropriate services. In

"Did he settle in alright?"

*Figure 10.1* The first day of school
*Source*: Wragg (n.d.), with kind permission.

some instances, lack of coordination between agencies results in delaying a child's placements. In other instances, differences in eligibility requirements between agencies leave some children and families unserved. Additionally, differences in curriculum and teaching style can negatively affect children's adjustment to a new program and their acquisition of new skills.

To minimize these risks, careful planning is required at the agency, direct service, and family levels. Following are some suggestions for each of these three levels.

- Interagency planning (agency level): Each agency serving young children and their families should develop a written transition plan outlining the activities involved in changing placement of a child and his or her family. These transition plans should be shared and compatible with those of other agencies. Some communities develop written agreements that identify *shared* philosophy, responsibilities, and resources.
- Program planning (direct service level): The direct service providers at the time of transition include (1) the sending program (i.e., the child's current placement), and (2) the receiving program (i.e., the child's next placement). The sending program staff should obtain basic information regarding the next placement in order to prepare

the child and family for the new program. Such information might include the program's philosophy, curriculum, schedule, and skills expectations. Exchange visits between programs is one suggested way of obtaining some of this information. When possible, the sending program should introduce the child to the skills that will be expected in the next environment and to the routine that will be experienced there. The sending program should also inform the family of differences in the level and type of family contact and support.

- Family planning (family level): Families should be given the opportunity to participate in all aspects of the transition process. They should be fully informed as to the anticipated sequence of activities and a timeline for completing the transition. They should be encouraged to visit the new placement option and meet with the new staff. Families can help prepare the child for the transition by taking the child for a visit to the new program, discussing the change, and fostering the development of skills that will be expected in the new setting.

Planning for transitions can provide the necessary "safety net" often needed as children and families take their first steps into new situations. Ideally, this safety net (i.e., assistance) should be there for the child and family as long as it is needed. This means that there should be overlap between the sending program and the receiving program and that the extent of this overlap should be determined on an individual basis. While a month or less of overlap may be sufficient for some families, others may require up to six months.

In addition to being flexible and responsive to individual families, transition should also include the following steps: (1) the completion of an evaluation of the child to determine current levels of performance and to identify special strengths and needs; (2) a discussion about future program possibilities (i.e., potential settings where the child might receive services); (3) visits to potential programs; (4) the selection of a program and a verification of eligibility; (5) the completion of an application for enrollment; (6) preparation of the child and the receiving program; and (7) monitoring of the child and family adjustment to the new program.

There follows a discussion that addresses several related concerns and offers some suggestions on how to prepare the setting (i.e., the receiving program) and the child for transitions and how to involve families in a meaningful way.

## *Preparing the setting*

As discussed earlier, inclusion means more than "allowing the child in" if he or she has the necessary skills. The message of inclusion is that "all children belong" and that the program will adjust to the child versus placing the demand on the child that he or she adjust to the program. Adjustment, or preparation, on the part of the receiving program may include any or all of the following activities:

• identifying and removing barriers to physical access (e.g., making the school, classroom, and learning centers wheelchair accessible);
• identifying and obtaining inservice training and technical assistance for the staff;
• identifying and obtaining special materials and equipment (e.g., communication boards, amplification devices, etc.);
• sharing of accurate information (e.g., information about the child, about program goals and procedures, etc.).

## *Preparing the child*

Skills needed for success in a program are sometimes referred to as "survival skills." Such skills are closely related to teacher expectations, especially in terms of independent work and social behaviors. To prepare a child for the next environment, it is important to have some under-standing of what these survival skills are.

Some interesting work has been done in the United States to identify survival skills for children in preschool (ages 3 to 5) and kindergarten (ages 5 to 6) classrooms. Such studies have looked at programs in different geographical locations and serving children from different ethnic and cultural backgrounds. In spite of these differences, skills identified as critical for success tended to be similar across programs. They also represent primarily social/communication and adaptive skills. The following is a list of skills that have been identified through various studies as survival skills at the preschool and kindergarten level (Noonan & McCormick, 1993):

• follows general rules and routines
• expresses wants and needs
• cooperates with/helps others
• complies with directions given by adult
• shares materials/toys with peers
• socializes with peers
• takes turns
• interacts verbally with adults

- interacts verbally with peers
- focuses attention on speaker
- makes own decisions.

It is important to understand that survival skills should not be considered behavioral *prerequisites* for participating in an inclusive program. They should, instead, be viewed as optimum goals. "A child's failure to demonstrate any one or all of the skills on a survival skills checklist should not prevent the child's transition to, and placement in, mainstream early childhood settings" (Noonan & McCormick, 1993, p. 361).

Another concern related to transition and survival skills is the fact that children who may have developed and demonstrated certain skills in one setting do not always use them in other, different settings – that is, they do not transfer the skills from one environment to another. For example, a child with communication problems may use signs and gestures to express needs and wants at home, but may not use these same skills at school. Another example would be a child with attention deficit disorder (ADD) who has learned to block out "distractions" at home (e.g., street noise, movement of family members throughout the house, etc.) but cannot attend to a task at school due to distracting sounds and movement around the classroom. Close observation and dialogue between sending and receiving programs and parents can lead to an early identification of this lack of transfer. Strategies can then be developed to address this concern before additional problems (e.g., secondary handicaps, poor self-concept, low expectations, etc.) develop.

Another major concern sometimes centers around differing expectations. Even though the survival skills presented above tend to be common across programs, it sometimes happens that a skill that is considered critical in one setting may not be so valued in another setting. This "mismatch" can lead to anxiety and stress for all involved – the child, parents, and staff. Johnson and Mandell (1988) addressed this concern in the area of social skills and related expectations. They developed and field tested an observational tool or survey that can be used to identify and address a mismatch in expectations and skills as a child moves from one program to another. A copy of this instrument (i.e., the SOME scale – Social Observation for Mainstreamed Environments) is presented in Figure 10.2 (pp. 200–201).

The SOME scale can be used to facilitate discussion between the sending and receiving programs and for identifying potential areas of concern. It can also be used to identify a child's strengths and to plan instructional strategies around both strengths and concerns. For example, the first item on the SOME scale refers to the child's ability to ask for help when needed. If the child does not demonstrate this skill, a minus (–) is recorded in the "Child's performance" column. If this skill reflects a skill considered essential by the teacher in the receiving program, a plus (+) is recorded in the "Classroom expectations" column. A minus paired with a plus reflects a mismatch. If this mismatch is not addressed prior to the child entering the program, related problems are likely to occur. Options for addressing this mismatch include (1) helping the child develop the desired skill and (2) working with the teacher to modify his or her expectations and procedures.

A mismatch, however, can also occur in the opposite direction – i.e., the child may have a skill that the teacher does not necessarily consider to be essential. In this case, there is a plus in the "Child's performance" column and a minus in the "Classroom expectations" column. This mismatch can be used to highlight a child's strength. If the skill is "plays well with others," the teacher can use this information to enhance the child's status with his or her peers – i.e., by arranging time and place opportunities to demonstrate this skill, by calling attention to the child's performance, etc.

To ease the transition of the child from one program to another, steps should be taken to lessen differences between the sending and receiving settings. If possible, it is also helpful to extend the transition gradually over time. This can happen more easily if both programs (e.g., Reception year and Year 1) are housed within the same building. This arrangement would allow for periodic visits of the Reception year class to the Year 1 class. Children would then have the opportunity to gradually familiarize themselves with the next year's classroom and teacher.

If the sending and receiving programs are not housed in the same building, field trips to the "new" school could still be arranged. To make the visit to the school as friendly as possible, the visit might include lunch or a snack, time for play outdoors, and participation in some fun group activities. After the visit, children should be engaged in a conversation about the experience and encouraged to role play the process of going to a new school.

### *Working with the family*

Parents have much to offer as well as much to gain by being involved in the transition process (Noonan & McCormick, 1993). The following are some of the ways in which parents can be involved:
- providing valuable information about their child, their goals and vision for their child, and ways in which they wish to be involved;
- teaching their child skills at home that will help their child to be successful in the new program (e.g., asking for help when needed, attending to a speaker, interacting with peers, etc.);
- providing emotional support for their child throughout the transition process.

Child's Name: _____   Date: _____

Individual(s) Observing the Child: _____

Individual Observing the Classroom: _____

Other settings in which child was observed: _____

Directions: In the first column, mark a plus (+) if the child usually exhibits the behavior, a minus (–) if the child tends not to exhibit the behavior. In the second column, mark a plus if the classroom teacher expects the children to exhibit the behavior, a minus if the behavior is not one of the classroom expectations. Use the third column for noting any related observations or concerns. In the fourth column, write in proposed resolutions to areas of concern; that is, in areas where the behaviors are expected but are not exhibited by the child.

| Behavior | Child's performance | Classroom expectations | Comments | Resolution |
|---|---|---|---|---|
| 1. Asks for help when needed | | | | |
| 2. Plays well with others | | | | |
| 3. Obeys class rules | | | | |
| 4. Attends to task for short periods of time | | | | |
| 5. Completes tasks with minimum adult assistance | | | | |
| 6. Initiates interactions with peers | | | | |
| 7. Initiates interactions with adults | | | | |
| 8. Observes other children | | | | |

| | | | | | |
|---|---|---|---|---|---|
| 9. Imitates other children | | | | | |
| 10. Makes simple decisions | | | | | |
| 11. Practices turn taking | | | | | |
| 12. Respects others' belongings | | | | | |
| 13. Respects others' feelings | | | | | |
| 14. Follows simple directions | | | | | |
| 15. Uses verbal vs. nonverbal means to express feelings | | | | | |
| Other | | | | | |
| Other | | | | | |

Recommendations: _____

Signatures: _____

*Figure 10.2* SOME Scale (Social Observation for Mainstreamed Environments)
*Source:* Johnson & Mandell (1988, p. 21), with kind permission.

Parents have identified some of the ways professionals can *help them* during the process of transition. The following are some of their suggestions:

- provide information about community services and parents' legal rights;
- provide information about what to look for in evaluating potential future placements (e.g., child–staff ratio, daily routine, etc.);
- identify "critical skills" their child will need to be successful in the next environment (i.e., new setting);
- reassure them that they (i.e., the professionals) will monitor the success of the child's transition and provide support as needed.

### The role of the teacher

The transition process places new demands on the teacher as well. While facilitating transition from one program to another can be quite interesting and rewarding, it can also be frustrating. The transition process often involves additional tasks for the teacher. For the sending teacher, such tasks may include the following:

- meeting with families to discuss and make plans for the transition process;
- visiting program sites with or without the families;
- sharing information with the receiving teachers;
- collecting information concerning teacher expectations;
- preparing the child for a successful transition (emotionally and through skill development);
- monitoring the child's adjustment to the new placement;
- serving as an ongoing resource to the family and receiving program.

The receiving teacher, too, has a special role to play in the transition process. Tasks associated with this role include:

- learning about the child's strengths, needs, special interests, and individual background;
- modifying the physical aspects of the classroom, as needed;
- adjusting the routine, instructional strategies, and expectations, as appropriate;
- establishing a relationship and communication pattern with the parents;
- providing feedback to the sending program.

## *Indicators of a successful transition*

The following statements summarize many of the "recommended practices" developed for smooth transitions. These statements might be used as "indicators" to evaluate the success of a child's and family's transition from one program to another.

- Interruption of needed services is avoided.
- The child, family, and service providers are given opportunities to prepare for changes that will occur.
- The child's strengths as well as needs are used as a basis from which planning occurs.
- Families are given information about their rights and the range of options available to them and their child.
- Families are enabled to provide input into their child's educational program.
- The most appropriate and most supportive environment is identified.
- The child is prepared (emotionally and through skill development) for the new environment.
- Continuity of curriculum and routine is facilitated from one setting to the next.
- The child receives support in the new setting.
- Families are offered support and opportunities for involvement throughout the transition process.
- The child's adjustment to the new setting is evaluated and adjustments are made, as necessary.
- There is ongoing communication and collaboration among professionals providing services to the child and family.

---

## Case study – Roy and Janis

### *Background information*

Roy is a Year 1 teacher in an inclusive education program. This is his second year of teaching. Janis is a paraprofessional assigned to Roy's classroom. She has worked as a paraprofessional for twelve years, with the last five years being in an early childhood classroom. Roy is firmly committed to an activity-based intervention model and looks for ways to foster individual child goals and activities through the naturally occurring events of the day. Janis, on the other hand, feels that the children with special needs would learn more efficiently through a direct instruction approach. She, therefore, gives frequent directives on what they should and should not do and constantly corrects them for "errors" in performance. For example, if a child says, "She taked it from me," Janis responds by telling him to say "She took it from me." Only after the child has repeated the "correct way" of expressing his message will Janis attend to his concern. If a child's goal is learning to write his or her own name, Janis will sometimes pull that child from another activity (such as painting or looking at books) to work on paper and pencil tasks.

Roy is not pleased with what Janis does. He has tried to explain the philosophy and guidelines of the activity-based intervention approach, but Janis remains unconvinced. She views Roy as being young and inexperienced. She also believes that what is currently being taught at the university in the teacher education program is just a trend that will soon be replaced with something else. She therefore continues to use the direct instruction approach. She often keeps records relating to the child's performance (e.g., "Jimmy wrote his name today with some hand-over-hand support") and will sometimes share her observations with the parents. Some of the parents think that Janis is "wonderful" because she works so hard on the children's instructional goals.

### Discussion

The "teaming" between Roy and Janis is dysfunctional. They do not share a common philosophy, their instructional strategies conflict, and the information they provide to parents often results in confusion and frustration. Both Roy and Janis are convinced that their way is the right way. Both want what is best for the children but fail to see that their lack of teaming is one of the major obstacles to an optimal learning environment.

Mrs. Lane, the program director, begins to sense the nature of the problem when she asks for Roy's opinion about an appropriate placement for Emily for the following year. Emily, a child with Down syndrome, is currently in Roy's class. Her developmental status is approximately two years below age expectations. Roy indicates that he feels Emily can go on to a Year 2 class in the same building, as long as the teacher understands the nature and extent of Emily's special needs and is provided with some assistance in making appropriate curriculum adaptations for her. Janis overhears this conversation and stops by the school office later in the afternoon to express her concern. Janis has been a friend of Emily's family since Emily was born and feels some "ownership" regarding her intervention program. Janis believes that Emily must first accomplish some of her current goals before she will be ready for Year 2. She suggests that progress toward these goals has been slow, due in part to the many "unrelated" activities she does in class.

Mrs. Lane asks Roy and Janis to meet with her the next day. She tells them that she is concerned about the lack of consistency in their approach to working with children with SEN. After some discussion about the issue, she asks each of them to review the school's philosophy and to relate their instructional strategies to this written statement. The school's philosophy statement starts with the following sentence: "All children have the right to an educational environment that recognizes and respects them as active learners and provides them with the opportunity to construct their own understandings about the world around them." Roy feels comfortable with this statement; Janis does not. Janis feels that not all children are capable of being active learners and constructing their own knowledge. It soon becomes evident that one of the major barriers to effective teaming for Roy and Janis resides in their differing philosophies of how young children learn. Mrs. Lane was wise to use the school's written philosophy as a source of comparison.

Mrs. Lane makes arrangements for Janis to spend a day in another classroom with an experienced teacher who can explain and demonstrate how the school's philosophy is reflected in individually appropriate instructional goals and strategies. Mrs. Lane then works with Roy to identify ways of making his approach more explicit. For example, she suggests that Roy display posters around the classroom to illustrate the learning potential of the different activity centers. She also asks Roy to devise a way of documenting progress toward individual child goals and objectives. Her third suggestion is that Roy develop a parent newsletter and use it to describe different aspects of the curriculum, including the value of play and child-initiated activities.

After six weeks, Mrs. Lane meets with Roy and Janis again. This time, the conversation focuses on self-identified professional development needs. Roy is interested in inservice opportunities that address in more detail the activity-based intervention approach and how to evaluate the effectiveness of this approach. Janis wants to learn more about ways to extend children's play in non-directive ways – that is, she wants to know how to challenge children's thinking and skill development through a more discovery-based approach. Once Roy and Janis became aware of the professional-development interests of each other, they began to share information and ideas about related resources. They also decided to use the classroom as a "bulletin board" to make a statement about the curriculum. One statement that is now displayed in large letters across the front of the room reads, "Young children learn through discovery." Photos and children's artwork posted around the room reflect children in the process of making their own discoveries.

# Part IV

# FOCUS ON THE CHILD

This section of the book presents information and ideas on how to make the learning environment and exploration opportunities accessible to all young children in the early years classroom. The primary focus is on the individual child with special educational needs and his or her unique strengths, needs, interests, learning style, and ways of interacting with other people and the physical environment. The discussion throughout this section is based on the understanding that curriculum for young children consists primarily of the physical and social environment *as they experience it*. It is also based on the understanding that for practices to be developmentally appropriate, they must also be individually appropriate (Bredekamp, 1997).

Children with special educational needs are, at least in some ways, at a different stage developmentally than many of their class-mates. The inclusive early years classroom must therefore provide learning opportunities that reflect a range of abilities. The material presented in the Chapters 11 and 12 is designed to provide some specific guidance on how this might be done.

# 11

# A CURRICULUM FOR EVERY CHILD

## The environment as curriculum

Curriculum might be defined in various ways. To some, curriculum refers to what is taught. This concept of curriculum focuses on "what is offered" versus "what is experienced." While "what is offered" (i.e., "a range of studies") may be an appropriate way to define curriculum for older students, it does not reflect the nature of young children and the ways in which they learn. For the young child, defining curriculum in terms of the environment *as he or she experiences it* would be more appropriate. This definition is consistent with the early childhood special education literature, where curriculum has been described as "the sum of that child's interactions (experiences) with the environment" (Wolery & Sainato, 1996, p. 132). It has also been referred to as "curriculum-is-what-happens" (McCracken, 1993).

For the young child with special educational needs, it is critical to consider that the nature of a disability can interfere with his or her experience of the environment as it is presented or arranged by the classroom teacher. This interference tends to diminish the child's learning opportunities in the classroom. Educators, therefore, cannot assume that the needs of every child can be met by creating a stimulating classroom environment and encouraging children to "learn on their own." No matter how enriching the environment appears to be, it is not enriching for the child who cannot access it for one reason or another. This is easy to understand in terms of a hearing or vision problem. If a child cannot hear the voices of her classmates and the teacher, the verbal environment will not be stimulating to her. Similarly, if a child cannot see the variety of materials available in the classroom, the visual environment will not motivate him or her to access the materials nor stimulate his or her thinking about how to use them. Other disabilities, too, can interfere with a child's *access* to an environment, often in less obvious ways than deafness or blindness. An attention deficit disorder (ADD), for example, can prevent a child from attending to specific stimuli in the environment.

The child with ADD may find it difficult to focus on such aspects of the environment as the teacher's voice, the details of a puzzle, the intricacies of dramatic play, etc. This child's difficulty in focusing or attending becomes a barrier to engagement with materials and people in the classroom, and thus limits his or her learning opportunities.

Recommended practices in early childhood special education call for both (1) the improvement of the child's skills to access the environment, and (2) environmental accommodations. At times, the pressure to "fix" the child (i.e., to improve the child's skills) overshadows the importance of making environmental accommodations. This is unfortunate, as the pressure on the child can lead to frustration on the part of the child, the parents, and the staff. Without appropriate environmental accommodations, the child's motivation and opportunities to become engaged with his or her environment will also be diminished.

Environmental accommodations for children with special education needs can address all or some of the following: the physical structure, the visual system, the schedule, the position of the teacher, and the use of adaptive equipment and materials. There follows a brief discussion of the first four of these factors. Adaptive equipment and materials are discussed in more detail in Chapter 12.

### The physical structure

The physical structure refers to the way space is organized, the furniture is placed, and the materials arranged. Generally, physical arrangements and facilities that are effective for typical young children will be suitable for children with SEN (NAEYC, 1984). For the benefit of all children, the physical structure of a classroom should be consistent with the desired learning activities and curricular goals. The physical structure should also serve as an easily read guide that helps the children to become or stay engaged in meaningful learning activities. While all children benefit from a well-organized physical environment, children with SEN can receive additional assistance by highlighting certain aspects of the organizational structure. Using tape to clearly define a circle on the floor is a type of organizational structure that can help children position themselves for such group activities as story time. The tape serves as a visual cue as to what it means to sit in a circle. An environmental accommodation that may be helpful to many children with SEN would be to use individual carpet squares as "position markers." While the tape alone defines the circle, it does not establish individual markers or boundaries. Use of the carpet squares, along with the tape, provides more definitive guidance. This may be especially helpful for young children with attention deficits, behavior problems, and visual impairments.

The following are some additional examples of how to highlight the organizational structure of the physical environment. These examples illustrate how the environment can be used as an instructional tool.

- Use pictures of items to label containers and shelves for the storage of materials. The shelves where blocks are to be stored, for example, could be marked with pictures of blocks.
- Use photos of individual children to mark their personal "cubbies" or storage areas. Such photos could also be used on individual work folders and/or book bags.
- Color code items and learning centers to correspond to appropriate use of materials. The "writing corner," for example, may be designated as the "blue area." A large blue banner might be used to label the area. Blue markings on items "belonging" to this area could help children to keep materials organized and provide guidance as to their appropriate usage. A blue dot on such items as pencils, rulers, staplers, paper punch, typewriter, stencils, etc. would suggest to the children that these materials all relate to the process of writing or working in an office.

Additional accommodations to the physical structure that may be required for children with SEN include greater space within the classroom. More space may be required to accommodate special equipment (e.g., wheelchairs, walkers, standing boards, etc.) and a larger number of adults (e.g., therapists, teacher assistants, etc.). Special attention should also be given to the "sturdiness" of equipment and materials. Shelves and tables, for example, must be sturdy enough to support children who have difficulty standing and maintaining balance. It is also important that clutter be minimized. Clutter can interfere with mobility, safety, and the engagement of children with SEN. Routes from one area of the room to another should be direct, should minimize cross traffic, and should be free of obstacles. For safety and easier access, doors should remain fully open. Sharp edges on furniture should be padded and broken materials should be repaired or replaced.

### The visual system

The visual system is closely related to and overlaps with the physical structure. It includes direction or guidance for the student as to what to do and when to do it. This can be especially helpful to children with SEN who have difficulty processing and/or following verbal directions. A visual system could be used for grouping children for cooperative activities, for specifying steps to be taken to complete an activity, and for providing guidance on how to move from one area to another. The following are examples of each:

- Children are often expected to work together with a partner or in a small group. Visual cues can be used to help keep children with their partner or group. Such visual cues might be symbols or pictures that they wear during the group activity.
- Many young children with SEN find it difficult to follow through on activities that involve a series of steps to complete, especially if these steps need to be followed in a specified order. Such activities may vary from how to make a peanut butter sandwich for lunch to how to operate a program on a computer. Visual cues in the form of drawings or pictures can be used to illustrate the steps to be taken.
- Cut-outs of footprints could serve as a visual system to guide children on how to move from one area to another. Such footprints might be used on stairways and hallways, for example, to show children how to "keep to the right" when using the stairs or moving through the halls.

### The schedule

The intent of inclusion is to integrate the child with SEN in the daily routine of the regular education classroom. This is in contrast to providing a special schedule for the child with a disability. However, to maximize that child's chances of success, some accommodations to the schedule may be necessary. These accommodations should be as nonintrusive and inconspicuous as possible. Some children with SEN need more time to complete a task than their classmates. Rather than rushing the child or doing the task for him of her, accommodations to the schedule should allow the additional time. For example, a child with a physical disability may be able to use the restroom on his or her own if given enough time. One accommodation to the schedule would be to allow him or her to start down the hall to the restrooms while the other children are still engaged in independent work in the classroom. It would be a mistake, however, to make a practice of always excusing the child from "clean up" activities or pulling him or her from a cooperative learning activity to accommodate the need for extra time to use the restroom. The extra time should not be viewed as a privilege or punishment, nor should it be the prerogative of only the children with SEN. Most children can benefit from individual accommodations to the schedule at times. These accommodations should be based on individual circumstances and needs and not on the designation of SEN.

### The position of the teacher

Where the teacher is in relation to the child with SEN and the way the teacher uses herself or himself to support or provide direction to the child is also an area that allows for environmental accommodation. If the goal is to enhance independent work, the teacher should provide greater distance between her or himself and the child. If, however, the child needs extra support and/or guidance, closer proximity would be appropriate.

## Individualized objectives

Developing individualized objectives is an important step in providing effective intervention for young children with special educational needs. Individualized objectives specify critical developmental skills to be taught. For young children with SEN, it is not an appropriate practice to simply wait for such skills to emerge (Peterson, 1987). Individualized objectives are determined, in part, by assessment results. The focus of assessment data, however, should not be on scores or the child's developmental age, but rather on what the child can do and how the child learns best.

Typical screening and diagnostic assessments do not yield the type of information most helpful to instructional planning. Additional assessment is thus required. This additional assessment is sometimes referred to as "instructional program planning assessment." Questions addressed during this assessment include the following:

- What can this child do independently? (i.e., What is the child's current level of functioning in each developmental domain?)
- What skills are in the process of being acquired? (i.e., What does the child do with support and assistance?)
- What critical developmental skills must the child attain? (i.e., What does the child need to learn to be more independent?)
- What seems to "work" with this child? (i.e., How does he or she learn best?)

The answers to these questions and other information obtained throughout the assessment process (including parental priorities) provide the necessary information for developing individualized objectives. These objectives should then be integrated into the instructional program. An important point to be kept in mind, however, is that while the objectives are individualized, the instructional program should be implemented in an integrated fashion. This means that the child with SEN is not pulled away from the regular routine of the classroom to work on his or her objectives. With an integrated approach, individualized objectives are embedded within the context of the broader classroom activities and with consideration to the development of the "whole" child in relationship to his or her environments.

The involvement of early childhood personnel is central to the effectiveness of assessment for instructional program planning. Early childhood personnel should be intimately involved in collecting and summarizing the information, making decisions about the collected information, and using that information (with other team members) to plan instructional programs.

At times, decisions to be made in program planning include placement decisions. Among the potential options, which one is most appropriate for the individual child? In addition to information about the child's abilities, needs, and learning styles, other information needed for determining the best placement for a child relate to the family's goals and priorities and the types of programs and/or classrooms available in the community. It is important to note that placement decisions need not always result in a program change for the child with SEN. If the child is already in an educational program, one potential placement is the child's current setting. In such cases, assessment for instructional program planning will include investigations into how the child's current setting might be adjusted to allow for the attainment of his or her individualized objectives.

### Different approaches

At one time, individualized objectives for children with SEN reflected a behavioral and clinical approach to intervention. With this approach, objectives focused almost exclusively on the child's weaknesses or areas of deficit. Direct teaching methods were then used to remediate these areas of weakness. Such methods were designed to push or pull the child up to the next developmental level. The following example illustrates this approach.

Through the assessment process, one of Tim's deficits was identified as the failure to use language to express needs or wants. A related objective was then developed – "At snack time, Tim will use words to ask for juice and a snack." To get Tim to perform this targeted behavior, the teacher decided to withhold refreshments at snack time until children requested them. If individual children did not request refreshments, she would prompt them to do so.

After introducing this new routine to the children, most of them had no trouble in requesting juice and a snack ("May I have juice and a cookie, please?"). Tim, however, did not make such a request. The teacher therefore told him to say, "Juice, please" and "Cookie, please." After several prompts, Tim repeated what the teacher modeled.

Some serious concerns related to this approach soon surfaced. Waiting for individual children to request refreshments diminished the social interaction and related discussion that had been occurring previously during snack time. Prior to this new "intervention technique," spontaneous conversations at snack time often focused on what the children had been doing earlier in the morning or what one of them had done the night before. Additionally, this "intervention technique" was calling attention to Tim's deficit. Most of the other children requested their refreshments without prompting and often with a complete sentence. Some of them, however, were beginning to say only what Tim said (i.e., "juice, please"). The teacher also noticed that Tim did not use language to express needs or wants during other situations that came up during the day. In other words, what Tim was doing at snack time did not carry over to other situations.

An alternative approach is to develop individualized objectives around broad competencies versus isolated behaviors. Instructional strategies to foster these competencies are then embedded within the daily routine with special attention to child-initiated activities. With this approach, the situation for Tim might have been different, as follows:

An individualized objective states that "Tim will use words and gestures to express needs and wants." Rather than "staging" times when Tim must demonstrate this skill, the teacher observes closely for naturally occurring situations when she can prompt, model, and call attention to the targeted behavior. She notices, for example, that at one point during the day Tim tries to put a tape in the tape player, but is having difficulty doing so. The teacher intervenes by saying, "Tim, do you need some help?" Tim nods his head to indicate "yes." The teacher then prompts Tim to say, "Please help me." Later, the teacher models the desired behavior. She walks over to Tim and says, "I need help hanging up this paper. Hold one side for me, please." She also uses a naturally occurring event to call attention to the targeted behavior. When Sandra asks for help in getting a lid off a paste bottle, the teacher refers her to Tim by saying, "My hands are wet right now. Could you ask Tim to help you?" After using these child-initiated or more naturally occurring strategies over a period of several weeks, the teacher notices that Tim is beginning to use words to express his needs and wants. She first notices this when Tim approaches her with a paper he had been working on. In trying to fold the paper, Tim accidentally tore it. Tim shows the teacher his paper and says, "Tape, please."

These two approaches to developing and fostering individualized objectives differ in a number of ways. The first approach represents a more deficit-oriented approach. It is based on specific skills and isolated behaviors. Related instructional techniques involve direct instruction and adult-initiated activities. The second approach represents a more developmental approach. It is based on broad competencies and context-oriented behaviors. Related instructional techniques include modeling, responsivity, and child-initiated activities. The first approach relies more on extrinsic rewards (e.g., a snack) versus intrinsic motivation (e.g., the ability to ask for and receive help when needed).

## *Developmental objectives*

Criteria for individualized objectives that reflect developmentally appropriate practices include the following:

- Be written broadly to allow for flexibility;
- Allow implementation within the context of the daily routine;
- Include skills that will increase opportunities for positive interactions with typically developing peers;
- Represent child-initiated versus teacher-directed behaviors;
- Be appropriate to the child's developmental level;
- Allow for generalization across settings and activities;
- Reflect current competencies as well as areas of concern;
- Serve a functional purpose;
- Include skills that will increase options for successful participation in future inclusive environments.

The objectives presented in Box 11.1 have been developed with the above criteria in mind. They have also been developed around the understanding that the young child is an active participant and interactor in the learning process and that he or she is always growing toward more independent functioning. While these objectives are categorized under the areas of language development, social development, emotional development, physical development, and cognitive development, they are all designed to support development as a whole. This list is by no means meant to be inclusive of all the skills or areas needed for healthy child development. Its purpose is to provide examples of objectives written from a developmental framework for intervention.

## *Embedding objectives in the daily routine*

Several planning strategies have been developed for incorporating individualized objectives within the routine of daily activities in an early education setting. Figure 11.1 represents one such planning tool. The idea of this matrix is to identify the daily routines and then match individualized objectives to the kinds of skills that can be learned or practiced during those times.

Another planning tool that might be helpful for fostering the development of individualized objectives is presented in Figure 11.2. This matrix is designed to help teachers zero in on individual children during different times of the day – that is, times of day that may be most conducive to learning or practicing targeted skills. The matrix presented in Figure 11.2 suggests that Bill may need special help or support during clean-up times. Bill may have difficulty staying on task or following directions. Clean-up times usually offer opportunities to practice such

*Box 11.1* Objectives reflecting a developmental framework

---

Language development
- Uses words and/or gestures to express needs and wants
- Uses descriptive words to add specificity to statements (soft, happy, etc.)
- Uses location words appropriately (in, on, under)
- Initiates verbal interaction with adults
- Initiates verbal interaction with peers
- Uses questions to obtain needed information
- Describes activities of self and others
- Participates in short conversations
- Follows simple directions
- Responds to simple questions

Social development
- Responds to invitation to play with another child
- Interacts with adults
- Interacts with peers
- Plays in pairs or small groups
- Understands and follows rules of fair play

Emotional development
- Responds to verbal redirection when frustrated
- Expresses pride in accomplishments
- Shows concern for others in a group

Physical development
- Runs around obstacles and turns corners
- Throws a ball with ability to direct
- Manipulates simple writing and art tools (pencils, pens, paintbrushes)
- Performs basic dressing tasks (buttons, zips)

Cognitive development
- Makes simple choices
- Attends to simple tasks for a reasonable length of time
- Explores multiple use of objects
- Predicts/anticipates probable outcomes and consequences
- Draws simple figures (stick figures, circles, letters)
- Matches pictures to simple objects

---

skills. This same matrix indicates that Center Time is a good time to foster some of Joe's other individualized objectives. Such objectives might relate to cognitive development and involve the development of such skills as problem solving, discriminating between similar objects, and seriation.

### Individualizing instructional practices

After individualized objectives have been developed and some thought has been given to how to foster the acquisition of the targeted skills, another important consideration relates to the level of intervention

217

Child's name: _____

| Individualized objectives | Motor | Communication | Cognitive | Social | Self-help |
|---|---|---|---|---|---|
| Daily routines | | | | | |
| Arrival | X | | | X | X |
| Bathroom | | | | | X |
| Large group | X | | X | | |
| Learning centers | | X | X | X | |
| Clean-up | | X | | | |
| Bathroom | | | | | X |
| Snack | | X | | | X |
| Outdoor activities | X | | | X | |
| Bathroom | | | | | X |
| Story time | | X | | | |
| Dismissal | | | | X | X |

*Figure 11.1* Embedding individualized objectives in the daily routine

and/or support needed by the child. Determining when and how to intervene requires careful observation of the child. It also requires observation
over time. One major focus of the observation should be on how the child
plays. If the child plays with active exploration and experimentation, the
level of direct adult involvement should be considerably different from
that required for a child who exhibits only low levels of play or repeats the
same play behaviors steadily over time. For the child with poor play skills,
the teacher may need to model new behaviors, introduce new materials,
or demonstrate an extension of the child's activity.

For children with SEN, it is important for the teacher to provide
opportunities for them to develop and practice skills related to their
individualized objectives. Many such opportunities tend to occur during
the regularly scheduled activities of the day – story time, self-help tasks,
social interactions, etc. At times, individual children may need prompting
or direction to encourage them to use materials or engage in activities

| Children's names | Bill | Joe | Kayla | Levi | Ann | George | Megan |
|---|---|---|---|---|---|---|---|
| Daily routines | | | | | | | |
| Arrival | | | | | X | | |
| Bathroom | | | | | | | X |
| Large group | | | | | | | X |
| Learning centers | X | X | X | X | | X | |
| Clean-up | X | | | | | | X |
| Bathroom | | | | | | | X |
| Snack | | | X | X | X | | |
| Outdoor activities | | X | | | | | |
| Bathroom | | | | | | | X |
| Story time | | | | | X | X | |
| Dismissal | X | | | | | | |

*Objectives*:
Bill – Follow simple directions; use location words appropriately
Joe – Explore multiple use of objects; initiate verbal interaction with peers
Kayla – Use spoon independently; use words to express needs and wants
Levi – Match pictures to simple objects; use descriptive words
Ann – Participate in short conversations; respond to simple questions
George – Respond to simple questions; show concern for others in a group
Megan – Perform basic dressing tasks; follow simple directions

*Figure 11.2* Individualized supports

directly related to their individualized objectives. For example, one of Carl's objectives may be to manipulate simple writing and art tools. Carl, however, rarely chooses to work at either the writing center or the art center. He spends most of his free-choice time using building materials or engaging in "car and truck" play. In this case, the teacher will need to be more directive at times in order to foster the development of the targeted skills. She can still do this, however, within the context of car and truck play. She might, for example, ask children to write their names on a "sign-up sheet" next to the learning center of their choice. She might also ask them to "check out" materials that they want to use. This strategy could assist all the children with organizational skills, while helping Tim with his writing skills.

Individualized objectives and related instructional practices should reflect a child's preferences for and interests in various toys, materials, and activities. In addition to closely observing children for information about their preferences and interests, parents and other family members should also be consulted. Activities and materials related to a child's preferences and interests generally motivate the child to become engaged in meaningful ways and serve as effective vehicles for accomplishing individualized objectives.

Individualized objectives and related instructional practices should also reflect an understanding of how the child responds to adults and peers. Through direct observation, teachers can identify the types of adult and peer behaviors which usually result in sustained interaction and positive reactions from the child. Teachers should also determine whether or not – or in what way – the child complies with adult requests. Does the child follow group instructions or only instructions that are given individually? Such information can help the teacher determine the kind and extent of support a child needs to participate in classroom activities. Another area of concern is whether the child imitates adults and other children. If the child does not imitate others, he or she may need to be taught to do so. Techniques that might be used to teach imitation include the following:

- Imitate the child and then wait for him to repeat your action: Position yourself very near and in front of the child. Wait for the child to perform an action. Imitate the child's action. Look expectantly at the child, waiting for him to repeat your action. If he does not, imitate his action again and then wait once more to see if he will repeat the action. After the child repeats the action, add something slightly new. Wait for the child to repeat this new version. For example, if Jerry pushes his hand down into the sand, you do the same. If he repeats this action, add a variation to it. You might do this by turning your hand over while it is under the sand and bringing it up with some sand cupped in your hand. Continue this back-and-forth game, where imitation is one of the elements that makes it fun.
- Prompt the child to imitate: A child can be prompted to imitate through verbal suggestions – "See what Janie is doing. Can you do what she's doing?" or "Jerry, it's your turn. Step up on the stage like Janie did."

### Monitoring progress

Once individualized objectives are developed and embedded into the daily routine, progress toward the accomplishment of the objectives needs to be monitored. Such monitoring is achieved most effectively through ongoing observations. Using a systematic approach for observations usually works better than just "watching the child."

Systematic observations require careful planning and consistency over time. There are many different formats that might be used for conducting systematic observations. Many teachers find that they need to try a variety of formats to identify the one that works best for them. Figures 11.3 and 11.4 present two different formats that might be considered.

The format presented in Figure 11.3 provides space for monitoring individualized objectives for an individual child over five different observation periods. A coding system makes it easy to record the level at which the child demonstrates performance. These levels include (1) independent performance, (2) performance with a verbal prompt, (3) performance prompted through modeling, and (4) performance with a physical prompt (e.g., holding the child's hand while he or she pours milk into a glass). An additional code allows noting that there were no opportunities to observe the desired behavior. Space for comments allows further descriptions of the behaviors observed. A teacher may choose to observe one specified day each week (for example, Friday). The form provided would then allow for one month's observation, with up to five observations during the month (for example, five Fridays). The form could be two-sided, with additional objectives listed on the back of the page.

Using the format presented in Figure 11.3 offers the following benefits:

- easy to use;
- directly relates to individualized objectives;
- allows for additional comments.

The format presented in Figure 11.4 is more open ended than that presented in Figure 11.3. This format uses anecdotal records – that is, notes about specific behaviors relating to the child's objectives. Each notation is dated and expressed in objective terms. Instead of saying that Henry was angry when he got off the bus, his specific behavior would be described (e.g., Henry pushed Tony and Cheri as he got off the bus).

Anecdotal records are meant to be brief, factual narrative accounts of observed behaviors and experiences. Anecdotal notes need to contain sufficient information to be informative, yet concise enough to be an efficient use of the observer's time. In addition to recording the date of an annotation, time of day and specific location might also be recorded. Enough detail should be provided so as to give an accurate description of the event – versus a judgment about what occurred. For example, noting that Tony was disruptive during story time provides very little factual information. A more descriptive notation would be: Tony left the circle

Child's name: _____ Date of birth: _____

*Key*: I = independent, V = verbal prompt, M = modeling, P = physical prompt,
O = no opportunity to observe

Objective 1:

| *Date* | *Level* | *Comments* |
|--------|---------|------------|
| _____ | O P M V I | _____ |
| _____ | O P M V I | _____ |
| _____ | O P M V I | _____ |
| _____ | O P M V I | _____ |
| _____ | O P M V I | _____ |

Objective 2:

| *Date* | *Level* | *Comments* |
|--------|---------|------------|
| _____ | O P M V I | _____ |
| _____ | O P M V I | _____ |
| _____ | O P M V I | _____ |
| _____ | O P M V I | _____ |
| _____ | O P M V I | _____ |

Objective 3:

| *Date* | *Level* | *Comments* |
|--------|---------|------------|
| _____ | O P M V I | _____ |
| _____ | O P M V I | _____ |
| _____ | O P M V I | _____ |
| _____ | O P M V I | _____ |
| _____ | O P M V I | _____ |

*Figure 11.3* Observation/documentation form

Child's name: <u>Ann Marie</u>                      Date of birth: <u>16 Feb. 1994</u>

Observer: <u>Jane Smith</u>

| *Use adult as positive resource* | *Use words to express needs and wants* | *Perform simple dressing tasks* |
|---|---|---|
| 3/2 Pulled on Jodie's sleeve and pointed to juice at snack | 3/12 Said "bike" to Nathan while watching him ride the bike during outdoor play | 3/9 Attempted buttoning coat at dismissal time |

*Figure 11.4* Anecdotal records

three times during story time. Each time, he went to the block corner and began taking blocks off the shelves.

Using the format presented in Figure 11.4 offers the following benefits:

- captures concrete facts to share with parents and other team members;
- assesses development of the "whole child," not just individualized objectives;
- can be helpful in identifying individual strengths, interests, and learning style;
- helps adults develop objective observation skills.

## Dimensions of diversity

While one of the basic understandings of this book is that young children with SEN are more similar to their typically developing peers than different, it is important to be aware and appreciative of the various ways in which they do differ. Varying levels of ability represent only one dimension of diversity. Other dimensions include cultural diversity and diversity in the way different children learn. To individualize instruction appropriately, teaching strategies must reflect an understanding of these two areas of diversity.

## *Cultural diversity*

Many reasons can be given as to why we should value diversity and teach our young children to do so. One reason is that children have a right to the valuing of diversity (Lane, 1984). They also have a right to know that their personal race, ethnicity, and culture are valued by others. What children experience at school (through both formal instruction and all other aspects of the school experience) gives them messages about whether or not their culture is understood and valued.

Too often, there are considerable differences between what children experience at home and what they experience at school. Such differences can greatly affect their performance and feelings of self-worth. As McCracken (1993, pp. 10–11) notes, "Most young children function quite well at home and in their own neighborhoods. They are relaxed, have friends, and feel as though they have some control over their lives." After they enter the unfamiliar environment of the school, their performance and self-esteem may drop considerably.

Teachers need to realize that differences between what children experience at home and at school can cause anxiety and negatively effect performance. "The greater disparity between home and school, the greater the anxiety for children" (McCracken, 1993, p. 10). To reduce this anxiety and maximize the child's chances of success, home and school environments should be fairly congruent. In order for this to happen, teachers must become "well-informed about, sensitive to, and responsive to cultural differences" (McCracken, 1993, p. 11).

Through a careful selection of classroom resources and teaching strategies, teachers can introduce familiar aspects of the child's community into the classroom. By merging school experiences with what the child experiences in his or her community, children become empowered as learners. "One of the principal aspects of empowerment is respect. Students are empowered when information is presented in such a way that they can walk out of the classroom feeling that they are a part of the information" (Hilliard, 1991/92, p. 29). If cultural differences are ignored – or worse – treated as deficits, the child and his or her family are likely to feel estranged from the program and less likely to benefit from it.

Culture is like a framework that "guides and bounds life practices" (Hanson, 1992, p. 3). Cultural diversity, then, refers to more than diversity in relation to race and ethnicity. It encompasses values, customs, and other dimensions of one's lifestyle, including family composition. Due to the great variability in family characteristics, it is important for early childhood professionals to acknowledge a broad, inclusive definition of family (Howard *et al.*, 1997). A broad definition recognizes that many families differ from the traditional nuclear family consisting of a father, mother, and their biological sons and daughters. Many children live in single-parent homes, in homes with blended families (i.e., with step-parents), in foster homes, in homes with adoptive parents, and in homes with extended family. Some live with gay or lesbian parents, some with grandparents, and some with parents who are teenagers. Thus, "terms such as 'traditional' and 'nuclear' are no longer meaningful for describing families" (Hanson & Lynch, 1995, p. 46).

It is not unusual for a child's family make-up to change several times over his or her growing-up years. The family's socioeconomic status may change as well. Many children will live in poverty for all or part of their early childhood years. Some live with abuse and neglect. In light of these many differences, teachers should use instructional activities that reflect an understanding of such differences.

Professionals who work with young children with disabilities tend to be in close contact with families at a sensitive time – that is, at the time of, or soon after, the family becomes aware of their child's special needs. Thus, while all professionals should work in a culturally competent manner, this becomes especially important for professionals working with young children with special needs. Cultural competence refers to the ability to honor and respect those beliefs, interpersonal styles, attitudes and behaviors both of families who are receiving services and the multi-cultural staff who are providing services (Roberts, 1990). Cultural competence is demonstrated in the following ways (Cross *et al.*, 1989):

- Acknowledging and valuing differences – this includes not only respecting the uniqueness of individuals, but also developing an understanding of how race, culture, and ethnicity influence families and children.
- Conducting a cultural self-assessment – this involves becoming aware of one's own culture and the way in which related cultural perspectives shape personal and professional behavior.
- Recognizing and understanding the dynamics of difference – this means understanding that factors such as racism, social status, and history influence the way individuals of different cultures interact with each other.
- Acquiring cultural knowledge – this involves becoming informed about different cultures, but also being aware of variations within groups.
- Adapting to diversity – this means matching practices to the needs and styles of family cultures. Identifying and using culturally unbiased assessment procedures is one example of adapting to diversity.

If professionals do not have knowledge of and respect for the language, lifestyle, beliefs, and values of the families they serve, they run the risk of being offensive or ineffective in their role as members of an early intervention team. Professionals must take care, however, not to assign certain characteristics to an individual just because he or she is a member of a certain ethnic group. Members of any cultural group will differ in how they reflect or identify with that group's cultural beliefs and practices. While some individuals hold a primary identification with one particular group, others do not. Some may identify primarily with one cultural orientation at work and another at home. Cultural identity, then, should be viewed as one of several factors contributing to an individual's practices and beliefs. Other factors certainly include age, gender, socio-economic status, level of education, and extent of family support. Thus, while early childhood professionals should be aware of and responsive to general cultural practices and preferences, they should also recognize that "as many differences exist within groups as across groups" (Hanson & Lynch, 1995, p. 54).

Professionals working with young children and their families should not only have an understanding and appreciation of cultural diversity but should also share this appreciation through their teaching. In the classroom, this is often referred to as multicultural education. Different approaches have been used to implement a multicultural curriculum. Approaches outlined by Grant (1997) include the following:

- The at-risk approach – the goal of this approach is to bring minority groups into the mainstream. The individual's own cultural group is considered to be at-risk because it is outside the mainstream.
- The human relations approach – the goal of this approach is for people to learn to get along with each other. It recognizes multiple groups in the "melting pot," and suggests that, in spite of these differences, we should be civil to one another.
- The single-group studies approach – the goal of this approach is to become more knowledgeable about individual groups. From this approach emerge such programs as African Studies, Asian Studies, Women's Studies, etc.
- The multicultural approach – the goal of this approach is to become aware of different points of view. It is based on the understanding that we live in a pluralistic society, and that our views of this society are shaped by our own cultural experiences.

Grant (1997) challenges the value of each of these approaches and calls for a recognition that all of education is multicultural. To avoid the mistakes often associated with the various approaches to multicultural education as outlined above, the following guidelines are offered.

- Use only accurate and fair portrayals of different cultures and individuals. Stereotypes should definitely be avoided. If historical presentations are used, they should be paired with contemporary presentations.
- Focus more on the everyday lives of people from different cultures versus their festivals and other special occasions.
- Use materials that are written and illustrated by people of the culture being described as much as possible.
- Use only terminology that is current and positive. Avoid all forms of condescending, patronizing, or dehumanizing terminology (e.g., savage, wild, etc.).
- Present people as unique individuals within a culture, rather than as the embodiment of a culture.
- Strive to diversify the staff. A program should include staff members who represent the ethnic, cultural, and language diversity of the children and families being served.
- Involve families in the program. "Programs that value children value their families" (McCracken, 1993, p. 65). Schools should invite families to share information and ideas regarding educational goals, learning activities, and community resources.
- Foster pride in each child's cultural heritage. Respect for each family's culture is essential for children to feel pride in themselves and in their heritage.

To implement the above suggestions, teachers should start by collecting information on the developmental characteristics and cultural experiences of all the children in the classroom. They should then select and arrange materials in their learning spaces that reflect the cultures of individual children and/or the neighborhood where they live. Once this is in place, teachers should closely observe the children's use of the materials and note related interests and questions that emerge. These observations should be used to plan new learning activities for the children. Such activities should link new concepts with those the children have already acquired. Thus, new learning will be related to what is already familiar to the child.

### Multiple intelligences

Intelligence is sometimes defined as the ability to learn and to know. One's intelligence is often measured or quantified in terms of performance on logical and linguistic tasks. This approach to defining and measuring intelligence suggests that intelligence is a single entity. Recent research, however, suggests that there are multiple intelligences or ways of knowing. The following seven intelligences were articulated by Gardner (1983):

- linguistic (having to do with language)
- logical–mathematical (most closely related to science and math)
- musical
- spatial
- bodily kinesthetic (having to do with bodily movement)
- interpersonal (having to do with relationships between and among people)
- intrapersonal (related to self-knowledge).

Gardner (1997) recently suggested an eighth type of intelligence – that of "naturalist intelligence." This intelligence is described as the ability to recognize important distinctions in the natural world.

Gardner's work has led to an increased understanding of the fact that all children are intelligent. A question that should guide educational programming for an individual child is not *whether* that child can learn, but *how* he or she learns best. To do justice to the different ways in which children learn, frequent opportunities relating to the development of each type of intelligence must be provided. This can be especially important for children with special educational needs. Just as their disability will tend to impede learning in some area(s) of development, their individual intelligence will enhance learning if appropriate opportunities are provided. As mentioned frequently throughout this book, to individualize a program means more than accommodating for areas of weakness. It also means providing opportunities for areas of strength.

The theory of multiple intelligences raises several significant issues related to special education. The following are five such issues that have been identified by Goldman and Gardner (1989).

- One issue emanating from the theory of multiple intelligences relates to the concept of being "learning disabled." To refer to a child as being learning disabled or as having a learning disability suggests there is only one kind of intelligence – that based on language and logic. The child's other potential areas of intelligence are not considered.
- The theory of multiple intelligences also reduces the impact of a child's deficit area, or area of disability, by focusing on other areas (intelligences) where the child does not have deficits. This theory further suggests that strength in one area can compensate for and even be used to teach effectively in an area of apparent weakness. For example, a child with difficulties in linguistics may be able to use some of his or her spatial skills to accomplish certain tasks usually associated with verbal ability. Such a child might draw a map instead of giving someone verbal directions.
- A third issue relates to assessment. Traditional assessment procedures emphasize linguistic and logical skills. Children whose skills

lie primarily in other intelligences are thus short-changed. Goldman and Gardner (1989) thus suggest that a new system of assessment should be developed and used so that individual abilities can be identified as fully as possible early in the child's academic career. Assessment based on the theory of multiple intelligences would seek to capture the expanse of human potential in all intelligences and identify each child's unique intellectual propensities.

- A fourth issue relates to school outcomes. An understanding of multiple intelligences suggests that the traditional idea of desirable school outcomes would have to be expanded to encompass a wider range of vocational and avocational roles. Achievement in standard academic areas would be just one of a number of goals. With this approach, the school could become a place where students can follow their own intellectual abilities and interests and be rewarded for doing so.

- Another issue relates to curriculum and instruction. The theory of multiple intelligences suggests that curriculum and instruction should be tailored as much as possible to the inclinations, working styles, and profiles of intelligence for each individual student. The theory also suggests that instructional programs should provide students with a wide range of materials and activities – i.e., a variety that fosters development across multiple intelligences versus the development of intelligence as a single entity. A classroom reflecting the theory of multiple intelligences would be furnished with engaging materials and activities that span the many realms of intelligence. Such materials would be open ended in design so that children have the opportunity to express themselves in their preferred form of expression. A classroom so equipped would maximize the chance of eliciting and fostering children's special abilities. It would expand and individualize the curriculum and thus create an environment that welcomes children with special needs. In summary, it would give all children the opportunity to develop and be recognized for their special abilities.

# 12

# EXPLORATIONS AND EXPERIENCES

Young children with disabilities have needs that are both similar to and unique from their typically developing peers. Because of the similarities, many of the teaching strategies used with typically developing children can also be used effectively with children with special educational needs. However, due to the unique needs of young children with SEN, adaptations may also be required. Without these adaptations, some children with SEN will be faced with serious barriers to experiencing and exploring the learning environment.

Generally, adaptations to accommodate a child with SEN should be kept to a minimum. To be consistent with the principles of normalization and the least restrictive environment, any adaptations that are made should be as unobtrusive as possible. This chapter describes some possible adaptations and suggestions on how and when to implement them in appropriate ways.

## Experiencing the environment

The process of learning is based primarily on experiences gained in interacting with the environment. While this is true for all people, it is critical to the learning process for young children. The environment constantly provides messages to the learner. These messages can be positive or negative. If the experiences are positive, learners are more likely to return to the activities and conditions they enjoyed. A major task of early childhood educators is to maximize positive experiences and minimize negative experiences so that children will be motivated to interact with their environment. The positive experiences will promote learning, boost self-esteem, and minimize undesirable behaviors.

### *Positive learning environments*

There are a number of factors to consider when creating learning environments for young children. While these factors are important for all young children, they are even more critical for children with special needs. A number of such factors are listed below, along with a brief discussion of each.

- Safety – a safe environment not only reduces accidents and injuries, but also fosters feelings of security. Children will be more likely to explore their environment if they feel safe and secure in doing so. Many young children with disabilities are faced with situations that make them more at risk for accidents and injuries than their typically developing peers. Such situations include problems with balance and motor control, seizure disorders, vision and hearing impairments, and hyperactivity.

  At times, parents and educators working with children with disabilities try to create environments that are devoid of all risks. This is not a good idea. An environment that is free of risk limits children's opportunities for novel experiences. Children need such experiences to stimulate exploration and, at times, to learn from their mistakes. As risk-taking plays an important role in learning new skills, teachers must be able to make informed decisions about what constitutes constructive risk versus what arrangements present undue danger.

- Accessibility – all children should have easy access to their environment. Accessibility fosters independence and feelings of competence. It also fosters active exploration. The needs of children with disabilities must be carefully considered in terms of accessibility. The arrangement of the environment should be such that it does not pose a handicap for children with SEN – i.e., it should not create barriers to their active participation and exploration. If the design of the environment denies participation due to inaccessibility, children will experience not only frustration, but are denied opportunities for active learning as well.

  Both the indoor and outdoor environments should be evaluated in relation to accessibility. Inside, children should be able to move about freely and have access to the same learning materials, spaces, and activities as their typically developing peers. A raised stage area in the classroom, for example, should be wheelchair accessible, so that a child with a physical disability can independently choose if he or she wants to be a "performer" on the stage or a part of the audience. Chances are that he or she will want to perform!

  Adaptations to the outdoor environment are often overlooked, resulting in children with physical disabilities becoming onlookers versus active participants during outdoor play. Gravel as ground cover, for example, can restrict the maneuverability of children in wheelchairs and children wearing leg braces. Wood shavings are a better alternative. Wood shavings are also impact absorbent, making the environment safer if children should fall. Outdoor dramatic play areas (such as play houses, theaters, etc.) should also be accessible for children who use wheelchairs or rely on adaptive equipment.

Children with physical disabilities should also have access to playground equipment. Bucket seats or straps can make swings more accessible for children with posture and balance difficulties. As illustrated in Figure 12.1, there are also swings that accommodate a child in a wheelchair. A fold-up ramp on this swing allows wheelchair access to the platform. Clamps then hold the wheelchair in place as the entire platform swings back and forth. Figure 12.2 depicts a slide designed for children with disabilities. By embedding the slide into an incline of the yard, children are not faced with the barrier of steps and are much less likely to get hurt in a fall.

Additional modifications for children with motor impairments might include straps on tricycle pedals, rails on climbing equipment, and ramps over barriers and uneven surfaces. An elevated sandbox and elevated garden represent other welcome adaptations for children in wheelchairs (see Figure 12.3).

Children with sensory disabilities (e.g., hearing and vision impairments) also tend to be left on the sidelines during outdoor activities versus being "in the thick of things." A lot of plastic equipment, for example, can cause static in students' hearing implants.

*Figure 12.1* Platform swing

*Figure 12.2* Slide embedded in yard

*Figure 12.3* Elevated flower bed

Wooden equipment would therefore be better. Sound features added to the playground can help orient a child with a vision impairment and make the play environment more interesting. Examples of sound features include wind chimes, bells, and equipment for drumming.

In 1970, an adventure playground designed specifically for children with disabilities was opened in Chelsea, London. This playground is referred to as the Handicapped Adventure Playground. An adventure playground is characterized by a wide variety of loose parts and open-ended materials. They often make provisions for animals as well (e.g., rabbits, pigeons, etc.). Children in adventure playgrounds are encouraged to build their own structures and arrange their own environment.

The purpose of the Handicapped Adventure Playground is to provide a specially designed and equipped playground for the enjoyment and sensori-motor development of children with mental, physical, and emotional disabilities. The response to the playground has been quite enthusiastic. Children with all types of disabilities have been able to come here and participate in a variety of fun and challenging activities. As they play in and explore this stimulating and challenging environment, these children develop not only new skills, but improved confidence as well.

Environmental yards and yards with a variety of natural features (e.g., gardens, hills, rocks, etc.) have also been used successfully with children with disabilities (Jordan et al., 1977; Wilson et al., 1996). The variety of sights, scents, and textures of such yards offers many opportunities for sensori-motor explorations and experiences. Children often respond by becoming engaged with their environment for extended periods of time, expanding their range of explorations, and using enhanced language to share the excitement of their discoveries with others.

Adaptations for accessibility both indoors and outdoors may involve changes in not only the physical environment but in communication methods as well. At times, the teacher may find it necessary to use alternative methods of presenting information and activities. For example, instead of just telling a child to mix water with the paint powder, the teacher may need to use modeling and/or physical assistance to communicate this message. Additionally, the teacher may need to teach the child to use alternative methods of communicating. This may be sign language, gestures, a communication board, communication software attached to a computer, etc.. It may also include more time to communicate, and special prompting on how to communicate.

Some children with severe physical disabilities may require a range of adaptive equipment to facilitate their therapy goals and to aid in accessing different aspects of the program. Equipment often used in this context includes wedges, wheelchairs, prone standers, posture chairs, and support bars. It is important for teachers to work closely with physical and occupational therapists and parents in the use of such equipment.

Adaptive equipment is any device that enhances the independence of an individual by controlling for abnormal postural responses. A towel roll is considered a piece of adaptive equipment when used with small children to provide support for sitting. Adaptive equipment can be a simple, homemade item (such as the aforementioned towel roll) or a very expensive and complicated device. Adaptive equipment is often used with children who have abnormal muscle tone, limited range of motion, decreased strength, and poor muscle control. The use of the equipment can help such children access their environment.

Proper positioning plays an important role in allowing children to interact successfully with their environment. Positioning means placing the child in certain postures that promote normalized muscle tone and improve functional skills. Adaptive equipment for positioning is necessary only when children are not able to position themselves correctly. Adaptive seating devices are often seen in programs serving young children with SEN. Proper positioning in sitting allows access to table activities and places children on the same level as their peers. A "corner chair," for example, is often used to provide support for a young child during floor activities. (See Figure 12.4 for a drawing of a corner chair.)

- Available space – the ratio of classroom size to the number of children served needs to be carefully considered in planning learning environments for young children. This becomes particularly important in programs serving young children with special needs. As already indicated, more space is often needed to accommodate wheelchairs and other adaptive equipment. More space is also needed to accommodate extra adults in the classroom, such as therapists, teacher assistants, parents, and volunteers.

  Extra space can also prove beneficial to children with behavior problems, children with attention deficits, and children with autism. Generally, stress and aggressive behaviors increase as the number of children in a particular space increases.

- responsivity – a responsive environment provides children with predictable and immediate feedback when they interact with their environment. Many toys for infants have high responsiveness. Crib mobiles, for example, often provide a visual and auditory response for any action done to it (touching it, pulling it, striking it, etc.). The

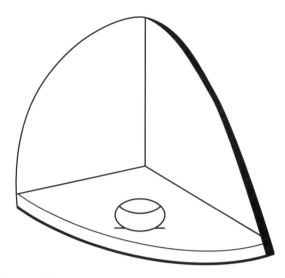

*Figure 12.4* Corner chair
*Note*: The corner chair provides support for a child who needs help sitting. The post, called an abduction block, helps to keep the child's legs apart.

infant's facial expressions and verbal reactions to such immediate feedback speak to the strength of a responsive environment.

An environment that provides immediate and consistent feedback helps children acquire a sense of power and security in controlling their environment. It is also highly motivating and tends to maintain engagement over time. Children who feel they cannot control their environment often develop "learned helplessness." Children develop this sense of helplessness when their attempts to control their environment are not successful. This tends to happen more frequently for children with disabilities.

Teachers can attend to the responsivity of the environment by choosing materials and planning activities that provide immediate positive reinforcement. They should also make sure that all materials and equipment are in good working order. If the battery in a flashlight is dead or the paint in a jar is dry, for example, children will experience frustration and disappointment when they try to use these materials. They will then be less inclined to try them again and possibly less inclined to try other materials as well.

### Promoting engagement

Engagement may be defined as "the amount of time a child spends in developmentally and contextually appropriate behaviors" (McWilliam, 1991, p. 42). The term "on-task" is sometimes used to describe a child's behaviors when he or she is engaged in instructional tasks. For an individual child, being engaged means being involved with the environment in a way that matches the expectations for a child of that developmental status and for that situation (McWilliam, 1991). Thus, engagement is exhibited in different ways by different children and in different circumstances.

A high level of engagement promotes learning and prevents or reduces behavior problems. Researchers have found, for example, that the longer a child is on-task the higher he or she scores in tests of achievement (McWilliam, 1991). As many children with SEN have difficulty establishing and maintaining engagement with their environment, an important goal of early intervention is to promote children's engagement in increasingly more complex and challenging ways.

Providing enticing, attractive environments often motivates a child to become engaged in a task or activity. Bailey and Wolery (1992) offer five suggestions for improving the initial attractiveness of activities and materials to facilitate engagement. These are as follows:

- Provide appealing materials. The appeal of materials can be enhanced by color (bright rather than drab), by size (extra large or extra small), and by sound. Three-dimensional objects are more appealing than two-dimensional. As already mentioned, materials that provide immediate feedback are also motivating. Materials tend to be more appealing if they match children's interest and level of development. Certainly novelty is another important factor. Novelty in the art center, for example, would be enhanced if the type of materials available were to vary periodically. One week, the children may have access to paint and large sheets of rectangular white paper. The next week, the art center might feature blue construction paper cut in the shapes of oceans, rivers, and lakes, along with a variety of "cut-outs" representing plant and animal life that live in the water. With available glue or paste, children could then create their own seascapes.

  One school developed a toy rotation plan to provide variety and enhance engagement (McGee *et al.*, 1991). They started by coding classroom materials according to dimensions of size, complexity, developmental level, category, and sensory quality. The inventory of materials were then divided into twelve sets, each containing ten items. Each set includes a mix of materials representing each of the above dimensions (i.e., size, complexity, developmental level, category, and sensory quality). Each completed set thus offers the following:

  1   A combination of items that vary in size and complexity (this is to avoid overwhelming the children with many large items and items with detachable parts).

2 Items that represent a range of developmental levels (this makes it possible for every student to experience success).

3 Items that address educational goals (each set includes at least one item in the following instructional categories: manipulatives, building materials, dramatic play objects, and visual motor materials).

4 Items that include a full array of sensory qualities (this makes it possible for each child's preferences to be met with each set).

Two such sets are in the room at any one time. Of course, there are other materials that remain in the room all the time (e.g., dolls, books, blocks, etc.), as they can be used in conjunction with the rotation materials. The rotation schedule is arranged so that more developmentally challenging materials are made available as the year progresses.

- Make participation a privilege rather than a duty. Engagement tends to be greatly enhanced when activities and materials are self selected. Making an activity something the children must do usually detracts considerably from their interest in it. When high-interest activities are self-selected and/or used as a reward for appropriate behaviors, engagement is generally not a problem.

- Give children immediate roles in activities. Children are not engaged when they are only passively involved in an activity (e.g., listening to a story, watching others perform, waiting for their turn, etc.). Engagement can be enhanced by finding ways to keep all children actively involved. During story time, for example, children could use puppets, stuffed animals, clothing props, etc. to take on roles of characters in the story. For other activities, children might be given roles as helpers, leaders, data collectors, or cheering squad. For all children, but especially for children with disabilities, roles must be designed to suit their individual skill level.

- Use instructions to initiate or prompt interactions. Children who are not engaged with materials or in an activity may need a specific command or prompt to get them started. For example, if Tonya is in the book corner with two or three other children, but is not looking at books or interacting with others, the teacher might say something like, "Tonya, did you see the book about dinosaurs that Anna is using? Can you find a book about dinosaurs, too?"

- Identify children's preference for materials. People tend to stay with materials and activities that are of interest to them. Some people like to play a musical instrument and may spend hours with that instrument. Others may enjoy tennis and spend as much of their free time as they can out on the courts. Activities that are not of interest, however, tend to get abandoned rather quickly. For some, this may be learning a second language or cooking gourmet meals. While the above examples relate primarily to adults, the same concept is applicable to young children. Young children are more likely to become engaged and to maintain engagement with materials and activities that are of interest to them.

Through close observation, teachers can identify the preferences of individual children. By then making the preferred materials and activities available, they can greatly enhance the child's engagement. The problem is that children with severe disabilities tend to have restricted preferences (McGee *et al.*, 1991). In such cases, identifying the sensory preferences, versus specific toy preferences, may be helpful. Some children respond better to items with strong visual characteristics, others prefer auditory toys, etc. Dramatic reductions in maladaptive behaviors have been achieved by using potent reinforcers that have been carefully selected according to each child's preferences (McGee *et al.*, 1991).

One school developed "hobby boxes" to hold individualized materials (i.e., materials selected specifically with regard to that child's strongest preferences, interests, and abilities) (McGee *et al.*, 1991). Each hobby box is marked with the child's name, and items stored in the box are marked with the child's initials. The hobby boxes are then stored on high shelves, within the child's view but out of his or her reach. This arrangement promotes social interactions with adults and verbal requests for materials.

Materials in the hobby boxes are only used if (1) the child requests them, or (2) the teacher presents the materials to the child when he or she is not engaged with other materials in the classroom. Non-engagement is not an option. Therefore, the collection of preferred materials in a child's hobby box makes it easier for the teacher to redirect the child who is not engaged.

## Additional teaching strategies

### Fostering interaction with the physical environment

Most typically developing young children learn to play with toys and materials without anyone showing them how to do so. However, some children with disabilities fail to become engaged with toys and other materials unless someone provides guidance and support. This may be in the form of modeling, prompting, and/or physical assistance. Children may also need assistance in staying with a play activity over time. Playing beside or with individual children, responding to or commenting on their playful actions, assisting them when needed, and providing toys that they prefer are ways to encourage more sustained periods of play. Providing "responsive" toys also encourages engagement over time. Responsive toys "react" or respond to the child's manipulation. Making noises and changing visually are examples of how toys might react to a child's manipulation. Tops spin and hum, soap bubbles form and float through the air, and clay changes shape.

As many children with SEN require assistance in becoming actively engaged with the environment, early childhood educators should identify ways to provide such assistance. At times, this means adapting toys and materials to make them easier for children with physical disabilities to manipulate or operate. Using battery-operated versus manually operated toys represents one such adaptation. The use of computer-assisted activities should also be considered. Additional ideas and suggestions are offered in a later section of this chapter under the heading "Aids to exploration" (p. 243).

### Fostering social interaction

Peer interactions are critical to the development of social competence in young children. "In fact, an increased affiliation with peers and a decreased reliance on adults appear to be major components of healthy social and emotional development in the preschool years" (McEvoy & Odom, 1996, p. 226). Yet, as was stated earlier in this book, young children with and without disabilities tend not to engage in high levels of interaction with each other unless they are encouraged and supported in doing so.

There are a number of factors that can influence the levels of social interaction between young children. One such factor relates to the types of toys and other materials provided. Some toys, for example, tend to foster particular types of behavior. Some toys encourage more independent and isolated play, while others encourage peer interactions. If a goal or individualized objective for a particular child focuses on learning to interact with peers, toys that promote social interactions should be provided. Such toys include dressing-up clothes for dramatic play, balls, wagons, trucks, and cars.

Group size can also influence the levels of social interaction between young children. Young children tend to engage in more social interactions where they are in small groups versus large groups (Wolery & Wilbers, 1994). For children with disabilities, this is especially true if peers in the small group are competent and skilled in the activities. At times, working in groups should be determined by the children themselves. At other times, it should be planned and arranged by the teacher. One special group arrangement used in educational settings is referred to as a cooperative learning group.

## Cooperative learning activities

Cooperative learning is a non-competitive teaching strategy in which children are divided into small groups for learning activities which have cooperative goals. This teaching strategy involves structuring activities that teach children to encourage one another, celebrate each other's successes, and work toward common goals (Johnson & Johnson, 1986; Noonan & McCormick, 1993). A primary purpose of cooperative learning is to foster cooperative interactions between children and to teach them the skills involved. It also tends to promote child engagement. For preschoolers, cooperative learning activities may be especially helpful in promoting social and communication skills of children with disabilities served in a typical early childhood setting.

Cooperative learning activities need to be carefully planned and teacher supported. If not, such activities can easily become situations of conflict, frustration, and confusion. To be educationally useful, a cooperative learning activity should involve children in something interesting and challenging. Children should be given the opportunity to make key decisions about how they perform group tasks. They should also be given the opportunity to judge their own success. Finally, cooperative learning activities should permit all members of the group to participate actively and successfully throughout the process.

Each child in a cooperative learning group has a clearly defined role, and each role is equally valued. For example, one child might serve as the reader for the group, while another child serves as the recorder. One child might be a timekeeper, while another is the group leader. Such an arrangement allows for active participation by children with varying abilities.

The teacher's role in cooperative learning activities is to teach cooperative skills so that the group can function effectively. Such skills include (1) asking for/offering help, (2) listening to others, (3) sharing materials and ideas, (4) taking turns, and (5) showing someone how to do something or helping them to accomplish a task. The teacher may also have to remind the children to stay near one another and to help each other. Additionally, the teacher should monitor the group carefully to see where assistance is needed. Finally, it is important for the teacher to provide positive feedback (e.g., "You really worked well together. I like the way you listened to each other"). Of course, it is also important for the teacher to carefully select the lessons and activities with which the children will be involved during the cooperative learning process. The lessons and activities must lend themselves to positive peer interactions.

## *Promoting independence*

A challenge of programs serving young children with special educational needs is establishing a balance between fostering independence (i.e., persuading children to do things on their own) and ensuring that they are not left out of some activities because of their lack of required skills. To promote participation, it is sometimes necessary to provide adult support and make special accommodations for children with SEN. If a child's disability keeps him or her from participating in an activity if help were not provided, such help should be given. The extent of the help, however, should encourage the child with SEN to do as much as possible on his or her own.

It is not only physical constraints that tend to impede a child's exploration and sense of independence. Social constraints can do so as well. Adults concerned with children's safety may unduly restrict access to certain experiences. They may do things for and to the children rather than allow them to explore, interact, and problem solve on their own. They may make unnecessary adaptations to the physical and social environment. This practice places control and responsibility for accessing the environment outside the realm of the child with a disability and within the control of other people. "This response runs counter to the most deeply held ideals of personal independence in our society" (Mettler, 1987, p. 478). It is therefore extremely important that adults avoid "overcontrolling" the environment for children with disabilities. (For a further discussion of this issue, see the final section of this chapter, pp. 250–251.)

## *Incidental teaching*

Incidental teaching involves teaching in the context of naturally occurring situations and is thus referred to as a naturalistic teaching strategy. It is designed to promote child engagement and skill acquisition across different developmental domains while the child participates in the daily routine of the classroom. Incidental teaching and other naturalistic teaching strategies are defined by the following characteristics:

- Teaching occurs in the natural environment in unstructured or semi-structured situations. Such situations often occur during play, predictable routine activities (i.e., snack time, clean-up, etc.), transitions from one activity to another, and routine group activities (e.g., circle time, story time, etc.).
- Individual teaching interactions are brief and distributed throughout the day.
- Individual teaching interactions are child-initiated. For example, if an individualized objective is to use more expanded language, the adult

would take advantage of the child's current communicative attempts to model more sophisticated language.

- Instruction uses positive reinforcement or activities that are re-inforcing to the child.

An incidental teaching episode begins when a child initiates an interaction in the context of naturally occurring routines and activities. The adult responds by modeling or prompting a more elaborated skill (i.e., a skill at a higher level than that demonstrated by the child). The following is an example: Joel, the target child, is having trouble opening his juice carton at snack time, but is saying nothing. The teacher enters the situation by saying, "Joel, ask Lorie to help you." Joel looks at Lorie and says, "Help me, please." Lorie opens the box for Joel. The teacher in this case prompted the target child (Joel) to use a more elaborated social/communication skill – that of asking for help. Joel was reinforced for his response by making Lorie understand his request and open the box for him. Incidental teaching is based on the understanding that daily activities that have a specific purpose (e.g., snack time is for eating) can also serve an instructional purpose (e.g., to promote fine motor and/or communication skills).

### Responsive teaching

Responsive teaching uses "social reinforcers" to foster desired behavior or the development of specific skills. Examples of social reinforcers include praise, hugs, and smiles. Further information about responsive teaching was presented in Chapter 5, along with an example of how this strategy might be used with an individual child.

## Aids to exploration

In addition to adaptive equipment (discussed above), other special adaptations are often used to modify the physical environment for children with SEN. Some of these adaptations are referred to as "assistive technology." All are designed to aid the child in his or her exploration of the environment.

### Assistive technology

Assistive technology can make it possible for children with disabilities to accomplish tasks that would otherwise be difficult or impossible for them to do. For example, a child who is unable to walk may use a wheelchair to get to the lunch room. If the lunch room is a long way from the classroom, the child may need a powered wheelchair to get there on time (i.e., when his or her class-mates get there). Another child who is unable to write with a pencil legibly or quickly enough to keep up with classroom work may have to use a computer for written assignments.

In each of these examples, there is a gap between the child's abilities and the skills needed to perform the required tasks or activities. Assistive technology provides the tools to bridge this gap, allowing many children with disabilities to participate meaningfully in regular education environments.

The term "assistive technology" covers a wide range of devices and services. They may be "low-tech," such as hand-held magnifiers and velcro strips, or more "high-tech" devices, such as computerized augmentative communication systems. The following is a list of different types of assistive technology, along with examples of each.

- Mobility devices – canes, walkers, manual or powered wheelchairs, scooters, adapted bikes, etc.
- Positioning devices – corner chairs (or floor sitters), standing frames, chair inserts, wedges, pillows, straps, etc.
- Self-care devices – adapted utensils, switch-operated electronic feeders, buttonhooks, velcro fasteners, toilet seats, etc.
- Computer access devices – trackballs, touch windows, switches, etc.
- Sensory aids – closed-captioned TV, text enlargers, speech output devices, magnifiers, tape recordings, Braille, large-print books, etc.
- Augmentative communication devices – spelling or symbol boards, picture cards, etc.
- Recreational devices – computer games, drawing and music software, beeping balls, etc.
- Architectural barrier removal – ramps, power door openers, special hinges, etc.

### Adapting toys and other learning materials

The selection of toys and other learning materials can enhance or hinder a child's success in a program. This is especially true for children with disabilities. Their unique motor, sensory, developmental, and normalization needs often put special limitations on the kinds of toys and other learning materials that will be useful to them. As it is often difficult to find materials that are "just right" for a particular child with a disability, adaptations to what is available must then be made. Mechanical adaptations are sometimes used to allow a child greater control and independent use of certain toys and learning materials. For example, adding a push switch to a wind-up toy makes it easier for the child to use the toy without assistance. Other materials can be modified by replacing buttons or ties on clothing with velcro and adding a "grip" to a pencil or pen for easier handling.

*Adaptive Play for Special Needs Children* (Musselwhite, 1986) is an excellent resource on how to appropriately adapt toys and other learning materials for children with disabilities. The following are ten different strategies that are offered.

- Stabilize – attach play materials to a steady surface.
- Enlarge – enlarge materials or key parts of materials to enhance visual perception and/or item manipulation.
- Prosthetize – attach additional parts for easier access for persons who are physically disabled or visually impaired (e.g., add "knobs" to wooden puzzle pieces).
- Reduce required response – minimize distance, range of motion, and/or complexity of response (e.g., use a plate switch rather than an on-off button).
- Make more familiar – select symbols that reflect the child's world.
- Make more concrete – reduce the abstract quality of an item (e.g., add pictures to graphic symbols).
- Remove extraneous cues – focus the child's attention on one quality at a time (e.g., if the task is shape recognition, avoid using multiple colors).
- Remove distracting stimuli – keep backgrounds in work areas simple (e.g., avoid multicolored materials and materials with designs).
- Add or enhance cues – increase visual and tactile stimuli.
- Improve safety and durability – avoid sharp objects and objects with sharp parts; protect objects from drool and other sources of dampness; increase the strength of toys.

### Adapting goals or outcomes

By adapting the goals or outcomes of an instructional activity, children with differing levels of ability can actively participate at their own level and meet their individual goals. For example, the goal of a science project for a student with developmental delays may be to stimulate and enhance language development. The goal of a typically developing peer working on the same project may be to learn a scientific principle. Another example might be for one child to use Cuisinnaire rods for sorting and learning colors, while other children are using the same materials to learn math concepts.

### Adapting tasks

Learning tasks can be adapted in a number of different ways, including the following:

245

- Time designations – adapt the time allotted for learning, task completion, and testing.
- Level of support – increase the amount of personal support by using a peer partner or providing extra adult assistance.
- Level of difficulty or complexity – simplify a task or the way in which it must be accomplished (e.g., kick a ball from a stationery position versus while running; use a calculator to figure math problems, etc.).
- Size – adapt the number of items that a child is expected to learn or complete (e.g., assign only five instead of ten spelling words).
- Output or performance – adapt how the student can respond to an instructional task (e.g., instead of answering questions verbally, allow the child to point to the correct response).
- Type of participation – adapt the extent to which a child is actively involved in a task (e.g., ask one student to hold a map while others point out locations).

### Expanding presentation of delivery system

Expand the ways in which instruction is delivered. This can be accomplished by using different visual aids, planning more concrete examples, providing hands-on experiences, and having students work in cooperative groups.

### Developing behavior support plans

For children who may need behavioral supports in order to participate in the regular class, behavioral support plans can be developed. Such plans are developed by the child's intervention team with input from a behavior consultant. They address the unique needs of the child and include provisions for obtaining appropriate resources (e.g., psychological counseling, etc.).

### Using aides/assistants

Using additional supports in the classroom, such as aides and assistants, enables students with disabilities to be integrated and successful. This practice has the added advantage of offering extra assistance to all the students in the classroom.

## Exceptionality appropriate practices

Exceptionality appropriate practices may be defined in several different ways. They may be defined as practices that provide the appropriate adaptations for children with disabilities. They may also be defined as specific adaptations for specific areas of disabilities. It is this second definition that forms the basis for this section of the chapter.

While special education is based on the principle of individualization (i.e., individualizing the program to the unique needs of each child), there are some guidelines related to adaptations for specific areas of disability. Thus, knowing the nature of a child's disability suggests the appropriateness of certain adaptations. These adaptations can form *part* of the child's individualized education plan.

Some suggestions for meeting the needs of children with various types of disabilities have already been presented, particularly in Chapters 4 and 5. Additional suggestions are presented below. These suggestions are offered as examples of exceptionality appropriate practices. There is some overlap between the areas.

### *For children with disabilities in the area of communication*

- Provide frequent visual cues (e.g., gestures, pictures, objects, etc.) to reinforce clarity/comprehension.
- Use specific terminology (e.g., use the names of things versus such pronouns as it, them, etc.).
- Expand on what the child says (e.g., "Ball. You want this big ball").
- Model the correct language usage and pronunciation versus correcting the child's "mistakes."
- Keep directions and explanations simple.
- Speak clearly and face the children when talking.

### *For children with motor difficulties*

- Organize the physical space to accommodate wheelchairs and other special equipment, as needed.
- Use elevated working areas that can accommodate children in wheelchairs.
- Use bolsters or other supports for floor activities.
- Use adaptive equipment, as needed, for positioning, support, and therapy goals.
- Use adaptive tools (scissors, spoons, pencils, etc.) as needed.
- Keep materials in open shelves which can be easily reached by children who are unable to stand and/or who are in wheelchairs.
- Provide adaptive seating to ensure that children will be at the same height as their peers.
- Avoid isolating children in their wheelchairs. Provide additional seating and positioning options (e.g., bean bag chair, corner chair, etc.).
- Make playground equipment and outdoor play activities accessible.

- Provide adequate time for completion of tasks.
- Arrange activities and instructional tasks so that minimal movements by the child produce effects on the environment.
- Be alert for subtle responses which indicate that the child is learning and communicating. Such responses might include smiling, changes in breathing, eye or head movements, etc.
- Organize the classroom to allow for privacy during change of clothing, toileting, etc.
- Make sure the child's adaptive equipment is in good working order.
- Use a TV tray or large cookie sheet with sides to provide boundaries for loose materials.

### For children with mental retardation and/or developmental delays

- Sequence learning activities and other tasks into small steps.
- Establish goals in relation to the child's developmental level.
- Provide frequent positive feedback.
- Allow extra time for learning and completion of tasks.
- Encourage interaction with and imitation of typically developing peers.
- Keep directions simple, sequenced, and organized.

### For children with attention problems

- Provide visual cues.
- Offer only a limited number of choices.
- Provide positive reinforcement for sustained attention.
- Introduce "calming" activities after vigorous play.
- Provide support during transition times (i.e., arrival, departure, and change of activities).
- Seat the child away from distractions (e.g., the classroom door, windows, etc.). Seat the child next to "good workers."
- Give only one direction at a time. Be specific and brief. Ask the child to repeat the direction to ensure that he or she understands.
- Establish and maintain a daily routine.
- Use interactive teaching styles and techniques. Encourage comments and questions. Move about the room. Provide opportunities for active involvement.

### For children with social/emotional problems

- Help the child learn to express feelings in appropriate ways (e.g., using words instead of actions).

- Provide extra structure to activities and use of materials (e.g., define physical space for activities).
- Allow a reluctant child to observe group activities until ready to participate.
- Help an aggressive child control behavior through consistent enforcement of rules.

### For children with hearing impairments

- Use vision as a primary input source. Provide visual clues (e.g., pictures, gestures, symbols, etc.) and remove visual barriers.
- Demonstrate (versus just talking about) new activities or tasks and use of new materials.
- Obtain the child's attention before speaking.
- Teach the child to watch the speaker's face.
- Position the child close to the speaker, the source of music, and other relevant sounds.
- Learn some sign language and teach signing to the whole class.
- Reduce the noise level of the room.

### For children with vision impairments

- Attend to the child's safety at all times without being too protective.
- Provide a variety of tactile, manipulative, and auditory experiences. Include objects that the child can feel – objects of different shapes, textures, pliability, etc. Use actual objects rather than representations of objects. Use toys that make sounds – music box, train with a whistle, etc.
- Introduce the child to changes in the environment verbally and through touch.
- Inform the child of what will happen next.
- Use hand-over-hand guidance when necessary so the child knows what is expected.
- Teach skills in the context of their natural occurrence (e.g., teach feeding skills at mealtimes while seated at the table).
- Present materials on a contrasting background (e.g., present light-colored materials on a dark surface).
- Make the child aware of your presence before touching him or her.
- Use the child's name when addressing him or her.
- Use the child's body as a reference point (e.g., "The book is on the floor by your foot").
- Develop a "buddy" system.
- Keep materials at the child's level.
- Encourage the child to examine materials tactily.

- Provide adequate lighting.
- Keep child's personal items in an organized storage unit that is easily accessible to the child.
- Keep walkways free of clutter.
- Teach the child to localize sounds.
- Provide familiar routines.
- Help the child to get comfortable with movement in space. Ensure his or her comfort and safety when moving or being moved. Provide motivation and physical guidance, as needed.
- Discourage self-stimulatory behavior (e.g., rubbing eyes, shaking parts of the body, etc.) by keeping the child involved in fun and meaningful activities.
- Use a TV tray or large cookie sheet with sides to provide boundaries for loose materials.

## Of special note

Much has been said about modifying the environment to foster independence and exploration on the part of children with disabilities. A word of caution, however, is in order. This caution relates to the message we give to children when we do things for them or exercise control over their environment. As already stated in various ways, children need to learn that *through their own efforts* they can affect the environment. Once children learn this, they will be more likely to interact with the environment with zest and joy.

Because children need to be encouraged to take initiative and responsibility for their own learning and experiences, they should be given opportunities to modify the environment in ways that work for them. Modifications to the environment should not always be external to the child (i.e., designed by the adults). For children to be independent (and to develop feelings of competence and self-esteem), they must encounter the world as it is and learn strategies to solve the problems they encounter. If modifications are required, changes can be made in either the physical or social situation or the children's own behavior. Children should have a say in whether or not their environment is modified and in what way. Sometimes, children's voices can be heard through what they say; at other times it may be through what they do.

Professionals and parents should thus be cautious about intervening too quickly and too often to modify the physical and social environment. Rather than promoting independence, such modifications may serve as a "hidden dependency trap" (Lang & Deitz, 1990) and lead to "learned helplessness." "If parents or professionals always modify the environment for the children, the children never learn how to control their environment" (Lang & Deitz, 1990, p. 3).

The extent and type of adaptations to be made should always be determined on an individual basis. The following are several questions that may be useful in deciding when to modify an environment and when to refrain from doing so.

- Is this adaptation necessary?
- How will this adaptation benefit the child?
- Is this adaptation age appropriate?
- Is this adaptation the least intrusive way to accomplish the purpose?
- Does this adaptation preserve the dignity of the child?
- What does this adaptation say to others about children with disabilities?
- Does this adaptation generalize to the natural environment – i.e., does it maintain its usefulness across settings and over time?
- Have the wishes and ideas of the child been considered in deciding whether or not – and in what way – to modify the environment?
- Does this adaptation say to the child, "You are not able"?

Inappropriate and useless adaptations and modifications deny the dignity of an individual by reinforcing society's belief that people who are disabled are incompetent (Lang & Deitz, 1990). Environmental adaptations that are imposed from without can easily interfere with the development of feelings of self-esteem and personal effectiveness. These two variables – i.e., self-esteem and personal effectiveness – must be carefully considered when attempting to create environments and provide experiences that facilitate independence.

Some adaptations and modifications are needed to enable young children with disabilities to experience success in the regular classroom setting. Teachers, however, must consider the potential dangers associated with the overuse of adaptations. They need to know that pervasive, long-term structuring of the physical or social environment conveys a negative message about children. Overprotection – or inappropriate and unnecessary adaptations – suggest that children with disabilities are unable to deal effectively with the world as it is. Rather than promoting independence and development, unnecessary adaptations tend to nurture dependent behavior.

Teachers who work with children with disabilities need to be aware of the physical barriers that such children face in interacting with the environment. They also need to be aware, however, of more subtle barriers that exist in certain language and social conventions which suggest to children that they are incompetent. The success of an intervention program should be judged, not in relation to how many adaptations were made, but in relation to how truly independent the child has become.

# GLOSSARY

**adaptation:**  A change made to better meet the needs of an individual.

**age appropriate:**  Experiences and/or learning environments that support predictable growth and development for typically developing children at specific chronological ages.

**anecdotal records:**  A brief account of a situation that provides a factual description of an incident, behavior, or event.

**arena assessment:**  The process of one professional interacting with a child to conduct an assessment, while other team members (including the family) observe and contribute.

**assessment:**  The collection of information through different types of procedures to better understand an individual, often in terms of development and learning.

**assistive device:**  Any specific aid, tool, or piece of equipment used to assist an individual with a disability.

**at risk:**  A condition that results in an individual having a greater chance of experiencing developmental, social, and/or academic difficulties.

**atypical development:**  Development that is outside the range of normalcy.

**augmentative communication:**  Any method of communicating without speech, such as using gestures, signs, picture boards, and electronic devices.

**behavior modification:**  Systematic, consistent efforts to change an individual's behavior. Behavior modification systems are often based on carefully planned consequences (i.e., rewards and/or punishments) for specific behaviors.

**biological risk:**  Conditions of bodily systems which make normal development problematic.

**bolster:**  A cylindrical piece of equipment (often made of foam) on which a young child is placed to help with positioning and to foster the development of muscle strength, balance, and protective reactions.

**cerebral palsy:**  Disorder of posture, muscle tone, and movement resulting from brain damage.

**Child Find:** A term sometimes used to refer to the process of identifying children with special needs.

**child-initiated activity:** An activity selected by a child with little or no intervention by another child or adult.

**chromosomal abnormality:** A genetic disorder caused by too few or too many chromosomes, or by chromosomes with extra or missing pieces.

**chronological age:** A child's actual age in years and/or months.

**collaboration:** Working toward and sharing a common goal.

**communication board:** An assistive device that allows individuals to point to pictures or symbols to communicate a message.

**community collaboration:** Different agencies within a community working together to provide more effective services.

**compensatory program:** A type of intervention program designed to offset poverty conditions experienced at home.

**conductive hearing loss:** A hearing loss caused by an obstruction in the auditory canal; partially or totally prevents sound waves from reaching the inner ear.

**congenital:** Presumed to be present at birth.

**criterion-referenced tests:** Evaluation tools which are specifically constructed to evaluate a person's performance level in relation to some standard (i.e., criteria).

**curriculum-based assessment:** An assessment of a child's abilities or behaviors in the context of a predetermined sequence of curriculum objectives.

**cystic fibrosis:** A chronic disorder often causing respiratory and digestive problems.

**developmental:** Having to do with the typical steps or stages in human growth and development before the age of 18.

**developmental age:** The age at which a child is functioning; based on assessment of the child's skills and comparison of those skills to the age at which they are considered typical.

**developmental delay:** A classification for children who perform significantly behind developmental norms.

**developmentally appropriate:** The extent to which a program and/or activity is appropriate for the age span of the children involved and is implemented with attention to the different needs, interests, and developmental levels of individual children.

**developmentally appropriate practices (DAP):** Curriculum which is appropriate to the age and individual needs of children.

**diagnosis:** An effort to find the cause of a problem by observing the child and considering the results of tests.

**disability:** An inability to perform certain tasks because of an impairment in some area of functioning.

**early intervention:** Services for young children with special needs or who are at risk.

**eligibility:** Determination of whether a child meets the criteria to receive services.

**engagement:** The amount of time spent in developmentally and contextually appropriate behaviors.

**environmental assault:** Conditions in the environment which put children at risk of developmental delay. Examples include toxic pollutants in the air, water, and food.

**environmental risk:** Conditions in the family or community that may lead to developmental delay.

**established risk:** The presence of a diagnosed physical or medical condition that is likely to lead to developmental delay.

**evaluation:** A comprehensive term which includes screening, assessment, and monitoring activities.

**exceptionality appropriate practices:** Specific adaptations for specific areas of disabilities.

**exosystem:** A network of societal structures, such as public and private service agencies, advocacy groups, and churches, which contribute to an individual's total environment.

**expansion:** A language stimulation technique in which adults expand a child's utterance by stating the child's idea in a longer phrase or sentence.

**expectations:** The level of behavior, skill, and participation expected of an individual. Expectations often vary from one setting to another.

**expressive language:** What is said or written to communicate an idea or question.

**family systems perspective:** The family is viewed as an interactive unit; includes the understanding that what affects one member affects all.

**fine motor skills:** Activities that involve small muscles, such as activities performed with the fingers and hands.

**functional skills:** Skills that will be immediately useful to the child and that will be used relatively frequently in the child's typical environment.

**generalization:** The integration of newly acquired information and skills and the application of these to new situations.

**gross motor skills:** Activities that use large muscles, such as running, climbing, throwing, and jumping.

**handicap:** A problem which an individual with a disability encounters when attempting to function and interact in the environment.

**hypertonic:** A condition in which muscles are tense and stretched; often related to spasticity.

**hypotonic:** Low muscle tone; usually characterized by weakness, "floppiness," poor posture, and hypermobile joints.

**incidental teaching:** Providing instruction in the context of play and other informal activities.

**inclusion:** The practice of including all children in the regular program.

**individual appropriateness:** Experiences that match each child's unique pattern of growth, personality, learning style, and family/cultural background.

**individualized objectives:** Specify critical developmental skills to be taught; based on an individual's current level of functioning.

**integration:** The practice of bringing together different groups which have previously been segregated (e.g., children with special needs and typically developing children).

**interagency:** Between agencies.

**interdisciplinary:** A model of team organization characterized by professionals from several disciplines who work together to design, implement, and document goals for an individual child. With this model, all members assess and/or provide direct services to the child.

**learned helplessness:** A belief held by an individual that he or she lacks control over life's events.

**least restrictive environment:** The most integrated placement in which a child may function successfully.

**legal blindness:** A condition where an individual's visual acuity is 20/200 or less in the best eye with correction and/or his or her peripheral field of vision is 20 degrees or less.

**macrosystem:** Cultural and legislative contexts in which other components of one's environment operate.

**mainstreaming:** The placement of a child with a disability in a program designed for children without disabilities.

**maturation:** The universal sequence of biological changes that occur as one ages.

**mesosystem:** The relationships among the components of an individual's microsystem. For young children with special needs, this usually includes the relationships between parents and teacher, therapist, and physician. It also includes the relationships between professions involved in serving the child.

**microsystem:** The setting in which individuals spend most of their time. For young children this usually includes the child's home, the homes of relatives and friends, and child care center or family day care home.

**morphology:** Rules for changing the form of individual words (e.g., from singular to plural).

**multidisciplinary:** A model of team organization characterized by professionals from several disciplines working independently who relate information to each other but do not coordinate, practice, or design a total educational program together.

**neonatal:**  The period from birth to 28 days of age.

**neurological:**  Refers primarily to the nervous system.

**nondiscriminatory:**  Not prejudicial. A nondiscriminatory test, for example, would not be prejudicial against a particular group of people (e.g., minority, disabled, etc.).

**norm-referenced tests:**  Tests that compare the performance of an individual against a group average or norm.

**normal curve:**  A bell-shaped curve which represents the theoretical frequency distribution of human characteristics (e.g., cognitive ability).

**normalization:**  A belief and practice based on the understanding that individuals with disabilities should experience patterns of life and conditions of everyday living which are as close as possible to the regular ways of life.

**open-ended materials:**  Materials which offer a wide range of opportunities for exploration.

**orientation:**  An awareness of spacial aspects of the environment, especially in relation to one's own body position in space.

**orthopedic:**  Refers primarily to bones and joints.

**otitis media:**  Inflammation of the middle ear; often results in a temporary fluctuating hearing loss.

**perinatal:**  The period around the time of birth.

**phonology:**  The sound systems of speech and language.

**positioning:**  Placing an individual in certain positions in an attempt to promote symmetrical body alignment, normalize muscle tone, and promote functional skills.

**pragmatics:**  The rules and conventions that govern how language is used for communication in different situations.

**prenatal:**  The period before birth.

**prevention:**  Efforts to keep a problem from occurring or from getting worse.

**primary prevention:**  Prevention efforts often focusing on the time before a child is born.

**prompt:**  An intervention technique involving a suggestion or command.

**receiving program:**  The program into which the child will be going.

**receptive language:**  The receiving of messages; language that is understood.

**reliability:**  A measure of whether a test consistently measures what it was designed to measure.

**residual hearing:**  The hearing ability remaining to an individual with a hearing impairment.

**residual vision:**  The visual ability remaining to an individual with a vision impairment.

**responsivity:** The quality of being responsive; responding readily.

**role release:** Mutual sharing of knowledge and expertise by professionals on a team which enables each team member to carry out responsibilities traditionally assigned to another member of the team.

**screening:** A process of identifying children who may need further assessment to determine special needs.

**secondary handicap:** A handicap that develops in response to the challenges faced by having a disability; for example, a child who is deaf is likely to have communication and social deficits as well.

**secondary prevention:** Efforts to prevent problems which have a high probability of occurring even though a disabling condition is not evident at the present time.

**semantics:** The meaning of words.

**sending program:** The program the child is leaving.

**sensory impairments:** Impairments related to the senses (i.e., hearing, vision, etc.).

**social toxicity:** Harmful aspects of the social environment (e.g., violence, poverty, etc.).

**spasticity:** The tendency to have sudden, involuntary contractions of the muscles.

**standard deviation:** A term used to describe how far a score is from the mean.

**standardized tests:** Tests which include a fixed set of items carefully developed to evaluate a child's skills and to allow comparison against a group average or norm.

**survival skills:** Those skills needed to be successful in the child's current and/or next environment.

**syntax:** Rules determining correct word order in sentences.

**teachable moment:** A situation that arises naturally in unstructured or semi-structured situations that provide a special opportunity for teaching a concept or skill within the context of what just occurred.

**teacher-directed activity:** An activity in which the adult initiates and continues to supervise what children do.

**tertiary prevention:** Providing services after a problem has occurred; the focus is on preventing secondary handicaps or related problems from occurring.

**total communication:** A combination of methods to communicate effectively in a given situation (e.g., sign language combined with oral expression).

**transdisciplinary:** A model of team organization characterized by professionals from several disciplines mutually sharing knowledge and expertise which enables each team member to carry out responsibilities traditionally assigned to another member of the team.

**typically developing child:** A child who is not identified as having a disability.

**validity:** A measure of whether test items measure what they were designed to do.

**visual acuity:** Sharpness of vision.

**walking ropes:** ropes running horizontally to assist people who are blind to move safely from one place to another.

# REFERENCES

Abramowitz, A.J., Eckstrand, D., O'Leary, S.G., & Dulcan, M.K. (1992). ADHD children's response to stimulant medication in two intensities of a behavioral intervention program. *Behavior Modification*, 16, 193–203.

Adeola, F.O. (1994). Environmental hazards, health, and racial inequity in hazardous waste distribution. *Environment and Behavior*, 26(1), 99–126.

Ainsworth, M.D.S. (1973). The development of infant–mother attachment. In B.M. Caldwell & H.N. Ricciuti (Eds.), *Review of child development research: Child development and social policy*. Chicago, IL: University of Chicago Press (pp. 1–94).

Ainsworth, M.D.S., Bell, S.M., & Stayton, D.J. (1972). Individual differences in the development of some attachment behaviors. *Merrill-Palmer Quarterly*, 18, 123–143.

Ainsworth, M.D.S., Blehar, M.D., Waters, E., & Wall, S. (1978). *Patterns of attachment: A psychological study of the strange situation*. Hillsdale, NJ: Erlbaum.

Allen, E.A., & Marotz, L. (1989). *Developmental profiles: Birth to six*. Albany, NY: Delmar.

American Psychiatric Association (1987). *Diagnostic and statistical manual of mental disorders* (3rd ed.). Washington, DC: APA.

Atwater, J.B., Orth-Lopes, L., Elliott, M., Carta, J.J., & Schwartz, I.S. (1994). Completing the circle: planning and implementing transitions to other programs. In M. Wolery & J.S. Wilbers (Eds.), *Including children with special needs in early childhood programs*. Washington, DC: National Association for the Education of Young Children (pp. 167–188).

Aylward, G.P. 1990). Environmental influences on the developmental outcome of children at risk. *Infants and Young Children*, 2(4), 1–9.

Bailey, D.B. (1991). Issues and perspectives on family assessment. *Infants and Young Children*, 4(1), 26–34.

Bailey, D.B. (1994). Working with families of children with special needs. In M. Wolery and J.S. Wilbers (Eds.), *Including children with special needs in early childhood programs*. Washington, DC: National Association for the Education of Young Children (pp. 23–44).

Bailey, D.B., & Wolery, M. (1992). *Teaching infants and preschoolers with handicaps* (2nd ed.). Columbus, OH: Merrill.

Bailey, D.B., Simeonsson, R.J., Yoder, D.E., & Huntington, G.S. (1990). Preparing professionals to serve infants and toddlers with handicaps and their families: an integrative analysis across eight disciplines. *Exceptional Children*, 57, 26–35.

Barkley, R.A. (1990). *Attention deficit hyperactivity disorder: A handbook for diagnosis and treatment.* New York: Guilford.

Batshaw, M.L., & Perret, Y.M. (1992). *Children with disabilities: A medical primer* (3rd ed.). Baltimore, MD: Brookes.

Bigge, J.L. (1991). *Teaching individuals with physical and multiple disabilities* (3rd. ed.). Columbus, OH: Macmillan.

Blahna, D.J., & Toch, M.F. (1993). Environmental reporting in ethnic magazines: implications for incorporating minority concerns. *Journal of Environmental Education*, 24(2), 22–29.

Bowlby, J. (1982). *Attachment and loss: Attachment* (2nd ed.). New York: Basic Books.

Bowman, B.T. (1992). Who is at risk for what and why. *Journal of Early Intervention*, 16(2), 101–108.

Bredekamp, S. (1987). *Developmentally appropriate practice in early childhood programs serving children from birth through age 8.* Washington, DC: National Association for the Education of Young Children.

Bredekamp, S. (1993). The relationship between early childhood education and early childhood special education: healthy marriage or family feud?. *Topics in Early Childhood Special Education*, 13(3), 258–273.

Bredekamp, S. (1997). NAEYC issues revised position statement on developmentally appropriate practice in early childhood programs. *Young Children*, 52(2), 34–40.

Bredekamp, S., & Copple, C. (Eds.) (1997). *Developmentally appropriate practice in early childhood programs* (Revised ed.). Washington, DC: National Association for the Education of Young Children.

Bricker, D. (1989). *Early intervention for at-risk and handicapped infants, toddlers, and preschool children* (2nd ed.). Palo Alto, CA: VORT.

Bricker, D., & Cripe, J.J. (1992). An activity-based intervention. Paper presented at Post Conference Workshop, Council for Exceptional Children Conference, Albuquerque, New Mexico.

Bronfenbrenner, U. (1979). *The ecology of human development.* Cambridge, MA: Harvard University Press.

Brown, N., & Kalbli, J. (1997). Facilitating the socialization of children with autism. *Early Childhood Education Journal*, 24(3), 185–189.

Bruder, M.B. (1994). Working with members of other disciplines: collaboration for success. In M. Wolery and J.S. Wilbers (Eds.), *Including children with special needs in early childhood programs.* Washington, DC: National Association for the Education of Young Children (pp. 45–70).

Brunquell, P.J. (1994). Listening to epilepsy. *Infants and Young Children*, 7(1), 24–33.

Bullard, R.D. (1994). Grassroots flowering. *The Amicus Journal*, spring, 32–37.

Burgener, G.W. (1980) Voice amplification and its effects on test taking performance (Doctoral dissertation, Southern Illinois University at Carbondale, 1980). Dissertaion Abstracts International, 41, 08A 3485.

Burgess, D.M., & Streissguth, A.P. (1992). Fetal alcohol syndrome and fetal alcohol effects: principles for educators. *Phi Delta Kappan*, 1, 24–30.

Chavis, F.F. (1992). Race, justice and the environment. *Nature Conservancy*, September/October, 38.

Chess, S., & Thomas, A. (1982). Infant bonding: Mystique and reality. *American Journal of Orthopsychiatry*, 52(2), 213–222.

Cioni, G., Paolicelli, P.B., Sordi, C., & Vinter, A. (1993). Sensorimotor development in cerebral palsied infants assessed with the Uzgiris-Hunt scales. *Developmental Medicine and Child Neurology*, 35, 1055–1066.

Clinton, H.R. (1996). *It takes a village*. New York: Simon & Schuster.

Cole, K.N., Dale, P.S., Jenkins, J.R., & Mills, P.E. (1991). Effects of preschool integration for children with disabilities. *Exceptional Children*, 58, 36–45.

Collin, R.W. (1993). Environmental equity and the need for government intervention: two proposals. *Environment*, 35(9), 41–43.

Cook, R.E., Tessier, A., & Klein, M.D. (1996). *Adapting early childhood curricula for children in inclusive settings*. Columbus, OH: Merrill.

Council for Exceptional Children (1988). Does early intervention help? *ERIC Digest* (#455). Reston, VA: Author.

Cross, K.L., Bazron, B.J., Dennis, K.W., & Issacs, M.R. (1989). *Towards a culturally competent system of care: A monograph on effective services for minority children who are severely emotionally disturbed*. Washington, DC: Child and Adolescent Service System Program, Georgetown University Child Development Center.

Dam, M. (1990). Children with epilepsy: The effect of seizures, syndromes, and etiological factors on cognitive functioning. *Epilepsia*, 31(4), 26–29.

Department for Education (DFE) (1994). *Code of Practice on the Identification and Assessment of Special Educational Needs*. UK: Author.

Department for Education (1997) *Excellence for all children, meeting special educational needs*, consultative Green Paper (October), HMSO.

Dichter, M. (1994). The epilepsies and convulsive disorders. In K.J. Isselbacher, E. Braunwald, J.D. Wilson, J.B. Martin, A.S. Fauci, & D.L.Kasper (Eds.), *Harrison's principle of internal medicine* (13th ed.). New York: McGraw-Hill (pp. 2223–2333).

Duckworth, E. (1987). *The having of wonderful ideas*. London: Teachers College Press.

Dunst, C.J., Mahoney, G., & Buchan, K. (1996). Promoting the cognitive competence of young children with or at risk for developmental disabilities. In S.L. Odom & M.E. McLean (Eds.), *Early intervention/early childhood special education*. Austin, TX: PRO-ED (pp. 159–196).

Dunst, C.J., Trivette, C., & Deal, A. (1988). *Enabling and empowering families: Principles and guidelines for practice*. Cambridge, MA: Brookline.

Dunst, D.J. (1993). Implications of risk and opportunity factors for assessment and intervention practices. *Topics in Early Childhood Special Education*, 13(2), 143–153.

Elkind, D. (1987). *Miseducation: Preschoolers at risk*. New York: Knopff.

Ensher, G.L., & Clark, D.A. (1986). *Newborns at risk: Medical care and psychoeducational intervention*. Rockville, MD: Aspen.

Environmental Protection Agency (1992). *Environmental equity: Reducing risk for all communities*. Washington, DC: Author.

European Commission Childcare Network (no date). *Quality in services for young children*. Author.

Failla, S., & Jones, L. (1991). Families of children with developmental disabilities: an examination of family hardiness. *Research in Nursing and Health*, 14, 41–50.

Fialka, J. (1994). You can make a difference in our lives. *Early On Michigan*, 3(4), 6–11.

Field, T., Widmayer, W., Greenberg, R., & Stoller, S. (1982). Effects of parent training on teenager mothers and their infants. *Pediatrics*, 69(6), 703–707.

Fuchs, D., & Fuchs, L.S. (1994). Inclusive school movement and the radicalization of special education. *Exceptional Children*, 60, 294–309.

Garbarino, J. (1977). Educating children in a socially toxic environment. *Educational Leadership*, 54(7), 12–16.

Gardner, H. (1983). *Frames of mind: The theory of multiple intelligences*. New York: Basic Books.

Gardner, H. (1991). The school of the future. In J. Brockman (Ed.), *Ways of knowing: Reality Club III*. New York: Prentice-Hall (pp. 199–217).

Gardner, H. (1997). *Education, information and transformation*. New York: Prentice-Hall.

Goldman, J., & Gardner, H. (1989). Multiple paths to educational effectiveness. In D. Kerzner and A. Gartner (Eds.), *Beyond separate education*. Baltimore, MD: Paul H. Brookes.

Goldstein, H., Kaczmarek, L.A., & Hepting, N.H. (1996). Indicators of quality in communication intervention. In S.L. Odom & M.E. McLean (Eds.), *Early intervention/early childhood special education*. Austin, TX: PRO-ED (pp. 197–221).

Grant, C. (1997). Why we need a multicultural teaching force. Paper presented for the "Enhancing Diversity in Education" Conference. Bowling Green, OH: Bowling Green State University (June 11, 1997).

Guralnick, M.J. (1990). Social competence and early intervention. *Journal of Early Intervention*, 14, 3–14.

Guralnick, M.J. (1994). Social competence with peers: Outcome and process in early childhood special education. In P.L. Safford, (Ed.), *Early childhood special education*. New York: Teachers College Press.

Guralnick, M.J., & Groom, J.M. 1988). Peer interactions in mainstreamed and specialized classrooms: a comparative analysis. *Exceptional Children*, 54, 415–425.

Haines, A.H., Fowler, S.A., & Chandler, L.K. (1988). Planning school transitions: family and professional collaboration. *Journal of the Division for Early Childhood*, 12, 108–115.

Hanline, M.F. (1993a). Facilitating integrated preschool service delivery transitions for children, families, and professionals. In C.A. Peck, S.L. Odom, & D. Bricker (Eds.), *Integrating young children with disabilities into community programs: Ecological perspectives on research and implementation*. Baltimore, MD: Paul H. Brookes (pp. 133–146).

Hanline, M.F. (1993b). Inclusion of preschoolers with profound disabilities: an analysis of children's interactions. *Journal of the Association for the Severely Handicapped*, 18, 28–34.

Hanson, M.J. (1992). Ethnic, cultural, and language diversity in intervention set-tings. In E.W. Lynch & M.J. Hanson (Eds.), *Developing cross-cultural competence: A guide for working with young children and their families*. Baltimore, MD: Paul H. Brookes (pp. 3–18).

Hanson, M.J. (1996). Early interactions: the family context. In M.J. Hanson (Ed.), *Atypical infant development*. Austin, TX: PRO-ED (pp. 235–272).

Hanson, M.J., & Lynch, E.W. (1995). *Early intervention*. Austin, TX: PRO-ED.

Harrington, M., & Meyers, H.W. (1992). Preschool programs for the hearing impaired: young children with hearing disabilities deserve special attention. *Principal*, 34–36.

Harrison, P.J., Lynch, E.W., Rosander, K., & Bordton, W. (1990). Determining success in interagency collaboration: an evaluation of processes and behaviors. *Infants and Young Children*, 3(1), 69–78.

Hilliard, A.G. (1991/92). Why we must pluralize the curriculum. *Educational Leadership*, December/January, 12–31.

Hoon, A.H. (1991). Visual impairments in children with developmental dis-abilities. In A.J. Capute & P.J. Accardo (Eds.), *Developmental disabilties in infancy and early childhood*. Baltimore, MD: Paul H. Brookes (pp. 395–411).

Howard, V.F., Williams, B.F., Port, P.D., & Lepper, C. (1997). *Very young children with special needs*. Columbus, OH: Merrill.

Hunt, J.M. (1961). *Intelligence and experience*. New York: John Wiley & Sons.

Johnson, D., & Johnson, R. (1986). Mainstreaming and cooperative learning strategies. *Exceptional Children*, 52(6), 553–561.

Johnson, J.E., Christie, J.F., & Yawkey, T.D. (1987). *Play and early childhood development*. Glenview, IL: Scott, Foresman.

Johnson, R.A. (1981). A review of existing programs and their relationship to a theoretical model for young language-impaired children with recurrent otitis media. Masters thesis. Bowling Green, OH: Bowling Green State University.

Johnson, R.A., & Mandell, C.J. (1984). *Individualizing parent and profesisonal partnerships*. Bowling Green, OH: Bowling Green State University.

Johnson, R.A., & Mandell, C.J. (1988). A social observation checklist for pre-schoolers. *Teaching Exceptional Children*, winter, 18–21.

Jordan, J.B., Hayden, A.H., Karnes, M.B., & Wood, M.M. (1977). Early childhood education for exceptional children. Reston, VA: The Council for Exceptional Children.

Kagan, S.L. (1991). *United we stand: Collaboration for child care and early childhood services*. New York: Teachers Collge Press.

Katz, L.G., & McClellan, D.E. (1991). *The teacher's role in the social development of young children*. Urbana, IL: ERIC Clearing house on Elementary and Early Childhood Education.

Kemple, K.M. (1991). Preschool children's peer acceptance and social interaction. *Young Children*, 46(5), 47–54.

Kemple, K.M., & Hartle, L. (1997). Getting along: how teachers can support children's peer relationships. *Early Childhood Education Journal*, 24(3), 139–146.

Kirchner, C. (1988). National estimates of prevalence and demographics of children with visual impairments. In M.D. Wang, M.D. Reynolds, & H.J. Walberg (Eds.), *Handbook of special education: Research and practice* (Vol. 3). Elmsford, NY: Pergamon (pp. 135–153).

Kochanek, T.T., & Buka, S.L. (1991). Using biologic and ecological factors to identify vulnerable infants and toddlers. *Infants and Young Children*, 4(1), 11–25.

Kopp, C.B., Baker, B.L., & Brown, K.W. (1992). Social skills and their correlates: preschoolers with developmental delays. *American Journal of Mental Retardation*, 96, 357–367.

Kostelnik, M.J. (1992). Myths associated with developmentally appropriate programs. *Young Children*, May, 17–23.

Lane, M. (1984). Reaffirmations: speaking out for children. A child's right to the valuing of diversity. *Young Children*, 39(6), 76.

Lang, M.A., & Deitz, S. (1990). Creating environments that facilitate independence: the hidden dependency trap. *Children's Environments Quarterly*, 7(3), 2–6.

Laybourn, A., & Hill, M. (1994). Children with epilepsy and their families: needs and services. *Child Care Health and Development*, 20, 1–14.

Leigh, J.E. (1983). Early labeling of children: concerns and alternatives. *Topics in Early Childhood Special Education*, 3(3), 1–6.

Lewis, M. (1984). Developmental principles and their implications for at-risk and handicapped infants. In M.J. Hanson (Ed.), *Atypical infant development*. Austin, TX: PRO-ED (pp. 3–24).

Linder, T.W. (1990). *Transdisciplinary play-based assessment: A functional approach to working with young children*. Baltimore, MD: Paul H. Brookes. Revised ed. 1993.

Linder, T.W. (1993). Transdisciplinary play-based intervention. Baltimore, MD: Paul H. Brookes.

Linton, G. (1995). The effects of sound field amplification on the academic readiness of kindergarten students. Doctoral dissertation. Bowling Green State University, Bowling Green, OH.

Lussier, B.J., Crimmins, D.B., & Alberti, D. (1994). Effects of three adult interaction styles on infant engagement. *Journal of Early Intervention*, 18, 12–24.

Lyons-Ruth, K., Alpern, L., & Repacholi, B. (1993). Disorganized infant attachment classification and maternal psychosocial problems as predictors of hostile-aggressive behavior in preschool children. *Child Development*, 64, 572–585.

McCracken, J.B. (1993). *Valuing diversity: The primary years*. Washington, DC: National Association for the Education of Young Children (NAEYC).

McDonnell, A., & Hardman, M. (1988). A synthesis of "best practice" guidelines for early childhood services. *Journal of the Division for Early Childhood*, 12, 328–341.

McEvoy, M.A., & Odom, S.L. (1996). Strategies for promoting social interaction and emotional development of infants and young children with disabilities and their families. In S.L. Odom and M.E. McLean, (Eds.), *Early intervention/ early childhood special education*. Austin, TX: PRO-ED (pp. 223–244).

McEvoy, M.A., Nordquist, V.M., Twardosz, S., Heckaman, K.A., Wehby, J.H., & Denny, R.K. (1988). Promoting autistic children's peer interaction in an integrated setting using affection activities. *Journal of Applied Behavior Analysis*, 21, 193–200.

McGee, G.G., Daly, T., Izeman, S.G., Mann, L.H., & Fisley, T.R. (1991). Use of classroom materials to promote preschool engagement. *Teaching Exceptional Children*, summer, 44–47.

McLean, M.E., & Odom, S.L. (1996). Establishing recommended practices in early intervention/early childhood special education. In S.L. Odom & M.E. McLean (Eds.), *Early intervention/early childhood special education*. Austin, TX: PRO-ED, pp. 1–22.

McWilliam, R.A. (1991). Targeting teaching at children's use of time. *Teaching Exceptional Children*, summer, 42–43.

Mandell, C., & Johnson, R. (1984). Screening for otitis media: issues and procedural recommendations. *Journal of the Division for Early Childhood*, 8(1), 86–93.

Mandell, C., & Johnson, R.A. (1985). Individualizing parent participation. Unpublished paper. Bowling Green, OH: Bowling Green State University.

Marlowe, M. (1986). Metal pollutant exposure and behavior disorders: implications for school practices. *Journal of Special Education*, 2(2), 251–262.

Mauk, J.E. (1993). Autism and pervasive developmental disorders. *Pediatric Clinics of North America*, 40(3), 567–578.

Meisels, S.J. (1985). *Developmental screening in early childhood: A guide*. Washington, DC: National Association for the Education of Young Children.

Meisels, S.J. (1991). Dimensions of early identification. *Journal of Early Intervention*, 15(1), 26–35.

Mettler, R. (1987). Blindness and managing the environment. *Journal of Visual Impairment and Blindness*, 81, 476–481.

Miller, P.S., & Stayton, V.D. (1996). Personnel preparation in early education and intervention: recommended preservice and inservice practices. In S.L. Odom & M.E. McLean, (Eds.), *Early intervention/early childhood special education*. Austin, TX: PRO-ED (pp. 329–358).

Morse, M. (1991). Visual gaze behaviors: considerations in working with visually impaired and multiply handicapped children. *Review*, 23(1), 5–15.

Musselwhite, C.R. (1986). *Adaptive play for special needs children*. Toronto, Ont.: Little, Brown & Company.

National Association for the Education of Young Children (NAEYC) (1984). *Accreditation criteria and procedures of the National Academy of Early Childhood Programs*. Washington, DC: National Association for the Education of Young Children.

National Association for the Education of Young Children (NAEYC) (1986). Position statement on developmentally appropriate practice in early childhood programs serving children from birth through age 8. *Young Children*, 41(6), 4–29.

National Association for the Education of Young Children (NAEYC) (1988). Position statement on standardized testing of young children 3 through 8 years of age. *Young Children*, 46(3), 21–38.

National Association for the Education of Young Children and the National Association of Early Childhood Specialists in State Departments of Education (NAEYC & NAECS/SDE) (1991). Guidelines for appropriate curriculum content and assessment in programs serving children ages 3 through 8. *Young Children*, 46(3), 21–38.

Neisworth, J.T., & Bagnato, S.J. (1996). In S.L. Odom and M.E. McLean, (Eds.), *Early intervention/early childhood special education*. Austin, TX: PRO-ED (pp. 23–57).

Nickse, R.S. (1990). *Family and intergenerational literacy programs: An update of the noises of literacy.* Columbus, OH: ERIC Information Series no. 342.

Noonan, M.J., & McCormick, L. (1993). *Early intervention in natural environments.* Pacific Grove, CA: Brookes/Cole Publishing Co.

Northern, J., & Downs, M. (1984). *Hearing in children* (3rd ed.). Baltimore, MD: Williams & Wilkins.

Odom, S.L., & McLean, M.E. (1996). *Early intervention/early childhood special education.* Austin, TX: PRO-ED.

Odom, S.L., & McEvoy, M.A. (1988). Integration of young children with handicaps and normally developing children. In S.L. Odom & M.B. Karnes (Eds.), *Early intervention for infants and children with handicaps: An empirical base.* Baltimore, MD: Paul H. Brookes (pp. 241–267).

Odom, S.L., & McEvoy, M.A. (1990). Mainstreaming at the preschool level: potential barriers and tasks for the field. *Topics in Early Childhood Special Education*, 10(2), 48–61.

Odom, S.L., McConnell, S.R., & McEvoy, M.A. (1992). Peer-related social competence and its significance for young children with disabilities. In S. Odom, S. McConnell, & M. McEvoy (Eds.), *Social competence of young children with disabilities.* Baltimore, MD: Brookes (pp. 3–36).

Ohio Department of Education (1989). *The early childhood identification process.* Columbus, OH: Author.

Osborn, J.J., Graves, L., & VonderEmbse, D.R. (1992). Project MARCS. Putnam County Schools, Putnam County, OH. Unpublished raw data.

Peterson, N.L. (1987). *Early intervention for handicapped and at-risk children.* London: Love Publishing.

Peterson, C.A., & McConnell, S.R. (1993). Factors affecting the impact of social interaction skills interventions in early childhood special education. *Topics in Early Childhood Special Education*, 13, 38–46.

Ramey, C.T. & Ramey, S.L. (1992). *At risk does not mean doomed.* Washington, DC: National Health/Education Consortium.

Ramey, C., MacPhee, D., & Yeates, K. (1983). Preventing developmental retardation: a general systems model. In L. Bond & J. Joffe (Eds.), *Facilitating infant and early childhood development.* Hanover, NH: University Press of New England (pp. 343–401).

Raver, S.A. (1991). *Strategies for teaching at-risk and handicapped infants and toddlers.* New York: Macmillan.

Ray, H., Sarff, L.S., & Glassford, F.E. (1986). Project MARRS. Walbash & Ohio Valley Special Education District, Norris City, IL. Unpublished raw data.

Report of Consensus Conferences (1987). *Access to prenatal care: key to preventing low birthweight.* Kansas City, MO: American Nurses' Association.

Roberts, R. (1990). Developing culturally competent programs for families of children with special needs (2nd ed.). Washington, DC: Georgetown University Child Development Center.

Rogers, S.J. (1986). Assessment of infants and preschoolers with low-incidence handicaps. In P.J. Lazarus & S. S. Strichart (Eds), *Psychoeducational evaluation of children and adolescents with low-incidence handicaps.* New York: Grune & Stratton (pp. 17–39).

Rogue, J.A. (1993). Environmental equity: reducing risk for all communities. *Environment*, 35(5), 25–28.

Rothbart, M.K. (1996). Social development. In M.J. Hanson (Ed.), *Atypical infant development*. Austin, TX: PRO-ED.

Sainato, D., & Carta, J. (1992). Classroom influences on the development of social competence on young children with disabilities. In S. Odom, S. McConnell, & M. McEvoy (Eds.), *Social competence of young children with disabilities*. Baltimore, MD: Paul H. Brookes (pp. 93–112).

Sainato, D., & Lyon, S. (1989). Promoting successful mainstreaming transitions for handicapped preschool children. *Journal of Early Intervention*, 13(4), 305–314.

Salisbury, C.L., Mangino, M., Petrigala, M., Rainforth, B., Syryca, S., & Palombaro, M.M. (1994). Promoting the instructional inclusion of young children with disabilities in the primary grades. *Journal of Early Intervention*, 18(3), 311–322.

Schweinhart, L.J., Barnes, H.V., & Weikart, D.P. (1993). *Significant benefits: The High/Scope Perry Preschool study through age 27*. Monographs of the High/Scope Educational Research Foundation No. 10. Ypsilanti, MI: High/Scope Educational Research Foundation.

Shonkoff, J.P., & Hauser-Cram, P. (1987). Early intervention for disabled infants and their families: a quantitative analysis. *Pediatrics*, 80, 650–658.

Shonkoff, J.P., & Meisels, S.J. (1991). Defining eligibility for services under PL 99–457. *Journal of Early Intervention*, 15(1), 21–25.

Simeonsson, R.J. (1991a). Early intervention eligibility: A prevention perspective. *Infants and Young Children*, 3(4), 48–55.

Simeonsson, R.J. (1991b). Primary, secondary, and tertiary prevention in early intervention. *Journal of Early Intervention*, 15(2), 124–134.

Skeels, H.M. (1966). *Adult status of children with contrasting early life experiences*. Monographs of the Society for Research in Child Development, 31(3), Serial No. 105).

Skeels, H.M., & Dye, H.B. (1939). A study of the effects of differential stimulation on mentally retarded children. *Proceedings and Addresses of the American Association on Mental Deficiency*, 44, 114–136.

Slavin, R.E. (1996). Neverstreaming – preventing learning disabilities. *Educational Leadership*, 53(5), 4–7.

Spitz, R.A. (1965). *The first year of life: A psychoanalytic study of normal and deviant development of object relations*. New York: International Universities Press.

Stevens, L.J., & Price, M. (1992). Meeting the challenge of educating children at-risk. *Phi Delta Kappan*, 1, 18–23.

Stile, S.W. (1996). Early childhood education of children who are gifted. In S.L. Odom & M.E. McLean (Eds.), *Early intervention/early childhood special education*. Austin, TX: PRO-ED (pp. 309–328).

Stoneman, Z. (1993). The effects of attitude on preschool integration. In C.A. Peck, S.L. Odom, & D. Bricker (Eds.), *Integrating young children with disabilities into community programs: Ecological perspectives on research and implementation*. Baltimore, MD: Paul H. Brookes (pp. 223–248).

Strain, P.S., & Danko, C.D. (1995). Caregivers' encouragement of positive interaction between preschoolers with autism and their siblings. *Journal of Emotional and Behavioral Disorders*, 3(1), 2–12.

Strain, P.S., & Smith, B.J. (1993). Comprehensive education, social, and policy forces that affect preschool integration. In C.A. Peck, S.L. Odom, & D. Bricker (Eds.), *Integrating young children with disabilities into community programs: Ecological perspectives on research and implementation.* Baltimore, MD: Paul H. Brookes (pp. 209–222).

Strain, P.S., Danko, C.D., & Kohler, F. (1995). Activity engagement and social interaction development in young children with autism: an examination of "free" intervention effects. *Journal of Emotional and Behavioral Disorders*, 3(2), 108–123.

*The Blade* (1997, March 30). Parents give up child with genetic disorder. Toledo, OH: Author.

Thommessen, M., Kase, B.F., Riis, G., & Heiberg, A. (1991). The impact of feeding problems on growth and energy intake in children with cerebral palsy. *European Journal of Clinical Health*, 45, 479–487.

Topping, K. & Wolfendale, S. (Eds.) (1985). *Parents and their children's reading.* Beckenham, Kent: Croom Helm.

UNICEF (1997). *The state of the world's children.* Oxford: Oxford University Press.

van Ijzendoorn, M.H., Juffer, R., & Duyvesteyn, M.G. (1995). Breaking the intergenerational cycle of insecure attachment: a review of the effects of attachment-based interventions on maternal sensitivity and infant security. *Journal of Child Psychology and Psychiatry*, 36, 225–248.

Vincent, L.J. & McLean, M.E. (1996). Family participation. In S.L. Odom & M.E. McLean (Eds.), *Early intervention/early childhood special education.* Austin, TX: PRO-ED (pp. 59–76).

Wachs, T.D. (1979). Proximal experience and early cognitive-intellectual development: the physical environment. *Merrill-Palmer Quarterly of Behavior and Development*, 225(1), 4–41.

Weiner, L., & Morse, B.A. (1988). FAS: clinical perspectives and prevention. In I.J. Chasnoff (Ed.), *Drugs, alcohol, pregnancy and parenting.* Lancaster, UK: Kluwer Academic Publishers (pp. 127–148).

Widerstrom, A.H. (1986). Educating young handicapped children. *Childhood Education*, 63(2), 78–83.

Williams, R. (1992). *Nobody nowhere.* New York: Times Books.

Wilson, R.A. (1988). The effect of sound field amplification paired with teacher training as an approach to language stimulation with Head Start children. Doctoral dissertation. Univeristy of Toledo, Toledo, OH.

Wilson, R.A. (1991, April). Including children with special needs. Presentation for the Toledo Area Association for the Education of Young Children Conference. Toledo, OH.

Wilson, R.A., & Aldridge, J. (1994). The Even Start initiative. In D.F. Lancy (Ed.), *Children's emergent literacy.* London: Praeger (pp. 217–235).

Wilson, R.A., & Reid, T. (1996). Environmental risk factors – a review of the literature. Unpublished data. Bowling Green, OH: Bowling Green State University.

Wilson, R.A., Kilmer, S., & Knauerhase, V. (1996). Developing an environmental outdoor play space. *Young Children*, 51(6), 56–61.

Wolery, M. (1994a). Assessing children with special needs. In M. Wolery and J.S. Wilbers (Eds.), *Including children with special needs in early childhood programs.*

Washington, DC: National Association for the Education of Young Ch. (pp. 71–96).

Wolery, M. (1994b). Designing inclusive environments for young children with special needs. In M. Wolery and J.S. Wilbers (Eds.), *Including children with special needs in early childhood programs*. Washington, DC: National Association for the Education of Young Children (pp. 97–118).

Wolery, M., & Sainato, D.M. (1996). General curriculum and intervention strategies. In S.L. Odom & M.E. McLean (Eds.), *Early intervention/early childhood special education*. Austin, TX: PRO-ED (pp. 125–158).

Wolery, M. & Wilbers, J.S. (Eds.) (1994). *Including children with special needs in early childhood programs*. Washington, DC: National Association for the Education of Young Children.

Wolery, M., Strain, P.S. & Bailey, D.B. (1992). Reaching potentials of children with special needs. In S. Bredekamp & T. Rosegrant (Eds.), *Reaching potentials: Appropriate curriculum and assessment for young children*, Vol 1. Washington, DC: National Association for the Education of Young Children (pp. 92–111).

Wolfendale, S. (Ed.) (1997). *Working with parents of SEN children after the Code of Practice*. UK: David Fulton Publishers.

Wragg, T. (no date). *Longman Parent's Guide to Key Stage 1 of the National Curriculum*. UK: Longman.

Yoder, P.J. (1987). Relationship between degree of infant handicap and clarity of infant cues. *American Journal of Mental Deficiency*, 91, 639–641.

Yoder, P.J., Warren, S.F., Kim, K., Gazdag, G. (1994). Facilitating prelinguistic communication skills in young children with developmental delays II: systematic replication and extension. *Journal of Speech and Hearing Research*, 37, 841–851.

Zametkin, A.J., Nordahl, T.E., Gross, M., King, A.C., Temple, W.E., Rumsey, M. J., Hamburger, S., & Cohen, R.M. (1990). Cerebral glucose metabolism in adults with hyperactivity of childhood onset. *New England Journal of Medicine*, 323, 1361–1367.

Zirpoli, T.J. (1995). *Understanding and affecting the behavior of young children*. Englewood Cliffs, NJ: Prentice-Hall, Inc.

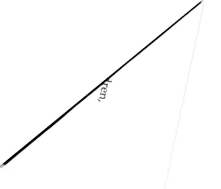

# INDEX